TECHNICAL MATTERS

Englisch für technische Berufe

von
Robert Kleinschroth
Malcolm McNeill
Dr. Steve Williams

in Zusammenarbeit mit
der Verlagsredaktion

Verfasser:	Robert Kleinschroth, Heidelberg
	Malcolm McNeill, London
	Dr. Steve Williams, Corio Bay Media, Melbourne
Berater:	Harald Berndt, Backnang
	Lothar Tomschi, Werder
Verlagsredaktion:	Merlene Griffin
Außenredaktion:	Oldham Publishing Services
Redaktionelle Mitarbeit:	Fritz Preuss, Ingrid Raspe (Wortlisten)
Layout und technische Umsetzung:	Sergio Vitale, vitaledesign, Berlin
Bildredaktion:	Gertha Maly
Umschlaggestaltung:	Sergio Vitale, vitaledesign, Berlin
Titelfoto:	GettyImages/Jonathan Knowles

Erhältlich sind auch:	Handreichungen für den Unterricht mit Audio-CD und Lehrer-CD ISBN 978-3-06-450649-7
Online-Ergänzungen unter:	www.cornelsen.de/matters

www.cornelsen.de

Die Internetadressen und -dateien, die in diesem Lehrwerk angegeben sind, wurden vor Drucklegung geprüft. Der Verlag übernimmt keine Gewähr für die Aktualität und den Inhalt dieser Adressen und Dateien oder solcher, die mit ihnen verlinkt sind.

1. Auflage, 1. Druck 2012

Alle Drucke dieser Auflage sind inhaltlich unverändert
und können im Unterricht nebeneinander verwendet werden.

© 2012 Cornelsen Verlag, Berlin

Das Werk und seine Teile sind urheberrechtlich geschützt.
Jede Nutzung in anderen als den gesetzlich zugelassenen Fällen bedarf
der vorherigen schriftlichen Einwilligung des Verlages.
Hinweis zu den § 46, 52 a UrhG: Weder das Werk noch seine Teile dürfen ohne eine
solche Einwilligung eingescannt und in ein Netzwerk eingestellt oder sonst öffentlich
zugänglich gemacht werden.
Dies gilt auch für Intranets von Schulen und sonstigen Bildungseinrichtungen.

Druck: Druckhaus Berlin-Mitte GmbH

ISBN 978-3-06-450648-0

 Inhalt gedruckt auf säurefreiem Papier aus nachhaltiger Forstwirtschaft.

VORWORT

Technical Matters orientiert sich an den Lehrplänen der Bundesländer für Berufsschulen.

Das einbändige Lehrwerk deckt nicht nur die grundlegenden Themenbereiche ab, die für die Ausbildung in technischen Berufen erforderlich sind, sondern bereitet auch auf die **KMK-Zertifikatsprüfung (Stufe II)** vor. Vorausgesetzt werden Englischkenntnisse, die der Stufe B1 des Europäischen Referenzrahmens *(Common European Framework of Reference)* entsprechen. Die *Extra material* in jeder Unit bieten Materialien zur Weiterarbeit auf Stufe B2 für leistungsstärkere Lernende, während Arbeitsblätter auf der Lehrer-CD in den Handreichungen für den Unterricht Trainingsmöglichkeiten auf Stufe A2 zur Verfügung stellen.

Technical Matters enthält zehn Units, die aktuelle Themen aus unterschiedlichen technischen Bereichen aufgreifen. Es ist möglich, einzelne Units auszulassen, jedoch wird empfohlen, wann immer Zeit und Lehrpläne es ermöglichen, die gegebene Reihenfolge einzuhalten, um einen kontinuierlichen Aufbau des Fachvokabulars zu gewährleisten. Landeskundliche Informationen über englischsprachige Länder werden ebenfalls vermittelt.

Die Sprachkompetenz der Schülerinnen und Schüler wird anhand zahlreicher Übungen zum Lese- und Hörverstehen geschult. Anhand motivierender Aufgaben, die von gelenkten Dialogen bis zu freien Diskussionen reichen, werden Hemmungen, sich in der Fremdsprache auszudrücken, abgebaut.

Fachvokabular und wichtige Redewendungen, die in *Language boxes* sowie in erweiterter Form im Anhang aufgeführt sind, werden anhand von Übungen gefestigt, um sie später handlungsorientiert *(Role-play, Partner files, Group activities)* anwenden zu können. Grundlagen der Grammatik werden zur Wiederholung angeboten.

Jede Unit enthält zwei Aufgaben, die auf die KMK-Zertifikatsprüfung vorbereiten sowie eine ganze Seite mit Aufgaben, wie sie in der KMK-Prüfung gefordert werden.

Jede Unit enthält auch einen *Webcode*. Schüler können diesen Code bei www.cornelsen.de/matters eingeben und zusätzliches Material gebührenfrei herunterladen.

Nach jeder zweiten Unit folgen zwei Seiten *Situations* deren Inhalte kompetenz- und anwendungsorientiertes Lernen fördern.

Im Anhang wird eine komplette KMK-Zertifikatsprüfung angeboten. Er enthält ferner *Partner files*, verschiedene Wortlisten, den erforderlichen Grundwortschatz, chronologische und alphabetische Wortverzeichnisse, ein deutsch-englisches Glossar und eine Aufstellung von nützlichen Redewendungen.

Der Verlag, die Autoren und die Berater wünschen Ihnen viel Erfolg und Freude bei der Arbeit mit ***Technical Matters***.

TABLE OF CONTENTS

UNIT	Title	Content
1	Talking about your company	Welcoming visitors Giving a presentation Describing a company
2	Describing your job and your workplace	Trades and workplaces A tour around a construction site Talking about jobs
	Situations 1	
3	Advising customers	Dealing with customer enquiries Making appointments and arranging visits Dealing with customer complaints
4	Planning a job	Choosing tools, equipment and materials Organizing resources Dealing with organizational problems
	Situations 2	
5	Using tools and instruments	Trades and tools Portable power tools Workshop machines
6	Troubleshooting	Identifying a problem Explaining and discussing a problem Dealing with a problem
	Situations 3	
7	Preventing accidents	Talking about safety rules Identifying hazards Describing an accident
8	Recycling	Identifying recyclable materials Describing a recycling process Discussing the pros and cons of recycling
	Situations 4	
9	Providing after-sales service	Types of after-sales services Understanding difficult technical texts Giving and understanding installation instructions
10	Applying for a job	Writing a CV Applying for a job Preparing for an interview
	Situations 5	

Appendix

KMK mock exam	121
Partner files	127
Useful phrases	133
Basic word list	141

TABLE OF CONTENTS

Language & skills	Grammar	KMK exam	Extra material	
Writing a summary Saying and writing numbers Reading for detail	Active and passive sentences	Leseverstehen Mediation	The future of cars is plastic	7
Describing a location Jobs, tasks and responsibilities Forming questions	Simple present and present progressive	Mediation	Two worker profiles	17
				28
Recording and collating customer information Comparing specifications Giving advice Making a written complaint	*Will*-future and *going to*-future	Mediation Produktion	Important facts about LED televisions	30
Discussing plans Describing and portraying statistics	Question formation	Hörverstehen Produktion Interaktion	How do you build a road?	41
				51
Describing the functions of tools Translating technical vocabulary Asking for and giving advice	Modal verbs	Interaktion	Using a combination square	53
Making notes Asking for help Describing a problem Giving and responding to advice	Simple past and past progressive	Mediation Produktion	Common universal motor problems	64
				75
How to deal with unknown vocabulary in technical texts How to avoid injury at work Describing the functions of safety equipment	Present perfect and simple past	Mediation Produktion	Accidents at work	77
Dealing with technical vocabulary Describing the properties of materials Understanding abbreviations used in texting and chat rooms	Sentences with *if* and *when*	Mediation Produktion	Plastic bottles	87
				97
Selecting information from a technical text Following installation instructions Using a flow diagram	Relative clauses	Hörverstehen Produktion	Heat pumps	99
Comparing and assessing job offers Presenting information clearly Understanding formal conventions Discussing personal attributes	Adjectives and adverbs	Interaktion	Writing your CV	109
				119

Chronological word list	147
Alphabetical word list	175
Basic technical vocabulary (German – English)	189
Common irregular verbs	190

Symbolerklärungen:

 Hörverständnistext auf der Audio-CD

 Prüfungsrelevante Übung

 Webcodes, die auf der *Matters*-Webseite (www.cornelsen.de/matters) eingegeben werden können, bieten weitere Materialien an, die zu eigenverantwortlichem Arbeiten motivieren.

Talking about your company

UNIT 1

- Welcoming visitors
- Giving a presentation
- Describing a company

1 Warm-up

Here are some industrial sectors that are important in Germany. Match the labels to the photos. (There are more labels than you need.)

Example: *Photo one shows power generation.*

> aerospace • automotive • chemical engineering • construction industry • consumer electronics • food and beverages • machine tools • power generation • textiles

2 Talking about companies

Work with a partner. Match the companies to the industrial sectors above. Some companies may be active in more than one sector.

Example: *Airbus is a company in the aerospace sector.*

7

UNIT 1 — TALKING ABOUT YOUR COMPANY

3 Welcoming a visitor

Rehau is a global group of companies with subsidiaries in Germany, the UK and other countries around the world. It produces polymer products for vehicles, buildings and a range of industries. Rehau's industrial customers are trained at the Rehau Academy in Rehau where they are taught how to use and install Rehau products. Sarah Köhler is meeting a new group of international customers at the Rehau Academy.

Copy the table below into your exercise book. Then read the dialogue and complete the table with information about the people.

Name	Firma	zusätzliche Infos
Steve Powell	Blade Electric	…

Powell Good morning. Steve Powell. I'm here for the training day on advanced plastics in industry.
Köhler Ah, Mr Powell from Melbourne, Australia?
Powell Yes, that's me.
Köhler Pleased to meet you, Mr Powell. I'm Sarah Köhler, the Academy co-ordinator. Welcome to Rehau.
Powell Thanks.
Köhler Can I introduce you to my colleague, Adnan Pamuk? Adnan is one of our field engineers. He's also an instructor at the Academy. That's why he's here today. Steve Powell – Adnan Pamuk.
Pamuk Hello, Mr Powell. Pleased to meet you. Glad you could make it.
Powell Thanks. Pleased to meet you too, Mr Pamuk.
Köhler Mr Powell is from Australia, Adnan.
Pamuk Really? That's a long way to come for a one-day training course.
Powell That's true, but my main reason for being here is the Frankfurt Motor Show. We have a stand there this year.
Pamuk I see. What company do you work for, Mr Powell?
Powell I work for a company called Blade Electric. We convert small production cars like the Hyundai Getz to run on electricity. So we're very interested in lightweight plastic components like the ones that Rehau makes.
Pamuk That sounds really interesting. We must have a chat later, over lunch, maybe?
Powell Yes, good idea.
Köhler Mr Powell, let me give you your name badge and a handout with information about today's programme.
Powell Thank you.
Köhler Please help yourself to tea or coffee.

TALKING ABOUT YOUR COMPANY

UNIT 1

4 Role-play: meeting and greeting

Form a group of seven.

Student A: You are an instructor at Rehau Academy. Welcome the participants, introduce yourself, then introduce them to each other.

Others: You are participants on the training course. Choose a name badge, then introduce yourself to A as that person. You can add extra information if you like. When A introduces you to other participants, make small talk.

Bruce Young
Field Engineer
Everglaze Windows

Amanda Kent
Automotive Technician
Blade Electric

Jack Fisher
Production Supervisor
AGM Industrial Tools

Phil Allum
Aerospace Engineer
EADS Astrium

Barry Hall
Product Design Manager
Comfort Furniture

Simon Jackson
Site Manager
Hydronic Heating Systems

LANGUAGE

Welcoming a visitor

Introductions
I'm … (*Name*).
I'm a/the … (*Stelle*).
I work for … (*Firmenname*).

Pleased to meet you.
Can I introduce you to … (*Name*)?

Making the visitor feel welcome
Welcome to … (*Firma*). Glad you could make it.
Let me give you a programme / brochure / handout with information about … .
Please help yourself / yourselves to tea or coffee / a drink.

Small talk
Where are you from? – I live/ work in … And you?
Did you have a good journey? – Yes, thanks. / No, the traffic was very heavy.
Awful/Lovely weather today, isn't it? – Yes, it is.
What's your room / hotel / hostel like? – Well, it isn't luxurious, but it's OK for a day or so.
Do you know Germany / this area? – No, I'm afraid not. / Yes, a little.

UNIT 1 — TALKING ABOUT YOUR COMPANY

5 A presentation

Rehau staff give the visitors a short presentation about the Rehau Group of companies. This is the handout from the presentation.

Rehau business activities
Rehau develops and supplies polymer-based products for a wide range of industries. As development partners we work closely with our customers through the whole concept, from raw material, design and construction to the production stage. Rehau comprises the following three business units:

Construction
Our uPVC window frames and doors are made to your specifications. Our products meet the highest Passivhaus standards in the construction industry.
Rehau flexible pipes for heating and plumbing are used in buildings all over the world. Our insulated pipes are used in renewable energy technologies such as biogas and heat pumps. Our heavy-duty pipe systems have many industrial and civil engineering applications.
Our plastic conduits make it easy and safe to manage data cables and electric cables in any building.

Automotive
Every third car built in Europe – and almost every luxury model – contains Rehau components. That includes exterior components such as bumpers, seals for doors and windows and internal components such as air conditioning hoses.
REHAU develops and produces complete windscreen and headlight washer systems - including water reservoirs, pumps and hoses.

Industry
REHAU provides components and complete systems for virtually all branches of industry. Our components are used in products as diverse as furniture, household appliances and the aerospace sector.
REHAU supplies the commercial and home-appliance industry with seals for refrigerators and freezers as well as components for washing machines, dryers, dishwashers, and cooking appliances.

Research and development
Our research and development department supports our three business units in their efforts to optimise products and add value for their customers.
Plastics alone cannot meet all the requirements of modern technology, so we combine polymers with both metal alloys and renewable raw materials such as wood, hemp, and jute.

Read the handout from the presentation, then copy and complete the following organization chart showing the structure of Rehau and its main business activities.

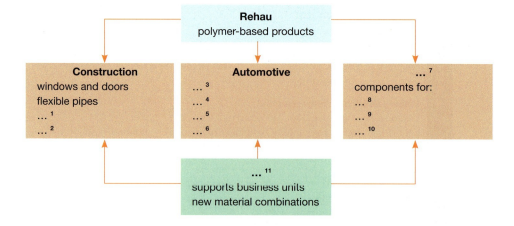

TALKING ABOUT YOUR COMPANY

6 Rehau's business activities

Sie glauben, dass die Firma Rehau ein wertvoller Geschäftspartner für Ihre Firma sein könnte. Schreiben Sie eine kurze Zusammenfassung von Rehaus Geschäftsaktivitäten für Ihren Chef.

> Beispiel: *Rehau stellt eine breite Palette polymerbasierter Produkte her. Die Firma ist in drei Bereichen tätig: …*

7 Introductions

02

Copy the following table into your exercise book. Then listen to the participants in the Rehau training course introduce themselves and their companies. Listen again and complete the table.

Company	Activities	Head Office	Size
Blade Electric	*automotive*	*Melbourne, Australia*	*small*
Skanska			
Keller Kitchens			
EADS			
Creda			
Superseal Plumbing			

8 A company profile

Schreiben Sie ein Profil Ihrer Firma für deren englische Website. Die *language box* wird Ihnen helfen. Schlagen Sie unbekannte Wörter in einem Wörterbuch nach.

LANGUAGE

Describing your company

We're a	small medium-sized large multi-national global …	company	in the	automotive renewable energy manufacturing …	sector.
We	supply provide	components electrical services plumbing services repair and maintenance services …	to	the automotive industry. customers in the … sector. …	

Our products are used in …
Our services are used by …
We're based in / near / 20 kilometres from … *(Ort)*.

UNIT 1 — TALKING ABOUT YOUR COMPANY

9 Company facts and figures

Sarah Köhler gives the participants some more information about Rehau's activities around the world.

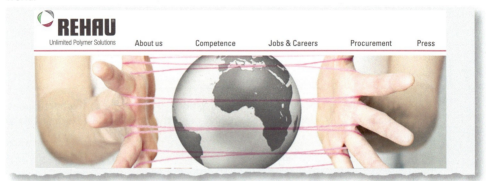

Copy the following summary into your exercise book. Then listen carefully and complete it with the correct numbers.

Rehau started with **three** [1] employees in … [2].

Rehau today:

Employees:	… [3] worldwide; … [4] in Europe
Training academies:	… [5]
Regions:	… [6]
Sales offices:	… [7] in … [8] countries
Plants:	… [9]
Administrative offices:	… [10]
Logistics centres:	… [11]
Apprentices Germany per year:	… [12]
Total apprentices Germany:	… [13]
Apprentices at Rehau plant:	… [14]

10 Working with words: parts of a company

Match the words 1–7 to the definitions a–g.

1 branch
2 distribution/logistics centre
3 head office / headquarters
4 plant/factory
5 Research and Development (R&D) / technical development centre
6 sales office
7 service centre

a This is a general word for any type of office that a company operates.
b This is the control centre of the company.
c This is where a company makes its products.
d This is where the company develops new products and production techniques.
e This part of the company makes sure that finished goods and raw materials get to the right place at the right time.
f This part of the company makes sure that its products continue to work properly.
g This part of the company sells products or services to customers.

TALKING ABOUT YOUR COMPANY

UNIT 1

11 Partner file: understanding numbers

Read the *language box* below, then work with a partner.

Student A: Turn to File 1 on page 127.
Student B: Turn to File 6 on page 130.

Saying and writing numbers

1.4	'one point four'	
100	'a hundred'	
104	'a hundred and four'	
1,000	'a thousand'	Be careful: English uses a point where German uses a comma, and uses a comma where German uses a point!
10,000	'ten thousand'	
100,000	'a hundred thousand'	1.4 = *eins Komma vier*
1,000,000	'a million'	1,400 = *tausendvierhundert*
1,000,000,000	'a billion'	

12 Presentation

Give a short presentation about your company. Include the following information:

- Company size
- Industry sector
- Company structure: divisions / departments / business units
- Main products/services
- Relevant figures/statistics

Illustrate your presentation with samples or photos of your company's products.

Wie man einen wirkungsvollen Vortrag hält

Vorbereitung

- Wichtig: Bereiten Sie sich ausschließlich auf Englisch vor. Ihre Präsentation wird dadurch überzeugender und authentischer als die deutsche Übersetzung.
- Notieren Sie stichwortartig, was Sie über das Thema wissen. Füllen Sie Wissenslücken durch Internetrecherchen.
- Geben Sie Ihrem Vortrag einen passenden Aufbau mit Einleitung, Hauptpunkten und Zusammenfassung.
- Überlegen Sie, welche visuellen Hilfsmittel Sie einsetzen können.
- Lesen Sie den Text mehrmals laut vor, um sich den Inhalt einzuprägen und einen selbstsicheren, flüssigen Vortragsstil einzuüben. Vereinfachen Sie schwierig auszusprechende oder lange Sätze.

Vortrag

- Lesen Sie den Text nicht ab, sondern sprechen Sie frei. Sie können Stichwörter auf Karteikarten als Gedächtnisstütze verwenden.
- Reden Sie langsam und ausdrucksvoll. Halten Sie Blickkontakt zu Ihren Zuhörern.

WEBCODE
TEMU0101

TALKING ABOUT YOUR COMPANY

GRAMMAR

Active and passive sentences

Active: *Carl Benz **produced** the first car with a petrol engine.*

Passive: *The first car with a petrol engine **was produced** by Carl Benz.*

- Die Passivform des Verbs (*produce*) wird mit einer Form von *be* und dem Partizip Perfekt (*past participle*) gebildet: *is produced, was produced, has been produced, had been produced*.
- Das Objekt des Aktivsatzes (*The first car with a petrol engine*) wird Subjekt des Passivsatzes.
- Das Subjekt des Aktivsatzes (*Carl Benz*) wechselt im Passiv an das Ende des Satzes und wird mit *by* angehängt.

13 Practice

A Partner A asks the questions. Partner B answers them using the passive form. Then swap roles.

Example: A: *Who produced the first car with a petrol engine?*
B: *It was produced by Carl Benz.*

Active	**Passive**
1 Who / found / the Rehau Company?	It / be founded / by the Wagner family.
2 When / they found / the company?	The company / be founded / 1948.
3 Why / they / name / the company 'Rehau'?	It / be named / after the town of Rehau.
4 How many apprentices / Rehau / employ?	463 apprentices / be employed / by the company.
5 Who / invent / the diesel engine?	It / be invented / by Rudolph Diesel.
6 Who / produce / the first battery?	The first battery / be produced / by Volta in 1800.
7 Who / make / the first balloon flight?	The first balloon flight / be made / by the Montgolfier brothers.

B Complete the sentences using the passive form of the verbs in brackets. Use your exercise book.

1 The new trainees (send) to the Rehau Academy by their firms.
2 They (meet) by Sarah Köhler, the Academy co-ordinator.
3 The trainees (teach) how to use and install Rehau products.
4 In Steve Powell's firm, cars (convert) to run on electricity.
5 Rehau plastic components (use) in this conversion.
6 Many car components (now make) of polymers instead of metal.

KMK exam practice

Rudolph Diesel – inventor and visionary

Rudoph Diesel was born in 1858 of Bavarian parents in Paris. After the outbreak of the war between Germany and France in 1870, the Diesels were forced to leave France and move to London. At the age of 13 his parents sent Rudolf to Augsburg to live with his uncle and improve his German. In 1873 he entered the Industrial School of Augsburg and decided to become a mechanical engineer.

Two years later he received a scholarship from the Royal Bavarian Polytechnic of Munich, which he accepted against the wishes of his parents who wanted him to find a good job and earn money. He became a brilliant engineer and started to develop various engines including a solar-powered air engine and a steam engine using ammonia vapour, which exploded and almost killed him. Soon after Daimler and Benz had invented the motor car, Diesel introduced the first diesel engine at the World Fair in Paris in 1898. It was fuelled by peanut oil – the first green fuel. In 1898 he founded an Engine Company in Augsburg which closed down after two years. In 1900 he founded a second company in London.

On 29 September 1913 Rudolf Diesel was aboard the steamer Dresden on an overnight voyage to England to attend the opening of an engine factory. He retired to his cabin after dinner. The following morning his cabin was found to be empty and his coat and hat were discovered on deck. On October 9, fishermen recovered a man's body floating in the North Sea. The belongings found on the body were later identified by Diesel's family.

There are various theories to explain Diesel's death. Did he commit suicide because of financial difficulties – a theory his family never accepted? Was he murdered by German agents to prevent his invention from falling into British hands? Or was he murdered by a killer hired by the oil industry who feared the competition of the green fuel? The only theory not advanced was the simple possibility that he had accidentally fallen overboard.

14 Rezeption: Leseverstehen

Erstellen Sie eine tabellarische Kurzbiografie von Rudolph Diesel.

Jahr	Kurzbiografie
1858	Rudolph Diesel wird in Paris geboren und wohnt dort bis 1870.

15 Mediation

Fassen Sie folgenden Text in eigenen Worten auf Deutsch zusammen.

> What is the main difference between the diesel and the petrol engine? In diesel cars the compression of the air created by the pistons is much higher than that of petrol engines. When diesel fuel is injected, it ignites when it comes in contact with the very hot compressed air. This means that spark plugs are not needed for the ignition. Why do diesel engines consume less fuel than petrol engines for the same amount of power? Friction and heat radiation cause about 7 % of the energy to be lost from both engines. However the petrol engine loses more energy with the exhaust gases. And at low temperatures petrol loses 29 % of its energy, diesel only 19 %. So petrol is a less efficient fuel than diesel. However, diesel cars need more energy to start the engine. This means the battery and the starter motor have to be more powerful than those in petrol engines.

Extra material

16 Reading for detail

Read the text then decide whether the statements below are true (T), false (F) or not mentioned in the text (NM).

THE FUTURE OF CARS IS PLASTIC

The use of advanced plastics in automotive engineering allows designers to develop unusual-looking and fuel-efficient vehicles. Porsche's Carrera GT is a good example.

Mechanical engineers at Porsche use a lightweight, high-strength aerospace material called carbon-fibre-reinforced plastic. It is used in the doors, bonnets, bumpers, chassis and also in support frames for the engine and transmission.

Paul Ritchie, CEO and engineer at Porsche Engineering Services:

'We test new materials in the Carrera GT. It's made essentially from reinforced plastic.'

Guan Chew, a mechanical engineer at Porsche Engineering Services in Troy, Michigan:

'With plastics you can design cars which are very bold. You can mould the plastics into very complicated shapes that you can't make in steel.'

An attractive appearance is not the only advantage of plastic.

Plastic can significantly reduce the weight of a vehicle – that improves its fuel efficiency. A Plastics Europe study shows that every kilo of plastic in a car replaces roughly 1.5 kilos of traditional materials such as steel.

Because car-makers can mould plastic easily, they can design components with more comfortable and ergonomic features. More aerodynamic shapes also mean better fuel efficiency. Less material is needed than with steel components, and the durability of plastics results in a longer, more reliable vehicle lifetime.

Car designers usually test new materials like plastic on high-end vehicles first. Once they know that the materials are efficient and cost effective, they start to use them in affordable consumer vehicles.

In the future, most car bodies may be 100% plastic, with no metal at all.

1 Plastic cars use less fuel than metal vehicles.
2 Plastic is not strong enough to be used in the chassis of a car.
3 The Carrera GT is the first Porsche vehicle to use this much plastic.
4 Mechanical engineers at Porsche claim that plastic cars are safer than metal ones.
5 Using plastics instead of metal can reduce the weight of car components by 33%.
6 Plastic cars don't last as long as metal ones.
7 Car designers use new materials in inexpensive vehicles first, then use them in expensive cars if they are successful.
8 Some cars are already made completely from plastic, with no metal parts.

17 Your opinion

Which is the most impressive car on the road today, from the technological standpoint? Give reasons for your opinion.

Example: *I think that the Tesla Roadster is the most impressive car on the road today. It can travel more than 320 km per battery charge and has better performance than many conventional sports cars.*

Describing your job and your workplace

UNIT 2

- Trades and workplaces
- A tour around a building site
- Talking about jobs

1 Warm-up

Match the labels in the box to the photos and describe what you can see.

Example: *Photo one shows a factory. There is/are … I can see …*

factory • office • foundry • workshop • laboratory • warehouse • building site

2 Jobs

Who works in the places above?

forklift operators • painters • joiners • IT specialists • steelworkers •
supervisors • scaffolders • builders • assembly line workers • bricklayers • lab assistants •
mechanics/fitters • welders • electricians

DESCRIBING YOUR JOB AND YOUR WORKPLACE

3 Everyday tasks

Test your partner. Then swap roles.

What do ... do?

1 builders
2 joiners
3 machinists
4 IT specialists
5 welders
6 painters
7 steelworkers
8 bricklayers
9 electricians
10 assembly line workers
11 lab assistants
12 forklift operators
13 supervisors
14 scaffolders

They ...

a organize the workforce.
b troubleshoot computer problems.
c work with molten metal.
d construct frames out of timber.
e build walls.
f move heavy loads from one place to another.
g repair and service machinery.
h help researchers.
i dig foundations.
j paint walls and ceilings.
k erect platforms outside buildings.
l install wiring and electrical appliances.
m perform one part of a manufacturing process.
n join metal parts together.

4 A guided tour

04

Listen to a conversation between a journalist and the site manager of a construction company. Then link these numbers with the things they refer to.

1	7	a	budget in pounds sterling
2	4,000	b	the total land area in square metres
3	760	c	the length of the swimming pool in metres
4	19,000	d	the time when the meeting takes place
5	45	e	office floor space in square metres
6	60,000,000	f	the number of swimming pools the journalist has ever
7	25		seen in a factory
8	0	g	factory floor space in square metres
		h	the progress of the construction work in percent

DESCRIBING YOUR JOB AND YOUR WORKPLACE

UNIT 2

5 A tour of the factory

Jeff Harrop shows Raphael Thomas around the factory, which is still under construction.

Read the dialogue and follow their route around the factory on the map on the next page.

Jeff My little portacabin is roughly where the car park will be. As you can see, the surveyors are already out with their levelling instruments, and we're removing the old road surfaces. Now, can you see that big cement mixer and the crane?

Raphael Next to the lorries?

Jeff That's right. They're laying the foundations for the assembly. It's the biggest part of the factory. It also houses the clean rooms, the paint and trim shops, the autoclaves, and the various workshops needed by the aerospace engineers. It consists of two floors, with a canteen on the ground floor. We'll take a look over there later. But there's not much to see at the moment.

Raphael Is that a warehouse on the other side?

Jeff Yes, a warehouse and the delivery bays. We're building them near the road, for obvious reasons. We'll have a storage facility for raw materials inside the warehouse.

Raphael What's going on over there?

Jeff Behind the trees? They're taking all the furniture into the administration block. We built that first. The company wants to use it a.s.a.p. Let's go and take a look, it's nearly finished.

They cross the building site and enter the admin block.

Jeff So here on the ground floor we have the reception area and a suite of meeting rooms. There's a large presentation hall at the end of this corridor. HR and finance are located on the first floor, and they're planning to have the other main departments – accounts, sales, marketing and so on – on the second floor. All the fancy furniture is going up in the service lifts to the third floor.

Raphael I guess the executive offices are up there.

Jeff You got it! The Chief Executive Officer has a very nice office.

Raphael What about Research and Development?

Jeff Well, Research and Development is pretty big, so they have a block of their own. It's between the assembly area and these offices.

Raphael You mentioned a crèche and some other facilities for the employees.

Jeff Ah yes! Sorry, I forgot, the crèche is through this door, next to the reception. The children should be near the employees after all. The recreation block is quite far off though, on the other side of the car park, directly opposite us. You can see it from the door. We're going to work on that last. We're putting in showers and changing rooms for the gym. It's quite luxurious.

They go outside again.

Jeff Anyway, that was a quick tour of the site. I just forgot to mention the training centre for apprentices and new employees. It's next to the recreation block, it's the bigger building.

Raphael Thanks, that was really interesting. I think I can find my way around now.

Jeff If you want to see anything else, just let me know. Now, let's get you some breakfast. The site canteen is right over here. One last thing – if you want to go to the toilets, they're on the left of the canteen entrance!

19

DESCRIBING YOUR JOB AND YOUR WORKPLACE

6 | Completing a site plan

Übertragen Sie den Plan des Baugeländes in Ihr Heft. Entnehmen Sie dem Dialog in Aufgabe 5 die fehlenden Wörter und setzen Sie diese in den Plan ein.

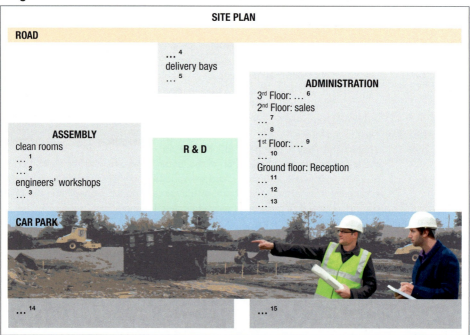

7 | A tour of your company

Sie erhalten die Aufgabe, für englische Besucher eine Führung durch Ihre Firma vorzubereiten. Simulieren Sie Ihre Führung vor der Klasse mithilfe einer Computer-Präsentation oder eines Lageplans.

> **TIP**
>
> ### Britisches Englisch und amerikanisches Englisch
>
> **Etagen**
> In Großbritannien heißt die unterste Etage *the ground floor*. In den USA nennt man sie *the first floor*.
>
> *British English (BE)*
> The reception is on the *ground* floor.
> The building is seven *storeys* high.
>
> *American English (AE)*
> The reception is on the *first* floor.
> The building is seven *stories* high.
>
> Einige Wörter sind auch anders:
>
> | | |
> |---|---|
> | lorry | truck |
> | lift | elevator |
> | toilet | rest room |
> | crèche | day nursery |

DESCRIBING YOUR JOB AND YOUR WORKPLACE

UNIT 2

8 Describing a location

Student A: Choose a location on the site plan and describe where you are.
Student B: Guess which part of the site your partner is describing. Then swap.

I'm standing	next to / beside	the assembly area.
	behind	the warehouse.
	opposite	the administration block.
	near	the executive offices.
	between	the ... and the ...
	far from	...
	on the left/right of	
	in	
	above	
	...	

Example:
A: I'm standing next to the car park.
B: You're standing in the administration block.
A: Right!

9 Parts of the building

A Read the speechbubbles and decide where these people are working.

reception • offices • cafeteria • meeting rooms • changing rooms • warehouse • delivery area • workshops

Andy:
I'm installing extractor fans to remove water vapour from the shower area.

Justin:
I'm extending the parking bays.

Carlos, Antony and Roger:
We're laying a concrete floor to support the heavy-duty workbenches.

Jules and Anita:
We're wiping dust from the windows, chairs and desks.

Seb:
I'm building a custom-made counter for the welcome area.

Carla:
I'm welding security bars to the window frames.

Anna:
I'm running an electricity supply through the wall for the presentation boards.

Mike:
I'm tiling the walls so they're easy to clean.

B Now ask your partner where the people are working.

10 Job titles

05

Listen to these people describing their jobs and then say what their job titles are.

Steve O'Donnell	pipefitter • bricklayer •
Martin Sanger	carpenter • health and safety
Santos Delgradia	manager • plumber •
Ying Hao	electrician • welder

21

UNIT 2

DESCRIBING YOUR JOB AND YOUR WORKPLACE

11 A building site

Describe the jobs on a building site in one sentence. The following language box may help you.

> **LANGUAGE**
>
> **Jobs, tasks and responsibilities**
>
> an architect • a bricklayer • a plumber • an electrician • a safety inspector • a site manager • a joiner • a surveyor • a decorator • a quantity surveyor
>
> design • mix • check • install • evaluate • supervise • construct • measure • hang • control
>
> buildings
> cement
> pipes for leakage
> plugs and wiring
> health risks and the use of hazardous materials
> employees and overtime
> timber frames
> precise distances, positions and angles
> wallpaper and painting
> costs

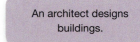

An architect designs buildings.

A plumber …

12 Questions and answers

Match Raphael's questions to Sheila's answers.

Raphael:
1 What are your responsibilities?
2 How long did you train for?
3 Are you fully-qualified or an apprentice?
4 Are you paid an hourly rate or a salary?
5 Which department do you work in?
6 What are you working on currently?
7 What is your job title?
8 Who is your boss / line manager?
9 Where did you train?
10 How many years of on the job experience do you have?

Sheila:
a Officially I'm the Logistical Support Officer, but everyone just calls me the logistics clerk.
b I'm in the materials section, I buy cement and things like that.
c Actually there's no certification for my role.
d I just learned it all on the job.
e I didn't do any formal training – but there was a trial period of six months when I started.
f I've worked here for six years.
g I get paid monthly.
h I make sure the building site is well equipped. If we run out of materials the work stops! But it's also bad if we buy things we don't use.
i The site supervisor, Angelo Carlucci.
j I'm drawing up a bulk order of cabling and insulation foam.

22

DESCRIBING YOUR JOB AND YOUR WORKPLACE

UNIT 2

13 Sections of a company

Before Raphael leaves the site, Jeff gives him some notes about the organizational structure of MGT.

Read his notes and complete Raphael's chart.

- MGT's operations boss is Carlo Fabruzzi. He's responsible for all MGT building projects. I report to the contracts manager, Michael Charles, and Mike reports to Carlo. We all work under Carlo.
- Marc van Tongeren makes sure there are no unauthorized people on the site. Obviously most of his work is done at night when nobody else is here.
- The lady who sorts out all our salaries is Janice Morrison. She doesn't work on site. Obviously, she's in the head office in Manchester with all the other human resources people.
- I think you met this guy – Jeff Harrop, that's me! I'm always on site, keeping an eye on things and bossing people around.
- Doctor Katerina Obedkova, you didn't meet her, at the moment she's visiting a conference in Prague. She's in charge of research.
- There are quite a lot of skilled labourers on the site. Joseph Wewerka supervises them. He's not very high up in the company, but he's one of the most important people. If Joe didn't organize the workers, nothing would happen. He does a lot of shouting, but it works!
- At the end of the day money controls everything, which means Lucas Fairfax has a lot of control, even though he's not a builder. He's better at pressing buttons than pulling levers – on his calculator!

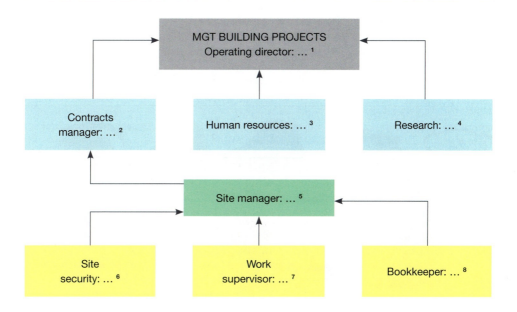

23

DESCRIBING YOUR JOB AND YOUR WORKPLACE

14 Role-play: talking about jobs

It's lunchtime in the MGT canteen. Raphael is moving from table to table and interviewing people.

Work with a partner and act out the following interview.

- **A:** I'm Raphael, a journalist. May I ask you a few questions?
- **B:** Yes, go ahead. By the way, I'm Tim.
- **A:** May I ask what your trade is?
- **B:** I'm an electrician.
- **A:** What job are you doing at the moment, Tim?
- **B:** I'm working in the recreation block. I'm installing extractor fans in the showers.

Now use this table to act out other interviews.

Name	trade	work place	jobs
Tim	electrician	recreation block	install / extractor fans / showers
Justin	builder	road / warehouse	extend / parking bays
Carlos	builder	factory	lay / concrete floor
Steve	joiner	reception area	create / custom-made counter
Martin	welder	warehouse	weld / security bars / windows
Doris	cleaner	administration building	wipe / dust / floors, furniture
Ying	electrician	conference rooms	run / electricity supply / lighting
Mike	tiler	recreation block	tile walls / toilets, showers
Santos	health & safety	building site	check / security measures
Tom	buyer	warehouse	buy / cement, bricks, timber
Peter	mechanic	workshop	clean / maintain equipment
Ron	scaffolder	building site	erect / platforms / outside buildings

15 Protective clothing and equipment

A Match the following protective clothing and equipment to the photos.

protective gloves • protective boots • safety glasses • safety helmet (AE: hard hat) • cup mask • ear protectors

1   2   3   4   5   6

B Now say why you should wear them.

You should wear (a) ... to

prevent / protect / avoid	your eyes from dust and sharp splinters. breathing in dust or harmful chemicals. injury to your feet. cuts and other injuries to your hands. your head from falling objects. your ears from loud noises.

WEBCODE
TEMU0201

DESCRIBING YOUR JOB AND YOUR WORKPLACE

GRAMMAR

Simple present and present progressive

1. I'm **working** for Siemens at the moment.
2. I **work** for Siemens.
3. The economy **is expanding**.
4. The economy regularly **expands** and **contracts**.
5. **Is** he **having** a meeting at the moment?
6. **Does** he always **have** a meeting on Tuesday mornings?
7. I don't **like** meetings, especially if they go on for too long.
8. The training course **starts** next Wednesday afternoon.
9. **Are** you **giving** a demonstration this afternoon?

- Das *present progressive* bildet man mit *am/is/are* + *-ing*. Es steht für Handlungen, die aus der Sicht des Sprechers noch andauern (1, 3, 5). Das *present progressive* wird oft mit Ausdrücken wie *now*, *currently*, *nowadays*, *at the moment* verwendet.
- Das *simple present* steht für Zustände, Gewohnheiten und allgemeine Aussagen (2, 4, 6). Es steht oft mit Zeitangaben wie *often*, *always*, *never*. In der 3. Person Einzahl (*he/she/it*) wird ein 's' an die Grundform des Verbs angefügt (4). Verben wie *need*, *like*, *want*, *hate*, *love*, die einen Zustand beschreiben, stehen normalerweise nicht im *present progressive* (7).
- Beide Zeitformen können auch ein zukünftige Bedeutung haben (8, 9).

16 Practice

Complete the text with the correct verb forms.

About Us

At MGT we ... ¹ (specialize) in healthcare and industrial facilities, commercial and educational buildings, telecommunications and data centres, as well as infrastructure projects such as waste-water treatment plants. Our projects ... ² (include) multi-million dollar car manufacturing plants and other commercial developments. We ... ³ (build) some of the most advanced facilities for our corporate, institutional and government clients.

More and more of our clients ... ⁴ (turn) to us for our innovative project management techniques. Our team ... ⁵ (offer) a single source solution for all of your construction needs. We ... ⁶ (have) the experience and personnel to provide the highest quality construction on schedule and within budget. We ... ⁷ (support) our clients from project inception to the opening of the fully operational facility, and always ... ⁸ (work) with clients to improve the cost effectiveness of our projects.

Current Projects

This year we ... ⁹ (expand) our activities in England. Despite a shrinking demand for large industrial buildings, we won a tender to build a new factory for Aeropart outside Birmingham, the first major construction project in the area for many years. We ... ¹⁰ (build) an industrial unit with a total area of 19,000 square meters.

17 Mediation

Sie sind Praktikant und assistieren Janice Morrison in der Personalabteilung von MGT in Manchester. Die Firma sucht dringend Konstruktionszeichner in Europa. Janice bittet Sie, nach der englischen Vorlage eine Stellenanzeige für deutsche Zeitungen zu erstellen. Eine wörtliche Übersetzung ist nicht erwünscht.

MGT is an expanding construction company that sets the pace in building state-of-the-art factories in Europe and the UK.
We are currently looking for junior draftsmen (m/f). Our company is located in Manchester, a city that offers many benefits including a high quality of life, all kinds of leisure activities and a short commuting time.

Qualifications:
- Fluency in English
- Vocational qualification and at least one year's work experience
- Proficiency in 3D CAD
- Experience in architectural and/or electrical design

Your responsibilities:
- Assisting the head of the design department
- Studying rough sketches and understanding the specifications
- Preparing drawings to scale with high precision
- Creating the drawings according to the standards and terms of MGT
- Generating final 3D models of construction parts
- Communicating with suppliers and customers

We offer:
- Excellent working conditions
- A competitive salary
- A generous benefits package
- One ticket p.a. for any Manchester United home match

Applications will only be considered if they contain a full CV.
If you are interested in applying, please send your résumé to
janice.morrison@mgt.com

Extra material

18 Two worker profiles

Read the texts and then say whether the statements below are true or false. Correct the statements which are incorrect.

Hello, I'm Jacek Kutrzeba, I'm a Polish painter and decorator. I moved to the UK in 2004 when the new rules for migrant workers began. Now I run my own company – we specialize in offices and workplaces.

Actually I'm still waiting to start on the Aeropart factory. I'm not going near the place with my paint pots until all that heavy equipment is out of the way and all the brick dust is swept up. One thing I know about wet plaster – it doesn't react well to dirt! I guess I'm lucky to be working for MGT. The contract will bring in enough work to last me and my team almost a year. I won the tender because of my work on a complex of offices for a drinks manufacturer in Portsmouth. It was a redecoration project, which we completed on time and within budget—if you can do that, you can guarantee future work. But I'm not saying it's OK to take short cuts—you can't compromise on quality. The construction industry is getting more and more competitive these days. There's no place for shoddy work.

Hi, my name's Trudi Caister, I'm an Australian plumber. I started working for MGT when I left my vocational college in Melbourne, but I did most of my training at home. My dad runs a plumbing firm so the business is in the family. When all the other girls were playing hockey and swimming, I was under the sink unscrewing the P-trap. Working for MGT is pretty good – we get big contracts for long-term building projects.all over the world, so you get to see all these different cultures. I've installed plumbing systems for factories in Canada, France and even China. Sometimes there's a lot of pressure, especially from all the deadlines, but with the Birmingham site we're having real problems with the budget. Our quantity surveyor won't get off our backs about it, but he's just doing his job.

The biggest challenge is the water supply. We're irrigating the premises with good, old-fashioned British rainwater! We're using it to flush the toilets and water the outdoor plants. The client also wants the mains water for the showers to be heated by waste energy from the factory, so the water has to be kept warm over quite a long distance. It's all part of the effort to go green, I suppose, but we're using up a lot of insulation. Luckily we have a technician who worked on the external water supplies in Siberian cities, so he's giving us some good advice.

1. Trudi's father works for a plumbing company.
2. She likes working for MGT because of the good contract she has with them.
3. She has to travel for work.
4. Normally the biggest problem for her is the work schedule.
5. The new factory will be energy efficient.
6. Jacek's company usually works in domestic buildings.
7. He needs to wait until the builders have left before he begins work on the factory.
8. He competed with other firms to work for MGT.
9. You can cut corners to complete work on time.
10. It's not easy to get work nowadays.

19 Your job

Write a profile about yourself. Include the following information:

> job title • department • usual responsibilities • current projects / tasks

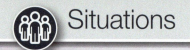

Situations

General information

Bill Taylor works for a traditional printing company that wants to introduce digital printing. Mr Taylor is visiting printing firms with a long experience of this technology. Today he's visiting Hummel Druck GmbH in Ulm. He has an appointment with Karl Schreyer, the managing director, at 9 o'clock.

1 The reception

Act out a dialogue using the information on the role cards.

Mr / Mrs …
Personal Assistant of the Managing Director
- Meet Mr Taylor at reception. Introduce yourself and welcome him to the firm.
- Show him to your office (next to the MD's office on the third floor).
- The MD is running a bit late. Explain why the visitor must wait and for how long. Offer refreshments. Give him a choice.
- Introduce him to the MD when he arrives.

Mr Taylor
Visitor
- Greet the PA.
- Accept the offer of refreshments. Choose what you would like.
- Make polite small talk with the PA.
- Introduce yourself to the Managing Director when he arrives.

Karl Schreyer
Managing Director
- Introduce yourself.
- Apologize for the delay. Explain what happened.
- Explain the plan for the morning:
  - presentation,
  - tour around company.
- Invite Mr Taylor to the conference room.

2 The presentation

Act out a dialogue using the information on the role cards and the Fact file.

Karl Schreyer
Managing Director
- Give Mr Taylor a short presentation of your company.
- At the end, invite the visitor to ask questions and try to answer them.

Mr Taylor
Visitor
- Listen to presentation and take notes.
- At the end, ask questions.

Fact file

1850	Herbert Hummel founded printing company: 12 employees
1892	Introduction of the four-colour Druckmeister
1975	World premier of the two-color Speedopress; 450 employees
1991	Development of digital imaging technology; 532 employees
1995	Branches in France, Brazil and Tokyo
2000	150-year anniversary of Hummel Druck; inauguration of Digital Printing Academy in Ulm; turnover of 3.7 billion Euro
2005	Record orders worth 4.79 billion Euro; 956 employees
2009	First German equipment supplier to the print media industry; steady increase of turnover to 6.2 billion Euro.
2010	Global recession; turnover falls to 4.2 billion Euro
2011	Turnover rises to 6.59 billion Euro; opening of assembly plant in China
2012	Record turnover of 9.89 billion Euro

Situations

3 The tour

Take over the roles below and act out dialogues using the information on the role cards.

Karl Schreyer
Managing Director

- Take Mr Taylor to these parts of the company and introduce him to people there:
- Sales Department (second floor of office block); Doris Baumann, sales manager
- Warehouse; Jürgen Riedl, manager
- Printing department; Brigitte Mergenthal, print technician
- Training centre; Rolf Degger, trainee

Mr Taylor
Visitor

- Ask the managing director questions about the places you visit on the tour. Take notes.
- Introduce yourself to the people you meet on the tour around the company. Ask them about their jobs. Take notes.
- Answer any questions your are asked.

Doris Baumann
Sales manager

- Introduce yourself.
- Explain what you do:
  advertising, marketing, dealing with customer orders, enquiries, complaints, lists of prices and services, costs
- Answer any questions the visitor may have.
- Ask Mr Taylor some questions.

Jürgen Riedl
Warehouse manager

- Introduce yourself.
- Explain what you do:
  buying supplies (paper, card, toner, office equipment), checking deliveries, storing supplies and products, packing, packaging, delivery
- Answer any questions the visitor may have.

Brigitte Mergenthal
print technician in printing department

- Introduce yourself.
- Explain what you do:
  create layout, enter text, add illustrations, photos, print and bind copies, send to warehouse, calculate price, call customer, delivery details
- Answer any questions the visitor may have.
- Ask Mr Taylor some questions.

Rolf Degger
Trainee at training centre

- Introduce yourself.
- Explain what you do:
  learn software programs for text, layout, data bank, printing systems, machines, customer relations, practical experience in printing department, warehouse, sales department
- Answer any questions the visitor may have.
- Ask Mr Taylor some questions.

4 The report

You are Mr Taylor, the visitor. Look at your notes and write a report about your visit to Hummel Druck GmbH. Illustrate your report with suitable photos from the Internet.

UNIT 3: Advising customers

- Dealing with customer enquiries
- Making appointments and arranging visits
- Dealing with customer complaints

1 Warm-up

A Match the photos to the customer types in the box.

> agricultural • commercial • heavy industrial • institutional / public sector • light industrial • professional • residential

B What types of customer does your company have?

Example: *Most of our customers are in the … sector.*

C What subjects will you need to give customers advice about when you are fully qualified?

- correct operation of equipment
- purchase and installation costs
- service and maintenance
- site assessment
- technical specifications
- other (describe)

D What details do you need from a potential customer when he or she contacts your company? Make a list, then compare ideas with your partner.

Example: *Customer's surname, …*

ADVISING CUSTOMERS

2 A customer enquiry

Elektro-Kieser GmbH in Schweinfurt designs, installs and tests electrical systems for light industrial, retail and domestic customers. The company receives a call from an English photographer, Clara Hooper, who is setting up a new business in the area. Receptionist Maria Wegener puts the call through to Klaus Kieser, the owner of the business.

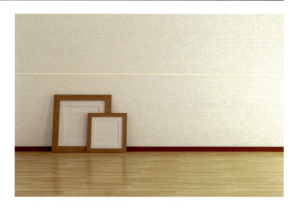

Read the dialogue then decide whether the statements below are true (T), false (F) or not mentioned in the text (NM).

Wegener	Elektro-Kieser, Wegener, guten Tag.
Hooper	Err, hello. Do you speak English?
Wegener	Yes, a little bit. How can I help you?
Hooper	I need advice about an electrical installation.
Wegener	I'll put you through to Mr Kieser. May I have your name, please?
Hooper	Yes, it's Hooper – Clara Hooper.
Wegener	I'll put you through, Mrs Hooper. Please hold the line.
Hooper	OK, thanks.
Kieser	Ms Hooper? Klaus Kieser here.
Hooper	Hello, Mr Kieser.
Kieser	I understand that you need an electrical installation, is that right?
Hooper	Yes, that's right. I'm going to open a new photo gallery and studio in Würzburg.
Kieser	Right. Could you describe your premises for me, please?
Hooper	Yes. I've leased some rooms on the ground floor of an old warehouse.
Kieser	And what do you need us to do?
Hooper	Well, it was an office before I took it over and it has fluorescent tube lighting. That's quite ugly and not right for a gallery. So I need someone to design a new lighting system.
Kieser	Yes, we can do that for you. We're specialists for lighting design and installation.
Hooper	Good.
Kieser	Is there anything else you need?
Hooper	Err, yes. I also need some extra power points.
Kieser	I'll take some details, then I'll arrange to come out and look at the site, if that's OK?
Hooper	Yes, thanks …

1 Ms Hooper intends to run a business in Würzburg.
2 There are no lights in the building yet.
3 Ms Hooper wants to display photographs in the building.
4 The building was formerly used to store goods in.
5 The building needs structural repairs.
6 Ms Hooper wants to install audio-visual equipment.
7 Elektro-Kieser designs and installs lighting systems for its customers.

ADVISING CUSTOMERS

3 Contact information for a new customer

Before you listen to the CD: What information does your firm need from a new customer? Design a form in your exercise book or on a computer.

Then listen to the conversation between Klaus Kieser and Clara Hooper and fill in your form.

4 Role-play: customer details

Use the zigzag diagram to role-play a telephone conversation between an electrical contractor and a new customer. The language in the box will help you.

Elektriker/in

- Fragen Sie nach den Wünschen des Kunden/der Kundin.
- Bitten Sie um eine Beschreibung des Gebäudes.
- Bejahen Sie die Frage: Sie sind in allen Aspekten der Elektroinstallation erfahren. Fragen Sie nach dem Firmennamen.
- Fragen Sie nach dem Namen des Anrufers.
- Bitten Sie ihn/sie darum, den Nachnamen zu buchstabieren.
- Sie brauchen eine Telefonnummer.
- Bedanken Sie sich. Ihr Chef wird sich bald melden.

Kunde/Kundin

- Sie brauchen eine Elektroinstallation in einem alten Gebäude.
- Es handelt sich um eine Lagerhalle mit ca. 1800 m² Fläche. Sie brauchen neue Leuchtstoffröhren (*strip lighting*). Fragen Sie, ob die Firma den Auftrag übernehmen kann.
- Die Firma heißt Logistic Solutions.
- Sie heißen Mike/Michelle Chambers.
- Antworten Sie.
- Ihre Handynummer lautet 0178 39133094.
- Bedanken Sie sich und verabschieden Sie sich.

LANGUAGE

Talking to a customer

I'll just take some details.
What's the best number to reach you on?
Yes, we can do that for you.
I'm afraid that's not our area.
I could come next Thursday.
How does … suit you?
Can we make it a bit later/earlier?

What's the address?
Do you have a fax number?
That won't be a problem.
I recommend that you try … instead.
How about on / next / the following … ?
I can't make that, I'm afraid.
Yes, (*Zeit*) on (*Tag/Datum*) will be fine.

! In English: 0438 279942 = 'oh four three eight, two seven nine (or double-nine) four two'

ADVISING CUSTOMERS

5 Making an appointment

Klaus Kieser arranges an appointment to visit Clara Hooper's premises. Listen and write down the date and time of the appointment.

> **TIP**
>
> **Wie Sie beim Hören mehr verstehen**
>
> Auch beim Hörverstehen macht Übung den Meister. Nutzen Sie daher jede Gelegenheit, Englisch zu hören. Folgende Tipps sollen Ihnen dabei helfen:
> - Lesen Sie die Aufgabenstellung vorher genau durch. Sie enthält bereits Hinweise, worum es im Text geht.
> - Nutzen Sie vorhandene Bilder. Sie liefern weitere Informationen zur Situation.
> - Konzentrieren Sie sich beim ersten Hören nur auf die Informationen, die für die Lösung der Aufgabe wichtig sind.
> - Hören Sie sich den Text ein zweites Mal an. Machen Sie sich Notizen und schließen Sie Informationslücken.
> - *Intelligent guessing*: Versuchen Sie, unbekannte Ausdrücke aus dem Kontext zu erschließen.
> - Geben Sie nicht auf und lassen Sie sich von zu schnellen Sprechern nicht entmutigen.

6 Partner file: arranging a site visit

Work with a partner to find a suitable day and time for a site visit.

Student A   Turn to file 2 on page 127.
Student B   Turn to file 7 on page 130.

7 Lighting options

Match the photos (a–d) to the descriptions (1–4).

a halogen lamp   b LED lamp   c light bulb   d fluorescent tube

1   This type of lamp makes light by heating a metal wire to a high temperature. They are cheap to make but very inefficient.
2   This type of lamp passes electricity through a gas-filled tube to make light. They are available as long, straight tubes or as short, curly tubes designed to replace a round bulb.
3   This type of lamp uses a thin tungsten wire in a gas-filled bulb. The gas allows it to operate at a higher temperature and give more light.
4   This type of lamp passes electricity through a solid semiconductor to make light. They operate at low temperatures and have no easily breakable parts.

ADVISING CUSTOMERS

8 | Customer requirements

Lesen Sie den Text und machen Sie sich stichpunktartig Notizen auf Deutsch zu den folgenden Fragen.

1. Warum will die Kundin die Leuchtstofflampen in ihrer Galerie ersetzen?
2. Welche drei Anforderungen stellt die Kundin an die neue Galeriebeleuchtung?
3. Warum schlägt Herr Kieser Dimmer vor?
4. Was macht Herr Kieser, bevor er die möglichen Lösungen mit der Kundin bespricht?
5. Welche Leuchtmittel schlägt Herr Kieser vor?
6. Welche Vorbehalte hat die Kundin gegen diese Lösung?
7. Wie versucht Herr Kieser die Kundin zu überzeugen?
8. Was verspricht Herr Kieser, um die letzten Zweifel der Kundin zu zerstreuen?

Hooper … Now, this large space is going to be the gallery. The another room, through that single door, is going to be my studio and office.

Kieser At the moment you've got fluorescent tube lighting. You want to take that out, is that right?

Hooper Yes, that's right. The tube lighting is wrong for a gallery. I'm going to need spotlights to display the photographs properly.

Kieser I see. So you want directional lighting. We'll discuss solutions in a moment. What else?

Hooper Well, I want to change the lighting level for different exhibitions. And maybe to have some lights less bright than others.

Kieser Right, you need a lot of control over the lighting. I suggest that you use dimmer switches. That way you can control the light levels precisely.

Hooper OK, good.

Kieser Is there anything else?

Hooper Well … we're an environmentally friendly business – I'm a nature photographer – so low power use is important.

Kieser So you need energy efficient lighting … Well that gives me a good idea of your requirements. I'll draw up a quick plan of your current lighting, then we can discuss solutions.

Hooper Great.

…

Kieser Right. Let's look at a lighting plan that will provide what you need. First of all, can I suggest that you use LED lighting?

Hooper Hmm … I'm not sure about that. Isn't LED lighting rather cold and harsh?

Kieser Oh, no. Modern LEDs are very versatile. The latest warm-white LEDs produce a very pleasant light.

Hooper Why LEDs, though? Why not compact fluorescent lamps?

Kieser Well, LEDs are up to 50 % more energy efficient than compact fluorescent lamps, and up to 90 % more efficient than tungsten halogen spotlights. They also generate very little heat.

Hooper Really? … Alright, that sounds good. How many will I need?

Kieser Well, the gallery space is eight by six metres, that's 46 square metres, so I suggest 24 LED lights. I'd suggest four parallel rows of six lights. The two central rows will be recessed downlights on one dimmer switch; they'll provide ambient light. The left and right-hand rows will provide directional light. They'll have a dimmer switch each. They will be track lights, so you can adjust the angle and position of each light to achieve the best lighting for the photos. What do you think?

Hooper Well, it sounds good in principle, but I need to see these LED lights in operation, because I'm still not sure they're exactly what I want.

Kieser I'll arrange that for you. We've just installed some for another customer.

ADVISING CUSTOMERS

UNIT 3

9 Drawing a lighting plan

Mr Kieser's lighting sketch shows the current layout of the lighting in Clara Hooper's premises. Use information from the dialogue in exercise 8 to draw a new lighting plan with the features that the customer wants. If you use symbols, you must also produce a key.

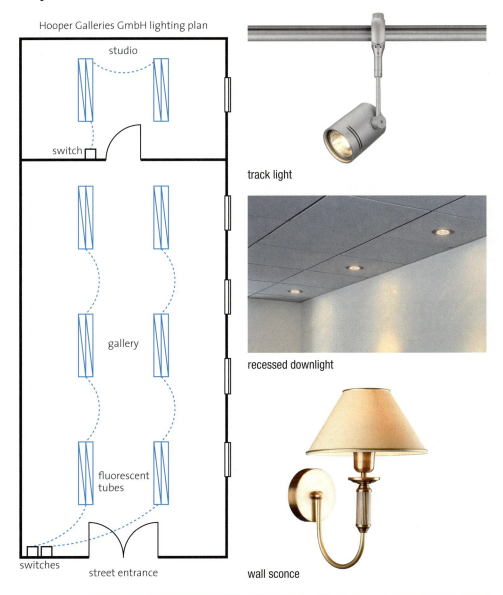

Hooper Galleries GmbH lighting plan — studio, switch, gallery, fluorescent tubes, switches, street entrance

track light

recessed downlight

wall sconce

TIP Sie können CAD-Symbole Online finden (Suchen Sie nach: symbols for lighting fixtures), z. B.: http://www.archblocks.com/archblocks-cad-blocks-and-products-previews/autocad-electrical-symbols-library-preview.

35

UNIT 3 ADVISING CUSTOMERS

10 Role-play: comparing specifications

Work with a partner to role-play a conversation between a factory owner and an electrical contractor. The language in the box below may help you.

Student A: You are the customer. You own a factory which uses 200 fluorescent tube lights. You want a more energy-efficient alternative but are concerned about the cost and labour of replacing all the lights at once. Ask questions about the costs and labour.

Student B: You are the electrical contractor. Use the information from the table to answer the customer's questions and convince him/her.

	fluorescent tube	LED tube
Price	€7.00	€60.00
Power	36 W	15 W
Power for 1 day (12 hours)	432 Wh (watt hours)	180 Wh
Power for 1 year	157.68 kWh (kilowatt hours)	65.70 kWh
Ballast power	18 W	not required
Total power for 1 year	236.52 kWh	65.70 kWh
Total cost @ €0.30 kWh	€70.96	€19.71
Total labour for 1 year	5 minutes (replace tube)	15 minutes (disconnect ballast and replace tube)
Total power for 10 years	2365.20 kWh	657.00 kWh
Total cost @ €0.30 kWh	€709.60	€197.10
Total labour for 10 years	50 minutes	15 minutes (no ongoing maintenance)

LANGUAGE

Advising a customer

Contractor
Can I advise you to … ?
If you only look at the upfront cost, …
On the other hand, if you take … into account, then …
If you compare power usage, you'll find that …
Over the course of a year, what that means is …
If we assume an electricity tariff of …, then …
Looking at the longer term, …
There'll be labour costs, too.
The … system is more suitable.
Yes, but it uses less power.
In a year you can save …
Because no further maintenance is required, …

Customer
I'm not sure about that.
Why do you say that?
What about … ?
Will it reduce my electric bill?
What about maintenance?
It sounds good in principle, but …
Really?
Please give me an estimate.
It's also more expensive.
How much will I save?
How much is that over ten years?
Alright, you've convinced me.

WEBCODE
TEMU0301

ADVISING CUSTOMERS

UNIT 3

11 A dissatisfied customer

KMK

Zwei Wochen nach Einbau der Beleuchtungsanlage reklamiert Frau Hooper, dass der Dimmer der versenkten LED Lampen ein lautes brummendes Geräusch macht. Herr Kieser überprüft den Dimmer und stellt einen Kurzschluss im Schalter fest. Die beiden anderen Schalter in der Galerie sind ebenfalls defekt. Er bittet den Hersteller per E-Mail um Ersatz.

Übertragen Sie Herrn Kaisers E-Mail in Ihr Heft und vervollständigen Sie es. Die Hinweise unten helfen Ihnen dabei.

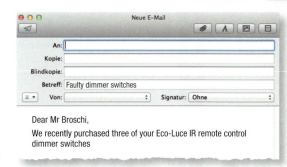

Betreff: Faulty dimmer switches

Dear Mr Broschi,
We recently purchased three of your Eco-Luce IR remote control dimmer switches

TIP: Wie man eine geschäftliche E-Mail auf Englisch schreibt

Betreff:	Eine kurze Beschreibung des Anliegens, z.B. *Faulty dimmer switches*
Anrede:	*Dear Mr Smith/Ms Smith* (Person bekannt)
	Dear Sir or Madam (Person unbekannt)
Haupttext:	Die erste Zeile immer mit einem Großbuchstabe anfangen.
	Den Text klar in Absätze gliedern, z.B.
	1. Absatz Hintergrundinfos
	2. Absatz Problembeschreibung
	3. Absatz Lösungsvorschlag
	Den Text mit einer Höflichkeitsformel abschließen.
Schlussformel:	*Yours sincerely/faithfully*
	Kind regards (weniger formell, immer häufiger gebraucht)
	+ Ihr Name, Stellung und Firma

LANGUAGE: Making a written complaint

Giving background information
We recently ordered … from you.
You recently installed … at our premises.

Describing the problem
Our customers complained that …
Our technician tested the … and found that …
The … proved to be faulty.
After installation, we found that …

Suggesting a solution
I am returning the … to you for inspection.
Please send us (a) replacement … as soon as possible.
Please refund the cost of the … .
Please send your engineer/technician to inspect the … without delay.

Polite phrases to finish off
Please do not hesitate to contact me if you require further information.
I look forward to hearing from you.

UNIT 3 — ADVISING CUSTOMERS

GRAMMAR

The *will-future* and the *going-to-future*

1. The lighting plan **will provide** what you need.
2. LED downlights **will give** your premises a modern look.
3. I hope that the lights **will bring out** the full quality of my photos.
4. **I'll find** those brochures for you. It **won't** (**will not**) **take** long.
5. Ms Hooper **is going to open** a new gallery.
6. Look at those dark clouds. There**'s going to be** a thunderstorm.

- Das *will-future* nimmt man für allgemeine Vorhersagen (1, 2) und für Vermutungen (3) über die Zukunft, oft nach Ausdrücken wie *I think*, *I believe*, *I'm sure*, *I hope*, *I suppose*, *I expect*, *perhaps*, *probably* …
  Das *will-future* steht ferner für spontane Entschlüsse, Angebote und Versprechen (4).

- Mit dem *going-to-future* spricht man über Absichten oder Pläne (5). Man verwendet es auch, wenn etwas sehr wahrscheinlich geschehen wird, weil es bereits Anzeichen dafür gibt (6).

12 Practice

A Complete the speechbubbles with the correct future form of the verb.

1. Hold on! I (help) you.
2. Careful! The books (fall). Oh, too late.

B Clara Hooper and her friend, Tom, are discussing the plan for the new gallery with Mr Kieser. Replace the verbs in brackets using a form of the future that fits best.

Clara I've made up my mind, Tom. I (open[1]) the photo gallery in Würzburg, not in Bonn.
Tom That's settled then. By the way, I think you (need[2]) at least four rooms.
Clara Look at the plan, I'm sure there (be[3]) enough space. And this room (be[4]) my office. What do you think?
Tom Hm … OK, perhaps you (not need[5]) more space for your office. What about the lighting?
Kieser I (draw up[6]) a quick plan of the lighting – it (not take[7]) a minute.
Clara Excuse me, Mr Kieser. Tom, (you/stay[8])? Didn't say you had an appointment with a customer? Just look at the clock, you (be[9]) late.
Tom Yes, I'd better hurry. I (call[10]) you later, dear. Bye. Bye, Mr Kieser.
Kieser Bye.
Clara Now, Mr Kieser, how many downlights do you think we (need[11])?
Kieser Well, it all depends whether you (have[12]) additional windows in the showroom.
Clara Hm … Herr Sander, the architect, isn't sure if he (be able[13]) to fit in extra windows.
Kieser So we'd better arrange a site meeting with Herr Sander first. Tomorrow I (visit[14]) the Light & Building fair in Frankfurt. But I (be[15]) free for the rest of the week.

KMK exam practice

13 Mediation

Sie nehmen mit mehreren Auszubildenden am „Leonardo Programm" bei Somar Electrics UK teil. Ein deutscher Teilnehmer gibt Ihnen folgenden Bericht mit der Bitte, ihm die technischen Daten auf Deutsch in einer Tabelle zusammenzustellen.

Vorgaben: 1. Sicherheit; 2. Energieeffizienz; 3. Geschwindigkeit; 4. Reichweite; 5. Aufladezeit; 6. Beleuchtung; 7. Funktion des Smartphones; 8. Beifahrersitz

You do it with a smartphone

For the first time Cathy is coming along to London. I fold out the pillion seat, the footrests automatically move into position. I place the smartphone in the mount which is in the centre of the handlebars and the immobilizer and the anti-theft protection are deactivated. I start the motor – you can't hear the slightest noise – and off we go. The smartphone is now the control and navigation centre. It shows that we've reached the top speed of 45 km/h. It also displays the range and the battery charge level. Thanks to the battery's capacity of 80 Ah, we could go on a day trip of 100 kilometers. We're going to have a picnic in Hyde Park and explore the smart drive kit which allows us to use online services. Should we forget where we parked the vehicle the GPS tracking app will help us identify its position.

Yes, we're talking about the new Daimler Smart escooter. Cathy is no longer afraid of joining me on my trips as she used to be when I still had the old scooter. She feels safer on the Smart escooter because it's equipped with ultra-modern safety features of a kind rarely seen even on modern motorcycles. These include an anti-lock braking system (ABS) specially adapted for a two-wheeler. There is the airbag integrated in the panelling beneath the handlebar. And a warning triangle is flashing in the rear-view mirror when vehicles are not visible in the "blind spot" of the rear-view. As to visibility, the front headlamp, the backlight and the brake light are equipped with state-of-the-art LED technology.

To brake the Smart escooter safely, just one touch suffices to retard both the front and rear wheel simultaneously. This task is performed by the wheel hub motor in the rear wheel, which normally propels the scooter forwards. When the brakes are applied, the motor becomes a generator whose resistance provides the required braking effect. The resulting braking energy is converted into electrical energy and stored in the scooter's lithium-ion battery. Unbelievable but true – there are even additional solar cells at the front. They support the charging of the battery while riding. Back home, I'll charge the battery at a household power socket. It'll take four to five hours. The charging socket is stored at the front while the charger itself is integrated in the scooter.

14 Produktion

Der Direktor von Somar Electrics will einen Teil der Dienstwagen durch E-Fahrräder (pedelecs) oder durch E-Roller (escooter) ersetzen. Jede Abteilung soll sich für eines der beiden Fahrzeuge entscheiden. Er gibt den Praktikanten folgenden Auftrag:

1. Erstellen Sie einen Bericht auf Englisch über Vor- und Nachteile der Fahrzeuge.
2. Geben Sie einen Rat für die Anschaffung.
3. Füllen Sie Wissenslücken durch Internetrecherchen.

Extra material

LEDs are an extremely useful lighting technology as they are low-power, low-heat and inexpensive to make. They are used in a wide variety of lighting applications, including TVs. This About.com article explains what is meant by 'LED TV'.

Important facts about 'LED' televisions
By Robert Silva

There has been a lot of confusion surrounding 'LED' televisions. To set the record straight, it is important to note that LED (light emitting diode) refers to the backlight system, not the chips that produce the image content.

LCD (liquid crystal display) chips and pixels do not produce their own light. In order for an LCD television to produce a visible image on a TV screen the LCD's pixels have to be backlit. 'LED' TVs use LED backlights with the LCD chips, rather than the fluorescent-type backlights used in older LCD TVs. They should properly be labelled LCD/LED TVs.

The are currently two main ways that LED backlighting is applied in LCD flat panel televisions.

One type of LED backlighting is called 'edge lighting'. In this method, a series LED backlights are placed along the outside edges of the screen. The light is then spread across the screen. The advantage of this method is that the LCD/LED TV can be made very thin. On the other hand, the disadvantage of edge lighting is that black levels are not as deep and the edge of the screen is often brighter than the centre of the screen.

The other type of LED backlighting is called 'full-array'. In this method, several rows of LEDs are placed behind the entire surface of the screen. The advantage is that these sets can use 'local dimming'. Local dimming means that each LED or a specific group of LEDs can be turned on and off independently, providing more control of brightness and darkness, depending on the picture being displayed. On the other hand, LCD TVs that use full-array LED backlighting are thicker than LCD TVs that use edge lighting.

If you are considering the purchase of an LED/LCD Television, find out which brands and models use the edge or full array method and take a look at each type when you go shopping to see which type of LED backlighting looks best to you.

The only true LED-only TVs are the ones you see in stadiums, arenas, other large events and on high-resolution advertising billboards.

15 Understanding the text

Read the text and decide whether the following statements are true (T), false (F) or not mentioned (NM) in the text.

1. In an LCD/LED television set, LEDs are used to form the image.
2. LCD images are not visible without a light source behind them.
3. LED-only television is not yet possible.
4. LCD/LED sets are usually more expensive than LCD-only sets.
5. Edge-lit sets are thinner than full-array sets.
6. 'Local dimming' means that the picture gets darker as the TV set gets older.
7. Full-array LCD/LED sets produce a better picture than edge-lit sets.
8. It is a good idea to compare different types of LCD television set before you buy.

16 Internet research

Go online to research another modern television technology, e.g. OLED TV, DLP TV.
Use the information to write a short article (not more than 120 words).
Remember to explain any abbreviations that you use.

Planning a job

UNIT 4

- Choosing tools, equipment and materials
- Organizing resources
- Dealing with organizational problems

1 Warm-up

A Identify the materials in these photos in German. Do you know the English names for these materials?

> aggregate • asphalt • cement • clay • gravel • limestone • sand

B Match the materials (1–7) with the descriptions (a–g).

1	Gravel	a	is used in blast furnaces to extract iron from its ore
2	Cement	b	is good for drainage
3	Asphalt	c	is sticky and viscous
4	Sand	d	is made of particles that are smaller than gravel but larger than silt
5	Aggregate	e	becomes hard when fired in a kiln
6	Limestone	f	improves traction on road surfaces
7	Clay	g	is combined with aggregate to form concrete

C Some of the statements above describe the characteristics (properties) of the materials. Other statements describe their uses. Copy this table into your exercise book and complete it.

Material	Property	Use
gravel		
cement		
…		

D Add the following materials to your table. Find out what their properties and uses are.

> ceramic • copper • glass • glue • polystyrene foam • silicon • steel

41

UNIT 4 PLANNING A JOB

2 Jörg's first jobs

Jörg Denzler is an apprentice civil engineer on exchange in the UK. His placement is with Cormack & Sons, a family business that specializes in pavements. The local council and a supermarket have contracted them for some jobs. Before the work starts, Mike Cormack gives Jörg a summary.

> Time frame: We start on Monday. On Friday our schedule gets hectic, so we need to finish the work on Thursday. We have four days to do three jobs!
>
> **1. Amersham Drive (Team A)**
> We have to replace the road surface and the binder underneath. It's 630m^2, an easy job. Straight, flat road – just lots of potholes. Should take us 2 days, max. It'll cost about £4 per square metre. We can recycle the old road surface to save money! One thing though: Lots of traffic on that road. Site safety is a priority!
>
> **2. The supermarket (Team B)**
> There's a wasteland near the new supermarket site. Lots of grass and weeds. We need to clear it and lay down some new paving blocks and make a parking area. It will take about 20 hours to prepare flat bedding, and 15 for the rest of the work. It will cost about twice as much as the Amersham Drive job. Team A and Team C will join this job when they finish their own work. I'm a bit worried about time. The work is precise. We can't make any mistakes!
>
> **3. The footpath (Team C)**
> The path is between a footbridge and a park. 56 metres of old tarmac. We need to replace it with concrete flagstones (50 x 50 x 3.5 cm) and edging. The ground is very uneven but the path is narrow – only two metres wide. We'll use 5 tonnes of sand to create a flat surface. I hope you enjoy screeding – we have to spread the sand all the way along the path. We can do it in 3 days unless it rains! It'll be about £10 per m^2 for materials and another £5 per m^2 for equipment and labour.

A Copy the table below into your exercise books and complete it with information from the text.

Site	Type of work	Duration	Cost	Problems
Amersham Drive				
the supermarket				
the footpath				

B Which job does each diagram represent? Produce a key (1–5) using the phrases in the box.

binder • bedding • edging • paving blocks • road surface • sand screeded to correct level

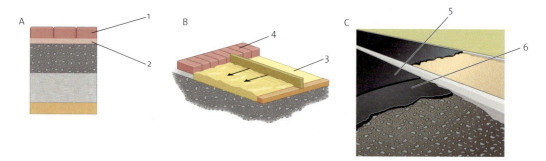

PLANNING A JOB

UNIT 4

3 The materials

Which paving materials do you think Mike will need for each job? Which are suitable/unsuitable? Read the descriptions and discuss with a partner.

 Concrete flags / slabs. Available in various colours, shapes and sizes. Reasonable prices. Quick and easy to lay. Ideal for pavements.

 Concrete block paving. Not usually bigger than 250 x 200mm. Midprice, and available in a range of colours and sizes. Must be laid correctly – can be time-consuming. Good for drives, paths, patios and commercial sites. Low maintenance and highly durable.

 Bituminous macadam. OK for roads, drives, larger footpaths and forecourts. Not suitable in gardens. Vulnerable to oil or petrol spillages which dissolve the binder. Relatively cheap, usually black in colour but also available in red and even green.

 Duckstones. Large, rounded pebbles, usually from a beach or river. Huge variety of size, shape and colour. Reasonable price. Very easy to lay. Low maintenance, but can be slippy when wet.

 Plain concrete. Cheap. Easy to lay, hard to get rid of. Ugly, but good for areas where a cheap, low maintenance pavement is required.

4 Tools and equipment

Identify the illustrations with the words in the box. Then choose the tools and equipment teams A, B and C will need for each job.

Example: *Team A will need …*

> block cutter • bulldozer • calculator • cement mixer • crane • jib • planing machine • ruler • theodolite • wheelbarrow

43

UNIT 4 — PLANNING A JOB

5 The plans

Mike gives Jörg a rough outline of the key tasks for each job. Decide which job they are part of and which team is responsible for the job. Then put the tasks in each outline into the correct order.

1
Establish a diversion for traffic
Relay binder and surface
Remove surface and binder
Melt down old surface material
Mark out site with cones
Apply road markings
Allow to cool and harden

2
Spread 100-150mm of concrete
Lay paving blocks in herringbone pattern
Apply bedding layer (mortar)
Mark out the paving area
Remove all weeds and organic matter
Dig out the area to a depth of 400mm

3
Lay paving flags
Place sand on prepared sub-base
Screed the sand to the correct level
Lightly compact the sand
Level out using shovels and rakes
Pile sand in mounds along path

6 Problems

It's day one of the job projects. Jörg has some problems to deal with.

Work with a classmate. Read the following situations and do the tasks below.

a Some residents of Amersham Drive email Jörg. They want to talk to Mike about the noise from the road works.
b The local school asks you to put more barriers up around the Park Road site, as it's close to their playground.
c Team A tells you the road has serious structural defects and will need much more work than was planned.
d Some of the block paving for the supermarket is damaged on delivery. They'll need more soon.
e The local council called and left a message. They're going to carry out a site inspection tomorrow and would like Mike to be there.
f Jörg forgot to remind Mike to pick up his children from school.
g One of the foremen is angry about his overtime and wants to meet with Mike.
h Jörg's partner left a voicemail message on his mobile. He doesn't know what it was about.

A Organize the problems into three categories: urgent, high priority, low priority.
B Which problem should Jörg tell Mike about first?

7 Explaining plans

Axel Schröder ist ein neuer Praktikant aus Deutschland. Sie sind Jörg und kümmern sich um ihn. Axel bittet Sie, ihm das Wichtigste von Mikes Planung (siehe Aufgabe 2) auf Deutsch zusammenzufassen.

44

PLANNING A JOB

UNIT 4

8 Bad news from the building site

KMK

A Übernehmen Sie mit einem Partner die Rollen von Jörg und Mike und besprechen Sie die Probleme. Tauschen Sie anschließend die Rollen.

Jörg	Mike
Amersham Drive: Schwieriger als vorgesehen. Vorarbeiter hat die Arbeit eingestellt. Anlieger über Lärm verärgert.	Jörg soll hinfahren und mit dem Vorarbeiter sprechen. Er braucht die Anlieger nicht anzurufen, solange die Arbeiten eingestellt sind. Er soll über Möglichkeiten zur Lärmdämmung nachdenken.
Park Road: Beschwerde der örtlichen Schule. Sie wollen mehr Sicherheitsabsperrungen vor dem Baugelände.	Jörg soll sich um die Beschwerde kümmern und das Problem mit dem Team besprechen.
Supermarkt: Viele Betonpflastersteine bei Lieferung beschädigt. Jetzt nicht genug vorhanden.	Jörg soll dem Lieferanten (Terry Garrick) sofort anrufen. Dieser soll die beschädigte Ware schnellstmöglich ersetzen.
Fußweg: Ms Carter vom Bauamt wünscht, den Bauplatz morgen um 10:30 Uhr zu besichtigen.	Jörg soll dabei sein. Bitte Ms Carter benachrichtigen und Termin bestätigen.

B Schreiben Sie ein kurzes Memo an Mike mit Vorschlägen zur Lärmdämmung.

C Übernehmen Sie mit einem Partner die Rollen von Jörg und Terry Garrick und führen Sie ein Telefongespräch. Tauschen Sie anschließend die Rollen.

D Verfassen Sie eine SMS-Nachricht an Ms Carter und bestätigen Sie den Termin.

9 Partner file: a change of plan

The current schedule needs to change. Look at the language box on the next page. Then work with a partner.

Student A: Turn to file 3 on page 127.
Student B: Turn to file 8 on page 130.

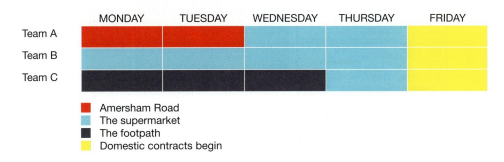

45

UNIT 4

PLANNING A JOB

> **LANGUAGE**
>
> **Discussing plans**
>
> Why doesn't Team A work with Team B?
> We need to finish Amersham Road by the end of the week.
> The supermarket is an urgent job.
> That will/won't work.
> That's a good/bad idea.
> Team C and Team B can work together.
> Three days is/isn't enough time.
> I think we'll need more/less time.
> How long do you estimate that the job will take?
>
> Team A could work with Team B.
> We must finish the job in four days.
> The footpath is not a top priority.
> How about …?/Why don't we …?
> Has anyone got any good ideas?
> Team C can join Team B.
> Two days is long enough.
> How can we speed up the work?
> That's probably long enough/too long.

10 The new plan

08

Mike discusses the problems on Amersham Drive with the council and tells Jörg how plans have changed. Listen and draw up a new schedule for the work.

11 Charts and diagrams

A Label the pictures with the words in the box.

bar chart • flow chart • Gantt chart • line graph • pie chart • table

1

2

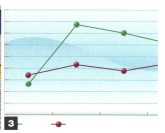
3

4

5

6

B Which diagram is best for:

1. organizing figures / statistics?
2. comparing levels?
3. showing changes over time?
4. showing stages / steps in a process?
5. planning a project?
6. displaying proportions?

WEBCODE
TEMU0401

PLANNING A JOB

UNIT 4

| 12 | **Talking about traffic** |

Look at the chart below and complete the sentences with a suitable verb. The language box below may help you.

Between 3am and 6am the traffic …¹ sharply. The traffic …² in the morning and the evening. After 6pm there is a sharp …³ in the amount of traffic. On Sundays the traffic …⁴ sharply in the morning and …⁵ in the afternoon. The traffic levels …⁶ throughout the week. The busiest time of week is 6pm on Mondays.

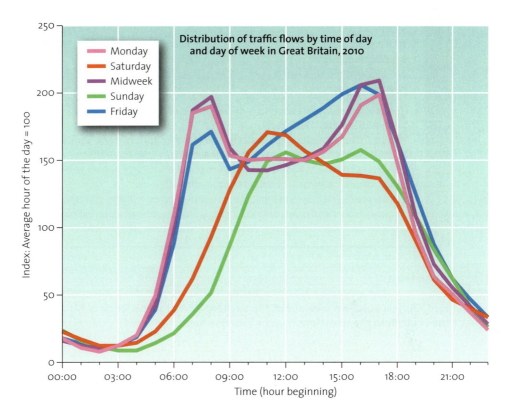

Describing graphs

to increase; an increase	zunehmen; eine Zunahme
to rise; a rise	(an)steigen; ein Anstieg
to decrease; a decrease	abnehmen; eine Abnahme
to drop; a drop	fallen, abstürzen; ein Rückgang
to change; a change	sich ändern; eine (Ver-)Änderung
to fluctuate; a fluctuation	schwanken; eine Schwankung
sudden, suddenly	plötzliche/r/s, plötzlich
dramatic, dramatically	dramatische/r/s, dramatisch
drastic, drastically	drastische/r/s, drastisch
steady, steadily	stetige/r/s, stetig

47

PLANNING A JOB

GRAMMAR

Question formation

1. Jörg **is** working at C&S.
   Mike **will** take Jörg out to the worksites.
   The job **could** be finished in June.

   Is Jörg working at C&S?
   Will Mike take him out to the worksites?
   Could the job be finished in June?

2. Mike **works/worked** at C&S.

   Does/did Mike **work** at C&S?

3. Jörg **did** a good job.
   He **had** a lot of fun.

   Did Jörg do a good job?
   Did he have a lot of fun?

4. Jörg **is/was** on exchange in the UK.

   Is/Was Jörg on exchange in the UK?

5. Who helped Tom?
   Who did Tom help?
   What caused the accident?
   What did the accident cause?

   Wer hat Tom geholfen?
   Wem hat Tom geholfen?
   Was verursachte *den* Unfall?
   Was verursachte *der* Unfall?

- Steht im Aussagesatz ein Hilfsverb (*be, do, have, can, will*), steht in der Frage das Hilfsverb vor dem Subjekt (1).
- Steht im Aussagesatz kein Hilfsverb, wird in der Frage eine Form von *do* vor das Subjekt gestellt. Das Vollverb steht im Infinitiv (2).
- Sind *do* und *have* Vollverben wird die Frage mit einer Form von *do* gebildet (3).
- Das Vollverb *be* wird nicht mit *do* umschrieben (4).
- Beachten Sie den Bedeutungsunterschied bei Fragen mit *who* und *what* (5). Fragen nach dem Subjekt (Wer oder Was?) werden ohne *do/does/did* gebildet. Fragen nach dem Objekt (Wen/Wem oder Was?) werden mit *do/does/did* gebildet.

13 Practice

Jörg fills in a questionnaire about the exchange programme. Look at his answers and then complete the questions in your exercise book.

1. you / company / from?
   I'm from Beckmann Construction.

2. you / study?
   I'm studying at the Mannheim University of Applied Sciences.

3. you / like best / about / the exchange?
   What I liked best about the exchange were the field trips and practical studies.

4. your / plans / for the future?
   I don't have any plans at the moment.

5. you / choose / our course?
   Because it wasn't too expensive or too long.

6. you / find out about / our course?
   A colleague told me about it.

KMK exam practice

14 Rezeption: Hörverstehen

Sie sind Linda Meissner, Praktikantin bei BIO POWER in Manchester. Drei Gruppen chinesischer Fachkräfte werden auf die Inbetriebnahme mehrerer Anlagen in China vorbereitet. Ihre Aufgabe ist es u.a., die Terminkalender zu führen. John Stone, Projektleiter in China, ruft sie am Mittwoch, den 4. Juli, 20.. an, um sich über den Stand der Dinge zu informieren.

Machen Sie Notizen zu den folgenden Punkten. Sie hören das Telefongespräch mehrfach.

1. End of test phase
2. Beginning and end of operator training
3. Arrival of maintenance trainer
4. Beginning of maintenance training
5. Beginning of supervisor training
6. Length of supervisor training
7. Return of participants to China
8. Opening date of first plant

15 Hörverstehen

Schreiben Sie eine Telefonnotiz auf Deutsch an Dr. Schneider.

TELEFONNOTIZ

Aufgenommen von:

Gesprächspartner:

Betreff: Inbetriebnahme der ersten Anlage BIO X3

Inhalt:

Datum:

Funktion:

16 Produktion

Sie holen Herrn Wang am Flughafen ab. Bitten Sie die Dame am Informationsstand um eine Durchsage auf Englisch mit folgendem Inhalt:

Durchsage für Herrn Jonathan Wang aus Peking.
Fluggesellschaft: British Airways; Flugnummer 4674
Abholung durch Linda Meissner
Treffpunkt: Meeting Point im Erdgeschoß

17 Interaktion

Übernehmen Sie die Rollen von Linda und Mr Wang, der kein Deutsch spricht.

Linda Sie erkennen Mr Wang, Sie stellen sich vor und begrüßen ihn. Heißen Sie ihn in Manchester willkommen. Fragen Sie, ob er einen guten Flug hatte und ob Sie ihn zum Hotel fahren dürfen. Sagen Sie ihm, dass ihr Auto auf dem Parkplatz steht.

Mr Wang Er freut sich, Lindas Bekanntschaft zu machen und bedankt sich, dass sie ihn abholt. Er bittet sie, ihn zum Marriott Hotel zu fahren. Zuvor möchte er sich noch ein paar Zeitungen kaufen.

Extra material

18 Understanding the text

A Match the highlighted words in the text with the following definitions.

a broken under a weight into small pieces
b protected from temperature change
c to get longer or wider without suffering damage
d inclined parts of a road / hills and slopes
e pressed to make the material more solid
f to last or endure
g stiff / unable to bend
h to lose control of a car's movement, especially on ice
i made stronger
j the opposite of "rigid"

How do you build a road?

Engineers need to plan the route of a new road carefully. It's important to know how many vehicles are going to use the road, how heavy they will be and how fast they are going to travel. These factors affect the design of the bends and gradients[1] too.

A normal car has little effect on a road surface. The volume of commercial traffic (HGVs especially) is most important. When we have all the data about the expected levels of commercial traffic, we can decide how thick the road needs to be to withstand[2] the daily pressure of the traffic.

Every road needs to possess certain qualities. It must be smooth and strong. It must resist weight, stretch[3], wear and skidding. To achieve this we build the road up in layers. But first the ground must be cleared, shaped (hills flattened, hollows filled in) and compacted[4]. When the ground is level, it must be rolled to make it completely firm. After we strengthen the ground with broken stone rolled into the surface, we lay the "pavement".

The lowest layer of the pavement, known as the sub-base, is made from crushed[5] stone or gravel and can be up to 600mm thick. Next comes the basecourse. The thickness of the basecourse is determined by the weight and volume of projected traffic. Finally comes the wearing course. It has to have some special properties. It mustn't stretch or crack, and it must be skid[6] resistant too. There are two kinds:

A concrete pavement consists of slabs or a continuous layer of concrete, sometimes reinforced[7] with steel. Because the material is rigid[8], the slabs have flexible[9] joints to allow for expansion/contraction caused by temperature changes, for example in summer and winter.

"Blacktop" pavement is different. The roadbase is 250mm of dense macadam, rolled asphalt, concrete or waterbound macadam. Mechanical pavers spread and roll the asphalt. The material must be hot so it is usually delivered to the site in insulated[10] lorries.

B Put the information in the text into a ten-stage flow chart in your exercise books.

Think about …

- The information you need before the construction of the road can start. (Stages 1–4)
  Stage 1: Calculate the volume of traffic.
  Stage 2: Calculate the …
  …
- The sequence of the road construction. (Stages 5–10)
  Stage 5: Clear, …

Situations

General information

Abbey Logistics is moving from a site in the town centre of Battle to a new and bigger site in a business park on the outskirts of the town. They are looking for tenants to take over the lease of their warehouse in the town centre. They have informed the town council and put adverts in various local and national newspapers. Since they are expecting a great number of applicants, they have installed a hotline call centre manned by three of their trainees.

1 At the call centre

Take over the roles below and act out telephone dialogues using the information on the role cards.

Roles A, B, C
Trainee / Call centre operatives
- Take the calls of potential tenants and answer their questions with information from the Fact File.
- Ask what the callers how they intend to use the warehouse.
- Fill out a memo for each caller. (If you don't understand something, ask the caller to say it again more slowly or spell it.)

CALLER MEMO
- Name:
- Position:
- Contact data:
- Call details:
- Action:

Fact file

Company	Abbey Logistics; 15, Market Road
Town	Battle: 6.300 inhabitants; 17 miles from Hastings
Object	Old warehouse in town centre; repairs needed; floor space 1600 m2; large parking lot
Location	7, High Street, two miles from railway station
Availability	from 8th of March
Lease	£2.300 per month
Site visits	Monday, Wednesday, Friday, 5:30 p.m. to 7:30 p.m., or by arrangement
Contact	For further information call hotline (Tel.: 01424 773 721) Monday to Saturday 8:30 p.m. to 6:30 p.m.

Role D
Caller: Ms Anne Dobson
- Give your personal data.
  Event manager
  44, London Road; Battle
  Mobile: 0172 85 67 03 22
- You are interested in the following details:
  availability, floor space, rent per month, condition of object.
- You'd like to use the warehouse for business conventions, trade fairs and rock concerts.
- Try to arrange a site visit for 5.30 p.m. on Thursday afternoon.

Role E
Caller: Mr Hugh Marculewicz
- Give your personal data.
  Private investor
  3, Wilton Crescent, Belgravia, London SW1X
  Mobile: 0175 52 83 46 33
- You need some information:
  - distance of Battle from Hastings
  - number of inhabitants of Battle
  - exact location
- You'd like to convert the warehouse into a modern multiplex cinema centre.
- Arrange a site visit for Friday afternoon.

Role F
Caller: Mr Gordon Amery
- Give your personal data.
  Property developer
  17, Ingles Rd, Folkestone, CT20 2RR
  Mobile: 0195 55 09 81 47
- You are interested in the following details:
  floor space, size of parking lot, location, sale price
- You'd like to convert the warehouse into a fitness centre and a super disco.
- Arrange to meet with a manager from Abbey Logistics to discuss a sale price.

Situations

2   A public meeting at the town hall

Take over the roles below. Follow the instruction on your role-play cards and act out a meeting.

Role A
Mr Fred Thornton, mayor of Battle
- Welcome the participants of the meeting.
- Explain why you / the town council are interested in the future use of the warehouse.
  attractive town centre, more visitors, income from business tax, volume of traffic, reactions of residents, local businesses, noise
- Ask participants to introduce themselves and describe their plans for the warehouse.

Role B
Ms Susan Lennox, managing director of Abbey Logistics
- Thank Mr Thornton for the warm welcome.
- Thank the potential investors for coming to the meeting.
- Present the warehouse, its location and the neighborhood. Use photos and a street map of Battle from the Internet.

Role C
Ms Anne Dobson, event manager
- Introduce yourself and say what you do:
  organize events: boxing, kick-boxing, wrestling, beauty contests, trade fairs, rock concerts
- Say what you want to do with the warehouse and give reasons why this would be good for local residents and businesses.
- Invite participants to ask questions and try to answer them.

Role D
Mr Hugh Marculewicz, private investor
- Introduce yourself and say what you do:
  investments in hotels, restaurants; owner of 6 multiplex cinemas
- Say what you want to do with the warehouse and give reasons why this would be good for Battle town centre, local residents and businesses.
- Invite participants to ask questions and try to answer them.

Role E
Mr Gordon Amery, property developer
- Introduce yourself and say what you do:
  buy land, build office blocks, houses, shops; owner of a disco in Hastings
- Say what you want to do with the warehouse and give reasons why this would be good for Battle town centre, local residents and businesses.
- You will need financial support from town council:
  - no-interest loan
  - no local taxes for … years
- Invite participants to ask questions and try to answer them.

Role F, G, H, I, …
local residents / businesses
- Introduce yourself:
- Name (Mr / Mrs / Ms …)
  - Local resident / address
  - Owner of …
  - Teacher at …
- Complain to mayor:
  - not enough information/ time
- Ask the three applicants (C, D, E) critical questions about:
  rebuilding /conversion, noise, traffic, jobs, costs, unfair competition, crime, …
- Sum up and say which plan you think is best (if any).

3   Local media

A   You are a reporter for a local radio station. Tell your listeners about the meeting and interview some of the participants.

B   Write a letter to the local newspaper either for or against one of the plans for the warehouse. Give reasons.

Using tools and instruments

■ Trades and tools   ■ Portable power tools   ■ Workshop machines

UNIT 5

1 Warm-up

A What do they use tools for? Use the language in the box to make sentences.

Example: *A bricklayer uses tools to cut and lay bricks.*

| A(n) | bricklayer
car mechanic
carpenter
construction surveyor
electrician
mechatronic technician
plumber
welder | uses tools
to | build
cut and lay
cut, shape and join
diagnose and correct
install and repair
measure | angles and distances.
bricks.
electronic control systems.
mechanical problems.
metals and alloys.
pipework.
timber.
wiring and appliances. |

B Discuss with a partner: What do *you* use tools and instruments for?

53

USING TOOLS AND INSTRUMENTS

2 Leonardo: a student-exchange programme

German apprentices from the Gewerblich-Technische Schule Augsburg are taking part in an exchange programme with students at Hereford College of Technology in the West of England. This morning, German exchange students Jürgen and David are being shown around the workshop by local engineering students Clara and Darren.

A Make a list in English of all the tools mentioned in the dialogue.

Clara OK, so this is our general engineering workshop. You'll find just about any hand tool here.
We've got a range of different hand-saws – hacksaws, crosscut saws, coping saws and keyhole saws …
Then there's all these chisels …

Jürgen Err, just a moment, please, Clara. I don't know the names of all these tools in English. What's this called, for example?

Clara That's a hacksaw. What is it in German?

Jürgen In German it's called a *Handbügelsäge* or a *Metallsäge* – a 'metal saw', because it's used for cutting metal. And this one?

Clara That's a crosscut saw, for cutting timber.

Jürgen We call it a 'fox's tail', a *Fuchsschwanz*.

Darren Weird. It doesn't even look like a fox's tail …

Clara True, but we have strange names for tools in English too. What about these chisels, for cutting steel? Why are they called 'cold chisels'?

David I think it's because they're used to cut cold metal, rather than hot metal. We call them *Flachmeißel* in German.

Clara Yes, that makes sense, I suppose … Anyway, where were we?

Darren Hammers.

Clara Oh, yes. Hammers. We've got a few claw hammers, but these ball-peen hammers are more useful for engineering classes … Here's a rack of screwdrivers. There are a range of Phillips and slot-head screwdrivers in different sizes …

Darren Don't forget the spanners.

Clara No, I was coming to them. We've got open, ring and socket spanners, and of course we've got a full range of sockets.

David What about torque wrenches?

Darren The very precise, electronic torque wrenches are reserved for special projects, because they're expensive. We can use these click torque wrenches, but they've been mistreated over the years, so they're not very accurate.

Jürgen That's a nuisance. Don't you have rules for using the tools?

Clara Yes, of course. But not everyone follows them, unfortunately.

B Work with a partner. Complete your list of tools with the German equivalents.

Drehmomentschlüssel • Fuchsschwanz • Flachmeißel • Tischlerhammer (mit Kuhfuß) • verstellbarer Drehmomentschlüssel • Kreuzschlitzschraubendreher • Kugelhammer • Laubsäge • Handstichsäge • Handbügelsäge/Metallsäge • Maulschlüssel • Ringschlüssel • Schraubenschlüssel • Schraubendreher • Steckschlüssel • Steckschlüsselsatz

USING TOOLS AND INSTRUMENTS

3 Workshop rules

Join the sentence halves to make rules for the use of hand tools in the workshop. There is one ending you don't need. When you have finished, listen to check your answers.

1 Always seek instruction
2 Only use tools
3 You must not use
4 A hand tool should
5 An edged tool must be
6 Do not sharpen the tool yourself
7 You must return the clean tool
8 Report all missing or defective tools

a without the permission of the workshop supervisor.
b have a securely fixed handle.
c to the workshop technician or supervisor.
d to its correct position in the rack.
e sharp and ground to the correct cutting angle.
f defective tools.
g leave tools on the workbench.
h for their intended purpose.
i before using an unfamiliar tool.

4 A mechatronics workbench

A Identify the items on Darren's workbench.

B Use the table below to say what each tool or instrument is for. Sometimes there is more than one possible answer. Try to find all of them.

Example: *A file is for smoothing wood or metal.*

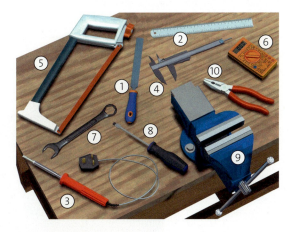

> ! I need a pair of pliers.
> *Ich brauche eine Zange.*
>
> Are these the pliers you need?
> *Ist das die Zange, die du brauchst?*
>
> a pair of …
> metal shears   *eine Blechschere*
> scissors   *eine Schere*

A(n)		is/are for		
file			bending	dimensions.
hacksaw			cutting	electrical circuits.
multimeter			gripping	metal or plastic.
pair of pliers			joining	nuts and bolts.
rule			loosening	objects.
screwdriver			measuring	screws.
soldering iron			smoothing	thickness.
spanner			testing	thin metal.
vernier calliper			tightening	wires.
vice				wood or metal.

USING TOOLS AND INSTRUMENTS

> **TIP**
>
> ### Wie man Fachvokabeln mit Hilfe des Internets übersetzt
>
> Wenn Sie eine Fachvokabel im zweisprachigen Wörterbuch nicht finden, können Sie natürlich in einem Online-Wörterbuch danach suchen. Werden Sie dort nicht fündig, sollten Sie nicht gleich aufgeben, sondern es mit ein paar Kniffen versuchen, z. B.:
>
> - einen deutschsprachigen Wikipedia-Artikel aufrufen und auf die englische Version umschalten.
> - bei Google das Wort durch Eingabe von Kontextwörtern (d. h. Wörtern, die normalerweise zusammen mit dem gesuchten Wort auftreten) suchen. Sie können auch versuchen, das englische Wort in deutschen Kontextwörtern zu suchen.
> - technische Seiten wie www.howstuffworks.com aufrufen, den Artikel für das Oberthema suchen und die englisch bezeichneten Teile anhand der Abbildungen erkennen.
>
> Sie möchten z. B. wissen, was „Entlötlitze" auf Englisch heißt. Rufen Sie den Artikel über Löten in Wikipedia auf und wechseln Sie zur englischprachigen Seite. Dort werden in dem Abschnitt über *desoldering* (Entlöten) auch *desoldering wicks* erwähnt. Die Google-Suche nach „*desoldering wicks* entlötlitze" bestätigt, dass es sich um das gesuchte Wort handelt.

5 Power tools

In der Cafetaria des College findet David im Tradesman Magazine einen Artikel über Elektrohandwerkzeuge. Er liest ihn, um sein technisches Englisch zu verbessern.

Lesen Sie den Zeitschriftenartikel auf der nächsten Seite. Machen Sie sich stichpunktartig Notizen auf Deutsch zu den folgenden Fragen.

1. Warum sollte der Profi preiswerte Heimwerkerwerkzeuge meiden?
2. Welche Vorteile haben Akku-Werkzeuge? Wann verwendet man sie?
3. Welche Extras sollte man beim Kauf einer Handbohrmaschine in Betracht ziehen?
4. Warum sind Säbelsägen bei Elektrikern und Bauarbeitern beliebt?
5. Welche Werkstoffe kann man mit einer Kreissäge schneiden?
6. Wodurch unterscheidet sich eine Elektrostichsäge von einer Säbelsäge?
7. Welche Einsatzbereiche hat eine Oberfräse?
8. Worauf sollte beim Kauf eines Elektrohobels geachtet werden?
9. Welche Arten von Heißklebepistolen gibt es?
10. Wie wird ein Nagelgerät angetrieben?

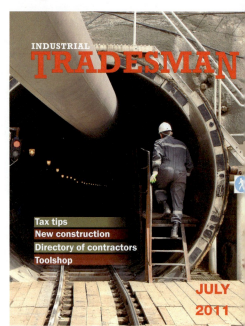

USING TOOLS AND INSTRUMENTS

UNIT 5

Portable power tools

Whether you are a DIY enthusiast or a professional, power tools are a vital part of your toolkit. Although there are lots of cheap tools on the market, it is worth paying a bit more for a good quality tool with a powerful motor and precision-made parts. Professional tools are designed for heavy-duty work and have a longer working life than hobby tools.

For light-duty work, a cordless, battery-powered tool may be a better option than one that requires access to mains voltage and has a flex that is easy to damage and may be a trip hazard in the workshop or on site.

Here are some of the tools that every craftsperson should have.

Power drill

A drill with a hammer action can bore holes in masonry and concrete. A drill with speed control, torque control and a reverse drive can also function as a power screwdriver so you don't have to buy a separate driver.

Router

This tool is used to cut slots and grooves and for shaping timber, hard plastics and soft metals. It can be adjusted to produce cuts of varying depth. There are hundreds of differently shaped bits which produce different profiles.

Reciprocating saw

The thin blade moves in a reciprocating (push-and-pull) motion. It can cut materials quickly, but it can't make precise cuts like a jigsaw. It is often used by electricians and builders on site to cut through walls.

Power planer

Planers are used to reduce the thickness of a piece of timber and give it a smooth surface. A planer has a flat steel plate and a wide blade. All planers should have a fine adjustment dial allowing you to remove just tenths of a millimetre from the surface of the timber.

Circular saw

The high-speed round blade is perfect for making straight cuts in timber; special blades are also available for cutting plastic, metal, masonry and even reinforced concrete.

Glue gun

Glue guns melt a stick of glue. The hot glue can stick together various materials, e.g. timber, fabric or plastics. There are different types of glue gun for high (190°C) and lower (120°C) temperatures.

Jigsaw

It looks similar to the reciprocating saw, but this is a precision tool that can cut complex shapes out of thin timber, plastic and metal. It is not suitable for making long, straight cuts. You must rest the saw on the material while you are cutting it.

Nail gun

Nail guns allow the carpenter to drive nails into timber or other materials far more quickly than with a hammer. Some nail guns use electricity, others use compressed air, a flammable gas such as butane, or even an explosive charge. All nailguns are dangerous – you must treat them with respect.

USING TOOLS AND INSTRUMENTS

6 Points to consider when choosing power tools

Complete the advice about choosing power tools using expressions from the box below. They are all in the text on the previous page.

> bits • blades • cordless • adjustment • heavy-duty • materials • powerful • precise • precision-made • professional • speed • toolkit • torque • working life

...¹ tools may be more expensive than hobby tools, but they can do ...² work and will have a longer ...³. Hobby tools have no place in the technician's ...⁴. More expensive tools have ...⁵ parts and will be more accurate. For ...⁶ and reliable work, that's what you need. Cheap ...⁷ may break off in the hole and cheap ...⁸ may shatter while you are cutting tough ...⁹.
...¹⁰ tools are more convenient than those which require a flex, but they are more expensive and may be less ...¹¹. Where a good finish is important, as in furniture making, you'll need tools which are capable of fine ...¹². For example, jigsaws should have ...¹³ control to cut different materials and power screwdrivers should have ...¹⁴ control to avoid overtightening.

7 Construction project

At Hereford College of Technology, a team of carpentry apprentices is working together on a construction project to build a garden shed.

Listen to the dialogue and decide which power tools they need for each stage of construction.

8 Role-play

Work with a partner and act out a dialogue. The language box below may help you.

Student A: You are the apprentice. Ask the supervisor for help with a job requiring a hand tool or a power tool.
Student B: You are the supervisor. Help the apprentice.

LANGUAGE

In the workshop

Apprentice	Supervisor
What tool should I use for this job?	You need to use a …
I need to … . What should I use?	You need a … for that.
Could you show me where the … is/are kept, please?	The … are kept in this toolstore / cabinet / drawer.
Could you show me how to adjust the speed, please?	Of course. Watch carefully: this is how you do it.
How do I adjust / change / set the …?	Look it up in the handbook.
… speed /torque /depth /direction?	Check the online instruction manual.
Thanks for your help.	You're welcome.

USING TOOLS AND INSTRUMENTS

9 Workshop machines

Which workshop machine should the apprentices use for the tasks below?

band saw   column drill   bench grinder   table saw

1 I need to remove these sharp burrs on the end of this steel pipe.
2 We need two metres of 60 x 60mm timber, but this timber is 120 x 60mm.
3 We need a 15mm diameter round hole in the bronze faceplate.
4 OK, now we need to cut a V-shaped section out of this steel tube.
5 The edge of this tool is damaged. It needs to be reground and sharpened.
6 We need to cut a centred groove along this piece of timber.

10 What's this for?

Use the language below to explain the function of each of the parts of the bench grinder.

Example: *The eye shield is used to protect your eyes.*

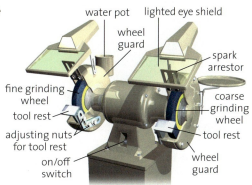

The … is used to	change	the piece that you are grinding.
	prevent	large amounts of material.
	cool	small amounts of material.
	protect	the angle of the tool rest.
	remove	the machine.
	start and stop	the cutting edge of the piece that you are grinding.
	support	the wheel coming into accidental contact with something.
	…	a fire in the workshop.
		your eyes.
		…

59

USING TOOLS AND INSTRUMENTS

11 How to use a column drill

KMK

Der Abteilungsleiter der Werkstatt führt einige neue Praktikanten in die Handhabung einer Ständerbohrmaschine ein.

Hören Sie seine Anweisungen und vervollständigen Sie Jürgens Notizen auf Englisch.

- *column drill speed chart*
  - *correct combination of ...* [1]
  - *on wall ...* [2]
- *Insert drill bits ...* [3]
- *Make sure ...* [4] *is centred in chuck.*
- *Place work on scrap piece of wood – no ...* [5], *protects ...* [6]
- *Clamp work with ...* [7]
- *Clear all objects ...* [8].
- *...* [9] *– use a cutting lubricant.*
- *Do not start column drill ...* [10]
- *...* [11]
- *Clean around drill.*

> **! Numbers**
>
> Be careful:
> four – fourteen – but: forty
> five – but: fifteen – fifty
> dt. 1 Milliarde = 1 billion
> 0 is pronounced nought, oh or zero.
> Points are used for decimals: 8.064
> (= Eight point oh six four)

12 Working with measuring instruments

Engineering projects require precise measurements. To take all the required measurements, engineering apprentices at Hereford College use both a vernier calliper and a micrometer.

digital vernier calliper

Give the following readings in numbers.

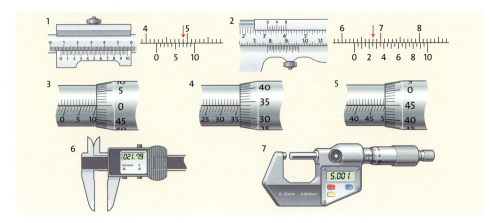

WEBCODE
TEMU0501

USING TOOLS AND INSTRUMENTS

TIP — Sprüche

He's not the sharpest tool in the box.	Er ist nicht das schärfste Messer in der Schublade.
If your only tool is a hammer, every problem looks like a nail.	Wer nur einen Hammer hat, für den ist jedes Problem ein Nagel.
A good craftsman doesn't blame his tools.	Ein guter Handwerker schiebt die Schuld nicht auf das Werkzeug.
You only need two tools in life: WD-40 to make things go, and duct tape to make them stop.	Eine scherzhafte Anspielung auf Stümperei (WD-40 – bekannte Schmierölmarke; duct tape – Isolierband)

GRAMMAR — Modals

1. The hot glue **can** stick together various materials.
2. The chuck key **could/might** fly out and injure somebody.
3. Your nailgun doesn't work properly. You **may/can** use my nailgun.
4. But you **must** put it back into my toolkit.
5. You **must not** use defective tools.
6. All planes **should** have a fine adjustment dial.
7. You **didn't have to** buy a separate driver.

Modals ändern die Bedeutung eines Satzes. Sie drücken aus, was man kann (1) oder könnte (2), was geschehen darf (3) oder muss (4), was nicht geschehen darf (5) oder geschehen soll(te) (6).

- *Must* steht nur im Present. Andere Zeiten bildet man mit der Ersatzform *have to* (7).
- *Must* not ist nicht das Gegenteil von *must*.
  You must be honest.   Du musst ehrlich sein.
  You mustn't lie.   Du darfst nicht lügen.
  You needn't do it.   Du musst es nicht tun.

13 Practice

Complete the sentences with a suitable modal verb.

1. (*Verbot*)
   Apprentices … use workshop machines without supervision.
2. (*Empfehlung; keine Möglichkeit*)
   There … be a torque wrench in here somewhere, but I just … find it.
3. (*keine Verpflichtung; Erlaubnis*)
   We … bring our own tools: we … use the college toolstore.
4. (*Möglichkeit*)
   Be careful: you … injure yourself with that tool.
5. (*Verpflichtung*)
   We … clean our workbenches at the end of the class.
6. (*nicht empfohlen*)
   You … buy cheap power tools because they won't last long.

KMK exam practice

Situation

Um den Teamgeist zu fördern, bucht Ihre englische Firma für zehn Manager (Männer und Frauen) ein fünftägiges Survivaltraining im schottischen Hochland. Sie und drei englische Praktikanten erhalten den Auftrag, als Vorhut Lager und Hütten aufzubauen. Sie dürfen nur Nylonseile, Plastikfolien und vier Werkzeuge mitnehmen.

14 Interaktion

Bilden Sie Gruppen und übernehmen Sie den Auftrag.

1. Sie überlegen welche Werkzeuge nötig sind und in welcher Reihenfolge Sie die Arbeitsschritte vornehmen.
2. Diskutieren Sie vor der Klasse erst Ihre Wahl der vier Werkzeuge und anschließend die Reihenfolge der Arbeitsschritte. Finden Sie einen Kompromiss.
3. Präsentieren Sie der Klasse Ihre Planung mithilfe einer Skizze. Beantworten Sie etwaige Fragen Ihres Lehrers und Ihrer Klassenkameraden.

15 Interaktion

A Einzelaufträge: Die Teilnehmer des Trainings dürfen entweder ein Swiss Army Knife oder ein Leatherman Multi-Tool mitnehmen. Erklären Sie der Klasse Ihre Empfehlung.

Swiss Army Knife	Leatherman Multi-Tool
small blade knife	clip point knife
large blade knife	serrated knife
tweezers	needlenose pliers
pliers with wire cutter	regular pliers
reamer with sewing eye	wire cutters
wood chisel	hard-wire cutters
magnifying lens	stranded-wire cutters
screwdriver & wire stripper	wire stripper
corkscrew	electrical crimper
fine screwdriver	screwdriver
mini screwdriver	large bit driver
cross-head (Phillips) screwdriver	small bit driver
scissors	scissors
hacksaw with metal file & nail file	diamond-coated file
straight pin	wood/Metal file
wood saw	saw
bottle opener	bottle opener
tin opener with small screwdriver	can opener
fish scaler with hook disgorger & ruler	ruler

B Zeigen Sie der Klasse ein Swiss Army Knife und erklären Sie die Funktion der Werkzeuge.

Example: *With the lens you can light a fire. It can also be useful if you're reading a map with small print.*

Extra material

Using a combination square

The combination square is a versatile instrument that has three different heads for different measuring tasks in the carpentry or engineering workshop. All three heads include a lock bolt to prevent slipping. The square and protractor heads also include a handy spirit level for checking that work is level.

Square head

The square head has a 90° square face and a 45° mitre face. It is a useful tool for scribing right angles and parallel lines. It has a scriber for drawing lines on metal and other materials. (On timber, a carpenter's pencil or craft knife may be used instead.) It can also be used as a depth gauge.

Protractor head

The protractor head permits accurate and quick reading of any angle. The direct reading scale is suitable for most purposes. For even more precise measurement, a protractor head with a vernier scale can also be used.

Centre head

The centre head accurately locates the centre of cylindrical or square work. Simply place the work between the jaws and scribe a line along the top of the steel rule. Rotate the work and repeat the process. For a piece that may not be completely round/square, scribe another line.

The illustration shows all three heads, but in use only one is mounted on the rule at a time.

Tip: Always make sure your square is clean and that it is located against a flat surface – burrs on metal or knots and bumps on wood will lead to an inaccurate result.

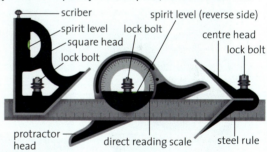

16 Understanding the text

Write notes in English of how the parts of the combination square can be used.

17 Your opinion

Are analogue instruments such as the combination square still useful in the workshop, or should they be replaced by digital electronic instruments? Give reasons for your answer.

UNIT 6

Troubleshooting

■ Identifying a problem   ■ Explaining and discussing a problem   ■ Dealing with a problem

1 Warm-up

A Match these phrases with the illustrations.

> an electrical fault • a blocked drain • a spillage • a burst pipe • damaged bodywork
> a bent nail • a leaking tap • mould

B Work with a partner. How would you solve these problems?

| How would you | deal with
sort out
repair
… | mould?
a bent nail?
an electrical fault?
a blocked drain?
a spillage?
a burst pipe?
damaged bodywork?
a leaking tap? |

> I'd
> dry/clean
> straighten/pull out
> turn off/fix/repair
> remove/replace
> …

TROUBLESHOOTING

2 Troubleshooting

Anna Dahlmann is a machine engineer from Passau. In her spare time she is developing an international troubleshooting forum. Amateurs and professionals use the site to exchange information about electrical equipment such as computers and household appliances.

A Which sections of the website are the following posts from?

① "Yesterday I turned it on and there was no picture. The power light indicated it was on, and I could hear sound, but there was nothing on the screen. Can any of you guys help?"

② "It made a loud vibrating noise this morning. It shook a lot so I turned it off. Now there is a funny smell inside (gas maybe??) The noise is driving me crazy, and my ice cream is melting! Help!!!"

③ "It was really weird – about twenty minutes after I turned it on it began to get extremely hot. Then it shut down automatically. It did that again this last night. The hottest part is just under the keyboard, near the DVD drive."

④ This error started without warning. Symptoms included not going into spin cycle or drain cycle. Age of unit: 2 years. No obvious breaks or leaks. Just a buzzing sound behind the control panel."

⑤ "About a week ago it started to work erratically. When I depress the trigger, sometimes the blade rotates but at other times it does not respond."

⑥ "I can use it with a USB connection, but when I try to use it wirelessly, the computer can't find it on the network. Every time I want to print something I have to pick up my laptop and go into another room."

B Which posts are they answering?

Eldi@Berlin
Have you tried a hard reset? (Unplug the set from the wall for more than four hours.). If that doesn't work, contact the manufacturer. It doesn't sound good! There are lots of issues with those models.

Techdude_67
Try uninstalling the software and reinstalling it. Follow the instructions exactly. Also check the configuration of your router.

StuffMender
Basically the unit isn't cooling down. The good news? It's not a serious problem. 9 times out of 10 overheating is caused by a dusty heat sink. Get a can of compressed air and blow it through the vent.

JimIlfixit
Yep – the other posters were right. This is a built-in alarm that sounds when your machine is off-balance. You need to get the drum rebalanced. Call a professional!

TROUBLESHOOTING

3 A new feature

A Anna discusses common computer problems with an American IT specialist.

Listen to part one of the recording. Are Anna's notes accurate and complete? Make any changes necessary in your exercise books.

> *Computer problems*
>
> *Overheating most common thing.*
> *People play computer games too long. The video card isn't good enough, not enough RAM. SOLUTION: get a better computer!*
> *Could also be dust blocking the fan.*
> *OTHER PROBLEMS: basically two kinds, hardware and software. Hardware problems are easier to solve than software problems. But they cost more.*

B Anna calls Larry back to clarify the information.

Listen to part two of the recording. Write the information missing from the table in your exercise books.

Problem / Symptom	Possible Causes	Solution
Blue screen of death	virus / hardware failure / and … ¹	Undo the last change you made before the error
Really slow PC	Programs running in background / fragmented hard drive	… ²
Programme not responding	… ³	Try waiting!
Can't connect to a network	Incompatible router / and … ⁴	Reset your router and restart the PC.
Blank screen	Faulty monitor cable / driver.	… ⁵

C Hören Sie nochmal Teil 2 an. Sind die folgenden Aussagen richtig (R), nicht im Text (N) oder falsch (F)? Begründen Sie Ihre Antwort und korrigieren Sie die falschen Aussagen.

1. Wenn ein blauer Bildschirm auftritt, kann es an einem defekten Treiber liegen.
2. Defragmentierung ist eine effektive Methode, um den PC schneller zu machen.
3. Manche Antivirusprogramme defragmentieren die Festplatte automatisch.
4. Auch mehr RAM macht den Computer schneller.
5. Wenn ein Programm nicht reagiert, sollte man es wiederholt anklicken.
6. Anna sollte sich einen kompatiblen Router kaufen.
7. Netzwerkprobleme löst man nicht durch Neustart des PCs.
8. Das Aktualisieren von Treibern sollte man einem Experten überlassen.

TROUBLESHOOTING

UNIT 6

4 Interaktion

Student A: Siehe File 4 auf Seite 128.
Student B: Siehe File 9 auf Seite 131.

5 Troubleshooting charts

Anna creates some charts like the one below for a fridge.

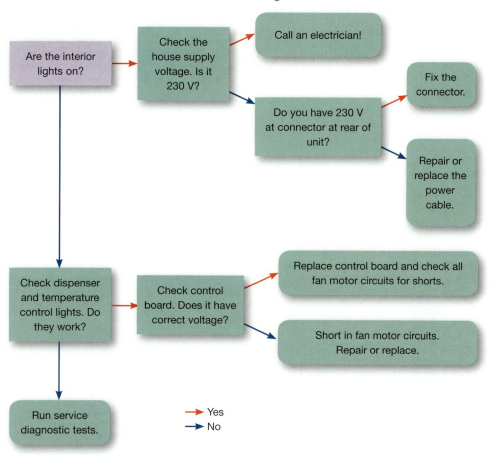

Read the website post and use the troubleshooting chart to find the correct solution.

Fridge failure!!

Hello troubleshooters! A couple of days ago my fridge suddenly died. The lights are still on inside, but the indicators on the temperature control have malfunctioned. I checked the power supply to the fridge and it was fine. The connector at the back of the fridge was OK too. However there seemed to be a problem on the control board. I tested the pins and there was no voltage …

TROUBLESHOOTING

6 Anna's computer problem

Anna has a problem with her computer and calls Larry for help.

Read the conversation with a partner. Use the correct questions from the box below.

a How do we do that?
b Do you have a backup?
c Is it recent?
d When did the problem start?
e What were the first indications something was wrong?
f Would that cause a crash?

Larry   …¹?
Anna   I'm not sure. I noticed it this morning.
Larry   …²?
Anna   The computer didn't start up when I turned it on.
Larry   There was a service patch this morning. Perhaps your computer automatically applied it.
Anna   …³?
Larry   It might do. We need to eliminate that as a cause.
Anna   …⁴?
Larry   You need to restore your computer to its previous state. …⁵?
Anna   Somewhere.
Larry   …⁶?
Anna   Yes, it's only a couple of weeks old.
Larry   That will do. Connect it to your computer and follow the instructions I emailed you.

LANGUAGE

Asking for and giving help

I'm afraid I've got a problem with my router / moped / laptop / …
Do you know anything about …? Can you help me with my …?
It isn't working properly / correctly. It …
The … is damaged / broken / defective. It's damaging my clothes / CDs / …
The first thing you must do is … Then you must / should …
Check / look at the … Turn the … on / off.
OK, I've done that. What's the next step? OK, I think I can manage that.

TROUBLESHOOTING

UNIT 6

7 Help from a friend

Margot, eine junge Frau aus Berlin, hat ein Problem. Sie ruft ihren Freund Maarten, einen Waschmaschinentechniker in Amsterdam an und bittet ihn um Hilfe.

Margot

Margot	Maarten
Begrüßen Sie Maarten. Sagen Sie ihm, dass du ein Problem mit deiner Waschmaschine hast.	
	Fragen Sie Margot, wann das Problem aufgetreten ist.
Sagen Sie Maarten, dass es sofort nach dem Kauf der Maschine angefangen hat.	
	Fragen Sie Margot, ob es ein neues Gerät ist.
Antworten Sie Maarten, dass es eine gebrauchte Maschine ist, die aber nur ein paar Monate alt ist.	
	Bitten Sie Margot, das Problem zu beschreiben.
Sagen Sie Maarten, dass die Waschmaschine nicht starten will.	
	Fragen Sie Margot, wer die Maschine installiert hat.
Antworten Sie Maarten, dass du die Maschine selber installiert hast.	
	Sagen Sie Margot, dass sie prüfen soll, ob der Stecker richtig eingesteckt ist.
Entgegnen Sie, dass der Stecker korrekt in der Steckdose eingesteckt und auch Strom vorhanden ist.	
	Sagen Sie Margot, dass sie überprüfen soll, ob der Wasserhahn für kaltes Wasser geöffnet ist.
Bestätigen Sie Maarten, dass der Wasserhahn offen ist.	
	Sagen Sie Margot, dass sie prüfen soll, ob ein Knick in dem Wasserschlauch ist.
Sagen Sie Maarten, dass es kein Knick gibt. Fragen Sie ihn, was man noch überprüfen könnte.	
	Sagen sie Margot, dass sie die Tür der Waschmaschine richtig fest zumachen soll und dann an der Kontrolllampe prüfen, ob der Türkontakt geschlossen ist.
Sagen Sie Maarten, dass du die Schritte befolgt hast und die Waschmaschine beginnt nun das eingestellte Programm abzuarbeiten.	
	Sagen Sie Margot, dass die Ursache der Türkontakt gewesen ist. Sie soll nach dem Waschen noch einmal nachsehen, ob der Kontakt sauber ist und ihn gegebenenfalls reinigen.
Danken Sie Maarten für die Hilfe. Laden Sie ihn zu einem Besuch ein, wenn er das nächste Mal in Berlin ist.	
	Danken Sie Margot und laden Sie sie zu einem Gegenbesuch ein.

69

TROUBLESHOOTING

8 Troubleshooting electronics

Identify the tools from the descriptions.

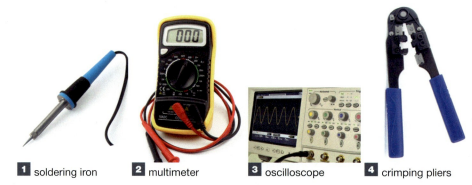

1 soldering iron 2 multimeter 3 oscilloscope 4 crimping pliers

A
This is a great piece of equipment, because it combines different functions in one unit. You just need to rotate the dial, and you can measure anything – voltage, current and resistance. There are two kinds, digital and analogue. This is obviously digital.

B
If you want to view the wave shape of an electronic signal, you need this. It's good for troubleshooting. Simply connect it to a circuit. If it's an unexpected pattern, you know something is wrong with the circuit.

C
I bought my first one when I was twelve. I used it to build my own radio. Paper needs glue, sellotape and staples. Circuit boards and leaking pipes need this little gizmo!

D
This tool removes the insulation from cables and wires. It also presses wires together so that they are easier to use as terminals.

9 Your tools

Work with a partner and act out dialogues.

Student A: Describe a tool or a piece of equipment you use for fixing or repairing. Explain what it does and where it is used.

> **TIP**
> **Ihre Beschreibung vorbereiten:**
> - Ein Foto im Internet suchen, ausdrucken und auf einen Zettel kleben.
> - Mit einem deutsch-englischen Wörterbuch die wichtigen Merkmale als Stichwörter auflisten.

Student B: Guess what your partner is describing. You can also ask questions. Then swap roles.

> How big/long/heavy is it? Can it also be used to cut wood/metal/…?

TROUBLESHOOTING

10 Trouble with cars

Work in teams. Choose the best answer to each problem in the car quiz.

1. The engine isn't running well. You can hear hissing. Something like air or steam is escaping. After the noise begins, the performance from the engine drops.
   a The engine is overheating. I'll check and repair the cooling system.
   b I'll ignore the problem and eventually it will go away.
   c I'll check the brake lines for leaking fluid.

2. As you accelerate, you hear a loud whirring from the engine. It gets worse as the speed increases.
   a I'll turn up the volume on my radio. Problem solved!
   b It's the alternator bearings. They need to be replaced.
   c It's only a loose fan belt. I'll stop the car and reattach it. Simple!

3. Whenever you change gears the transmission makes a loud grinding noise.
   a The car is out of oil. I'll go to the petrol station, buy some more, and refill the engine.
   b The clutch is worn. I'll take the car to a garage and pay for a new one.
   c A bit of noise is normal. It's a machine, not a mouse!

4. You see blue smoke coming out of your exhaust, and you are running out of oil more quickly than usual.
   a I have a leak in the oil tank. I'll patch it up with a soldering iron.
   b Somebody blocked my exhaust with a banana. I'll get a coat hanger, straighten it, and remove it.
   c The valve seals on my engine are cracked. I'll buy replacements.

5. Nothing happened this morning when you turned the key in the ignition.
   a I got a hammer and hit the ignition box a few times. The old solutions are the best.
   b I thought it was a faulty ignition switch. I turned the key to the ON position. Sure enough, the warning lights on the dashboard didn't light up. Problem: broken switch.
   c Yes, it was great. I didn't have to go to work.

6. Your steering wheel is slipping a lot, even when you hold it still. It doesn't have full control of the wheels.
   a It's a worn power steering belt. I'll replace it.
   b I have sweaty hands. I'll ask my wife for driving gloves this Christmas.
   c It's these roads. It has nothing to do with my beautiful car.

7. When you applied the brakes you heard a loud screeching noise.
   a I'll take a yoga class to help me relax in stressful situations.
   b I'll replace the brake fluid – there's none left.
   c Obviously my brake pads are worn. I have to replace them before I damage the brake discs.

8. Your car is getting fewer miles per gallon.
   a The spark plugs aren't working efficiently. I'll check the insulation for cracks.
   b The car headlights are using too much petrol. I'll turn them off when I don't need them.
   c I'll write a letter to the government. Someone needs to complain about the quality of the petrol.

Now turn the book around and check your answers.

21–24 points	You are the next Schumacher. The road is your kingdom.
14–20 points	If you get a flat on the motorway you could probably deal with it. Probably.
8–13 points	Do you know what a car looks like? Next time take the bus.

WEBCODE
TEMU0601

UNIT 6

TROUBLESHOOTING

GRAMMAR

Simple past and past progressive

1 Two weeks ago, Anna **bought** a second hand washing machine.
2 She **installed** it herself, **put** the laundry in, **opened** the water tap and **switched** it on.
3 Anna noticed that water **was leaking out** and that the machine **was making** a noise.

- Das *simple past* gebraucht man für Situationen, die in der Vergangenheit abgeschlossen wurden. Es steht oft nach Zeitangaben wie *yesterday, last month, a week ago* (1).
  Es steht ferner für aufeinanderfolgende Ereignisse in der Vergangenheit (2).
  Das *Simple past* bildet man durch Anhängen von *-ed* an den Infinitiv der regelmäßigen Verben.

- Das *past progressive* gebraucht man für Handlungen, die zu einem Zeitpunkt oder in einem Zeitraum der Vergangenheit schon, gerade oder noch im Verlauf waren (3).
  Das *past progressive* bildet man mit *was/ were* + der *-ing*-Form des Verbs.
  I / He / She was working. You / We / They were sleeping.

11 Practice

A Put the verbs in brackets into the correct past form.

Yesterday evening I ... ¹ (drive) back home through the Peak District in one of the company's latest prototypes . I ... ² (feel) safe and comfortable in the driver's seat which had front and seat-mounted side airbags. I ... ³ (enjoy) the music in the almost soundproof cabin. It ... ⁴ (get) dark and foggy and soon it ... ⁵ (begin) to rain. "What's that in the middle of the road? A person, or what?" I ... ⁶ (hit) the brakes and ... ⁷ (swing) the steering wheel to the right, but too late and the car ... ⁸ (skid) along the slippery road and into a tree. I ... ⁹ (get) out. Thank goodness! It was only a deer. I ... ¹⁰ (start) the engine again but it ... ¹¹ (not/run) well. I ... ¹² (can) hear a hissing sound. Something like air or steam ... ¹³ (escape). I ... ¹⁴ (switch) the engine off. After some minutes I ... ¹⁵ (put) the key back in the ignition and ... ¹⁶ (turn) it. Silence. The car radiator ... ¹⁷ (still/steam) like a kettle. So I ... ¹⁸ (phone) the police on my mobile. Fifteen minutes later they ... ¹⁹ (arrive) and ... ²⁰ (take) some photos. A breakdown lorry finally ... ²¹ (tow) me back home.

B Complete the report to the insurance company.

Dear Sir

I would like to report an accident which ...¹ (occur) yesterday, 5 March, 2012. It ...² (take) place near Ashbourne in the Peak District at approximately nine p.m. It ...³ (rain), so I ...⁴ (drive) the car at a moderate speed, about 30 mph when suddenly I ...⁵ (see) a deer. It ...⁶ (run) into my path. This was at the junction Derby Road and the High Street. I ...⁷ (apply) the brakes, but the result was that my car ...⁸ (turn) sideways and ...⁹ (hit) a fence post and then ...¹⁰ (skid) off into a tree. There ...¹¹ (be) considerable damage to the side and the front of the car. The enclosed photos ...¹² (be) taken by the police. The police case number is PRX/2-7862-97763.

Best regards
Ted Hunter

Recall MVCK 2012/120742; Vehicle identification number MVCK 7278196702

Dear Sir or Madam

Recently there have been rumours about sticking brake pedals in our Multi Van CK from the 2012 model year. These rumours have not been confirmed by any of our dealers nor have accidents caused by brake failures been reported so far. If you have not experienced any problems with your brakes so far, you can be certain that your Multi Van CK is safe to drive.
However, we take the issue very seriously and advise you to call your local dealer without delay to request a service date for Recall MVCK 2012/120742. Please provide your dealer with the VIN of your vehicle which is printed at the beginning of this letter. We have authorized our dealership to check and service the brake system. This is free of charge (including parts and labour). The inspection is estimated to take three hours.
This offer extends to other Multi Van CK vehicles from the 2012 model year in your possession which you might have bought second hand. In case you have sold the above mentioned vehicle (VIN MVCK 7278196702), please inform the new owner.
We apologize for any inconvenience this precautionary measure may cause you and thank you for your attention to this important matter.

Sincerely

Jim Usinto
Nuyotashi Service Division Europe

12 Mediation

Sie sind in Ausbildung bei einer Logistikfirma. Ihr Chef bittet Sie, ein deutsches Memo an Herrn Horst Diemer, den Leiter des Fuhrparks, zu schreiben. Ihr Memo soll folgende Informationen enthalten:

- Anlass des Memos
- Das Problem
- Behebung des Problems

13 Produktion

Ihr Chef bittet Sie ferner, Mr John Dobson, Chef der Niederlassung in Dover, durch eine kurze E-Mail von der Rückrufaktion zu informieren. Ihre E-Mail soll folgende Informationen enthalten:

- The problem
- Action to be taken
- Service offered by Nuyotashi
- Time involved

Extra material

14 Monthly focus

Every month Anna highlights a particular topic for more advanced users. This month the topic is electric motors.

COMMON ELECTRIC MOTOR PROBLEMS

Noise/Vibration
Whenever noise or vibration are found in an operating motor, the source should be quickly isolated and corrected. What seems to be an obvious source of noise or vibration may be a symptom of a hidden problem. Noise and vibration can be caused by a misaligned motor shaft or can be transmitted to the motor through the power transmission system. They can also be the result of electrical or mechanical imbalance in the motor. After checking the motor shaft alignment, disconnect the motor from the load. If the motor then operates smoothly, look for the source of noise or vibration in the driven equipment.

Dry/worn bearings
This can cause a tight or frozen motor. The result could be squealing during operation, reduced speed and power, and overheating. Running a motor in this condition may eventually lead to burnout. Lubricate the motor on a scheduled basis, following the manufacturer's instructions. This ensures optimum bearing life. Clean the lubrication equipment and fittings before lubricating. Dirt introduced into the bearings during lubrication probably causes more bearing failures than the lack of lubrication. Excessive lubricant can find its way inside the motor where it collects dirt and causes insulation deterioration.

Brushes/Commutators (DC Motors)
Observe the brushes while the motor is running. The brushes must ride on the commutator smoothly with little or no sparking and no brush noise (chatter). Stop the motor. Check that the brushes move freely in the holder and the spring tension on each brush is equal. Make sure that the commutator is clean, smooth and has a polished brown surface where the brushes ride. Replace the brushes if there is any chance they will not last until the next inspection date.

A Read the text. Are the following statements true or false? Correct the false ones.

1. Noise or vibration in the motor always indicates a problem with the motor itself.
2. Before you disconnect the motor from its load, you should check the motor shaft alignment.
3. If a motor is not moving a possible cause is dry bearings.
4. Running a dry motor will reduce the efficiency of the motor, but will not cause long term damage.
5. Lack of lubrication is not the main cause of bearing problems.
6. You cannot use too much lubrication.
7. A small amount of sparking is normal and expected in an operational motor.
8. You only need to replace seriously damaged brushes.

B Write a similar text about technical problems you face at work. Include information about:

- problems
- causes
- symptoms
- solutions
- tools

Situations

Home Repair Services Ltd.

We offer a round-the-clock service for all of London. Locked yourself out? Washing machine needs fixing? Kitchen flooded? Whatever your problem is, we can fix it. Wherever you live in London, one of our highly experienced handymen can be ringing your doorbell in less than an hour after your call.

Hourly rates: from 6 a.m. to 6 p.m.: £89;
before 6 a.m. and after 6 p.m.: £129;
Sat, Sun: £149
Call our hotline: (02) 8000-9191

1 In the call centre at Home Repair Services

Follow the instruction on the role-play cards and act out the phone calls.

Call centre operative
- Take down caller's personal data and fill in the caller memo.
- Ask what the problem is.
- Arrange an appointment.
- Say when the expert will arrive at the site.
- Explain the costs involved.

HRS - Caller memo
Time of call:
Name of caller:
Address:
Telephone:
Problem:
Appointment:

Caller 1
Mr Bela Lugosi, 24, Linhope Street, London NW1 4SA; Mobile: 01789-5062298

- You call on Saturday, 4.35 p.m.
- You are partly disabled and you need help to hang the pictures and fix the lamps in your new flat. The walls and the ceiling are made of plasterboard.
- Ask when the handyman will arrive.
- Enquire about the charges.

Caller 2
Mrs Gladys White, 7, Wilton Crescent, London SW1X, Mobile: 01755-2834633

- You call on Sunday, 20.45 because your bathroom drain is blocked.
- Ask when help will arrive.
- Enquire about the charges.

Caller 3
Mr Tony Spencer, 24, Melcombe Street, London NW1 6AG; Mobile: 01727-3195214

- You call on Monday, 9.35 a.m.
- You've bought a sat-receiver with a parabolic dish. You need help to install it.
- Ask when the craftsman will arrive.
- Enquire about the charges.

Situations

2 At the door

The handymen drive to the customers' homes in a small van. Before they ring the doorbell, they take the tools and the equipment from the van that they think they'll need. Make a list of tools for each job and explain why these tools are needed.

plunger electric drill torch

antenna cable flexible auger multimeter spirit level

pipe wrench plasterboard screws crimping pliers antenna connectors

teflon packing tape bucket

3 Customers' letters

- You are Mrs Gladys White. You would like to thank the young lady who unblocked your bathroom drain last Sunday. She was friendly, cheerful and worked so quickly. Can she come and install your new washing machine? (Suggest a day and a time.)
- You are Mr Tony Spencer. Write an email to Home Repair Services and complain about
  - time between call and arrival (1 hr 30 mins) of the handyman;
  - charges where higher than agreed by phone.

Preventing accidents

UNIT 7

- Talking about safety rules
- Identifying hazards
- Describing an accident

1 Warm-up

Match the warning signs (1 – 10) with the places (a – j).

a the door of a storeroom for aerosols and cleaning fluids
b in front of an open inspection shaft
c the bottom of a scaffolding rig
d in front of an area of wet cement
e under a crane
f a tin of heavy-duty cleaning agent
g near a high-voltage power cable
h a workshop grinder
i in a storage area or a warehouse
j the gates of a construction site

2 Warnings

Listen to the six dialogues and match them to six of the signs above.

15

UNIT 7

PREVENTING ACCIDENTS

3 | Safety training

Macintosh Construction PLC is an international construction company and their European headquarters is in London. On their first working day new employees have to do a safety training course with Charlie Dunbar, the safety officer. His job is to prevent accidents.

Read this hand-out from the safety officer and then choose the correct headings from the box below.

> CONFINED SPACES • EXCAVATION WORK • HIGH-RISK SITUATIONS •
> LIFTING • PLANT • PPE • TRAINING AND SUPERVISION • WORK AT HEIGHT •
> WORK ON POWERED SYSTEMS

9 GOLDEN SAFETY RULES

1 …
Do not start up or shut down equipment or installations without using the appropriate, written operating procedure.

2 …
When driving a vehicle, always obey traffic regulations both on- and off-site.

3 …
Do not carry out any work you are not qualified to do. Do not use any power tools you are not qualified to operate unless an experienced and qualified worker is present.

4 …
Do not access installations or perform work without wearing general or task-specific personal protection equipment.

5 …
Do not walk or stand under a load while lifting is taking place.

6 …
Do not perform work without checking that the power (mechanical, electrical, hydraulic, thermal, radioactive) and product supply has been rendered inoperative.

7 …
Do not enter a tank or vessel until isolation has been verified and the atmosphere checked. A qualified and properly-equipped safety attendant (standby worker) must be nearby.

8 …
Take precautions to prevent ground movement. For example, machinery must be positioned at a set distance from the excavation and trench walls must be stabilized.

9 …
Do not work on scaffolding or roofs without a safety harness.

TIP

Sparen Sie Zeit beim Nachschlagen unbekannter Vokabeln und Redewendungen:
- Lesen Sie den Text mit einem Partner. Einige Vokabeln lassen sich oft aus dem Kontext erschließen.
- Notieren Sie nur die unbekannten Wörter, die für das Textverständnis notwendig sind.
- Vergleichen Sie Ihre Liste unbekannter Wörter mit denen anderer Klassenkameraden.
- Einigen Sie sich auf die Übersetzungen, die dem Text angemessen sind.
- Schlagen Sie verbleibende unbekannten Wörter nach und wählen Sie den treffendsten Vorschlag des Wörterbucheintrags.

LANGUAGE

Singular nouns
- Nomen ohne Mehrzahlform:
  The scaffolding is secure.
  (Ebenso: *oil*, *grease*, *gravel*.)

Plural nouns
- Nomen ohne Einzahlform:
  These metal shears are sharp.
  (Ebenso: *pliers*, *goggles*.)
- Nomen mit beiden Formen:
  Our European headquarters is / are in London.

PREVENTING ACCIDENTS

UNIT 7

4 Explaining safety rules

Erkläre die folgenden Regeln einem deutschen Kollegen, der Englisch nicht versteht.

WORKSHOP SAFETY RULES
- Walk, don't run.
- See and be seen.
- Keep strictly to the yellow walkways.
- Never distract anyone who is operating a machine.
- Always keep your workplace clean and tidy.
- Understand all the safety signs and obey them.
- Make sure that in an emergency you know how to …
  - stop your machine.
  - sound the alarm.
  - find the first-aid kit.

5 A quiz

A Work with a partner and identify the safety equipment (1 – 16) with the words in the box.

a	cup mask	i	helmet
b	ear protectors	j	machine guard
c	equipment cage	k	overalls
d	face shield	l	padlock
e	gloves	m	reflective jacket
f	goggles/ safety glasses	n	respirator
		o	safety boots
h	harness	p	siren
		q	welding visor

What's number …?

It's a / an / pair of …?

B Discuss who needs the equipment and why. The language below may help you.

A	carpenter	needs to wear …	because he/she works	on roofs/ladders.
	metalworker	needs to use …		on scaffolds.
	painter			with loud machines.
	welder			in enclosed spaces.
	mechanic		as a protection against	noise / dust / gas.
	…			sparks / splinters.

6 Talking about dangers in your workplace

Halten Sie einen Vortrag auf Englisch über die Gefahren in Ihrem Beruf. Wie kann man sie vermeiden?

PREVENTING ACCIDENTS

7 | Site safety

The final part of the induction is about improving site safety. Look at the illustration and discuss the potential hazards and how they can be prevented. The language box may help you.

LANGUAGE

Preventing accidents

| Stacks of | bricks
pipes
timber
… | shouldn't be | too high.
too near trenches.
unsecured.
… |

| Drivers of plant machines should | obey traffic rules.
be properly qualified.
signal when reversing.
… |

Construction workers must wear … at all times.

| A safe construction site should have | high security fences.
security gates.
warning signs.
an emergency siren.
a first-aid station.
barriers around excavations and trenches. |

PREVENTING ACCIDENTS

UNIT 7

8 A bad fall

Sven Olsen is a mechanic. Pedro Hernandez finds him lying on the ground.

A Look at the illustrations and role-play a dialogue with a partner. Use the key words under the illustrations.

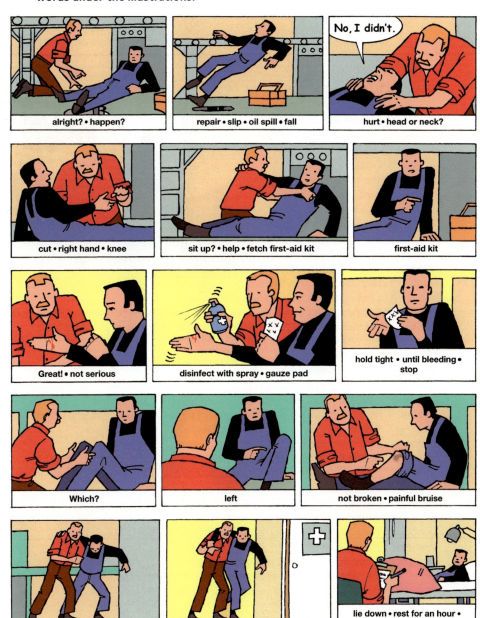

B Now listen to the dialogue on the CD and check it with your dialogue.

PREVENTING ACCIDENTS

9 A serious accident

Charlie Dunbar, the safety officer at Macintosh Construction, is telling Gerry Webster, the site manager, about a more serious accident.

A Work with a partner and complete the dialogue with words or expressions from the box. Then act it out.

> bricklayer • bruises • for • hospital • insurance company • licence • platform •
> safety harness • training course • unfair • wheel loader • witnesses

Webster	When did it happen, Charlie?
Dunbar	At 3.25 this afternoon, according to the …¹.
Webster	Tell me what happened exactly.
Dunbar	The driver of a …² backed into the scaffolding on the south wall of building B. One of the bricklayers fell off the …³ and broke his leg.
Webster	Who was the driver?
Dunbar	Luigi Manfredi. He has been with us …⁴ four years and he's a careful driver.
Webster	Well he wasn't careful today, was he? Has he got a …⁵ to drive the wheel loader?
Dunbar	Of course he has, Gerry. You know I wouldn't let anyone …
Webster	OK, Charlie. No offence intended. Who was the …⁶?
Dunbar	Terry Bates, a local lad.
Webster	Was the scaffolding properly secured?
Dunbar	Yes.
Webster	So why did this brickie fall off the damn thing? Wasn't he wearing a …⁷?
Dunbar	No, he told me that he had just taken it off because he was having a break.
Webster	The silly sod! Didn't he have a …⁸, Charlie?
Dunbar	Of course he did!
Webster	Well he didn't learn much, did he?
Dunbar	I think you're being a bit …⁹, Mr Webster. You can lead a horse to water, but you can't make him drink!
Webster	Sorry, Charlie. I know it isn't your fault. But I've got to deal with the …¹⁰ and explain things to headquarters in London.
Dunbar	You'll have my accident report in an hour or so, Gerry.
Webster	Thanks, Charlie. What …¹¹ is the Bates lad in?
Dunbar	Croyden General. I've called them and they told me that he has no other injuries apart from the broken leg and some painful …¹². Luckily he only fell three metres.
Webster	He has more luck than sense, if you ask me.

B Complete the compound nouns with a word from the box.

1 site …
2 wheel …
3 safety …
4 training …
5 insurance …
6 accident …

> company • course • harness • loader •
> manager • report

PREVENTING ACCIDENTS UNIT 7

10 A visit to the doctor

Sie sind in der Praxis von Dr. Keen. Sie hatten einen Arbeitsunfall. Spielen Sie den Dialog mit einem Partner. Die *language box* wird Ihnen helfen.

Arzt/Ärztin

Begrüßen Sie den Patienten. Fragen Sie, was ihm/ihr fehle.

Patient/Patientin

Sagen Sie, dass Sie eine tiefe Wunde im rechten Arm hätten.

Fragen Sie, ob es ein Haushalts- oder ein Arbeitsunfall war.

Antworten Sie, es sei im Lager ihrer Firma passiert.

Fragen Sie, wie der Unfall passiert sei.

Sie hätten Kartons mit einem Messer geöffnet. Das Messer sei ausgerutscht.

Untersuchen Sie die Wunde. Sagen Sie ihm/ihr, der Schnitt sei zwar lang, aber nicht tief.

Fragen Sie, ob die Wunde genäht werden muss.

Sagen Sie, dass nur drei Stiche nötig seien und dass sie ihn/ihr sicherheitshalber eine Tetanusspritze geben müssten.

Fragen Sie, ob er/sie Sie krankschreiben werde.

Sagen Sie, er/sie solle mindestens vier Tage zu Hause bleiben.

Fragen Sie, wann Sie zur Nachuntersuchung kommen sollen.

Sagen Sie, er/sie solle sich an der Aufnahme einen Termin für nächste Woche geben lassen.

Sie bedanken sich und verabschieden sich.

LANGUAGE

What's the problem?

work accident
household accident
long cut
not deep
only… stitches
for at least … days
reception
ask for an appointment

I'm afraid I've got a …

deep wound
storeroom
knife slipped
Will you have to stitch it?
Are you going to write me off sick?
When should I come back for a check-up?
Thank you, Doctor.
Goodbye

WEBCODE
TEMU0701

PREVENTING ACCIDENTS

GRAMMAR

Present perfect and simple past

Das **present perfect** bildet man mit **has/have** und dem Partizip Perfekt (3- Form des Verbs).

1 **I've (have) worked** here for four years / since March 2009.
2 Ted **has** just **spoken** to the boss. They**'ve (have)** never **had** such an argument.
3 **I've (have) lost** my helmet. **Have** you **seen** it?
4 **Did** you **mislay** your goggles again? Where **did** you last **see** them?
5 The other day, Sven **slipped** on an oil spill and **cut** his hand.

- Man gebraucht das *present perfect* für Situationen, die in der Vergangenheit begonnen haben und bis zum Zeitpunkt des Sprechens andauern (1). Zeitangaben stehen oft nach *since* (Zeitpunkt) und *for* (Zeitspanne).
  Adverbien wie *just, only, often, already, never* stehen zwischen **has/have** und dem Verb (2).
- Man verwendet *present perfect* auch für Ereignisse, die für die Gegenwart wichtig sind. Ein Zeitpunkt bleibt unerwähnt oder ist unbekannt (2, 3).
  Weitere Details (wann, wo, wie) stehen im *past tense* (4).
- Das *simple past* steht ferner für Situationen, die in der Vergangenheit abgeschlossen sind (5).
  Es steht oft nach Ausdrücken wie *yesterday, last year, three days ago, the other day*, usw.

11 Practice

A Write down the correct verb forms, then role play the dialogue with a partner.

Tom
Oh dear! What …¹ (*you do*) to your face, Tom?
How …³ (*it/happen*)?
…⁵ (*you/see*) a doctor yet?
I …⁷ (*lose*) my right thumb ten years ago.
I …⁹ (*cut*) it off with a circular saw. A trainee …¹⁰ (*ask*) me a question and I …¹¹ (*be*) distracted for a moment.
Yes, that's why the health and safety manager …¹³ (*call*) for a meeting.

Fred
I …² (*have*) an accident on the way to the workshop.
A biker …⁴ (*knock*) me over.
Not yet. …⁶ (*you/ever/have*) an accident?
How …⁸ (*it/happen*)?
Well, there …¹² (*be*) far too many accidents in this workshop recently.

Why? …¹⁴ (*there/be*) another accident?

B Complete the reader's letter to a magazine with either the present perfect or past tense form of the verbs in brackets.

Last year I …¹ (*work*) at Uncle Jim's garage during the school holidays. He …² (*be*) very pleased with me. "You're the best apprentice I …³ (*ever/have*)," he said. And I …⁴ (*dream*) of becoming a mechanic ever since. My parents …⁵ (*tolerate*) this interest as a hobby, but they …⁶ (*never/take*) it seriously. Last month I …⁷ (*apply*) for a place at the Harley Davidson agency. Yesterday I …⁸ (*receive*) an invitation for an interview. My Dad …⁹ (*see*) the letter. We …¹⁰ (*just/have*) a terrible argument. He …¹¹ (*try*) to persuade me to stay on at school, pass the final exams and then go to a university. "A mechanic! That's not a job for a girl!" But I …¹² (*always/be*) good with my hands and he knows that, too. So far I …¹³ (*never/do*) anything that my parents …¹⁴ (*not/do*) want. But maybe now the time …¹⁵ (*come*) to do what I want. I …¹⁶ (*often think of*) leaving home, but I …¹⁷ (*not/make up*) my mind yet. Please, what do you think I should do?
Yours sincerely
Peggy Cameron

KMK exam practice

Excerpt from a scooter service manual

Motor scooter safety depends on the roadworthiness of the scooter and the care taken by its driver. As a new scooter driver you should make yourself familiar with the scooter before you go on the road. Remember that your scooter is designed for town use only. You are not allowed to drive on the motorway.
Excessive speed is the main cause of accidents. Respect the speed limits and never go faster than is safe under the prevailing road conditions. Take care not to slip on road marks or on wet or icy roads. Traffic rules require that the driver and any passenger on the pillion seat must wear crash helmets.
You must also switch on the lights when in motion. It is also recommended that you wear gloves, safety goggles to protect your eyes and bright clothes so that you are better visible to other drivers. Be particularly careful at intersections, car park entrances and exits. And do not rely on the rear-view mirrors, they allow only a partial view of what is going on behind you. Know where their blind spots are and check them frequently.
Optional luggage carriers are designed to transport lightweight objects (maximum 4 kilos). Make sure that the weight is distributed evenly and that loads are securely fastened.
To guarantee the road safety of your scooter it is essential that you follow the service and maintenance plan. If the scooter is not serviced regularly, you might lose your insurance cover in the case of an accident and the manufacturer's guarantee in the case of a breakdown.

12 Mediation

Ihr Freund hat einen Motorroller in Großbritannien gekauft. Er versteht die englischen Sicherheitshinweise nicht. Schreiben Sie für ihn eine deutsche Kurzfassung mit den wichtigsten Punkten.

1. Versicherungsschutz
2. Zuladung
3. Straßenverkehrsordnung
4. Schutzkleidung
5. Unfallverhütung

13 Produktion

Die meisten Unfälle passieren zu Hause. Wie lassen sie sich vermeiden? Schreiben Sie einen kurzen Bericht auf Englisch.

Die folgenden Stichwörter sind als Anregung gemeint:

- Typische Unfallsituationen und deren Folgen
- Unfallorte: Flur, Küche, Bad, Schlafzimmer etc.
- Unfallvermeidung durch Achtsamkeit
- Technische Hilfsmittel zur Unfallverhütung

Extra material

14 Accidents at work

Read the following texts from the website of the Health & Safety Executive, UK. These questions have been removed from the articles. Put them back in the correct place. The key words in brackets can help you.

- **a** Do people use unlit areas such as paths or yards in the dark?
- **b** Do you have the most appropriate equipment for the job? It may often be safer to use a tower scaffold or mobile elevating work platform than a ladder.
- **c** Do you choose equipment that is suitable for its working environment, e.g. waterproof or dustproof?
- **d** Might temporary work such as maintenance or alterations take place? It could introduce hazards such as trailing cables.
- **e** Do you work near or under overhead power cables? There are essential safety precautions to follow.
- **f** Can the work be done using long-handled tools or by bringing it down to ground level?
- **g** Do you dig in the street, pavement or near buildings? Knowing the proper precautions for avoiding underground cables is essential.
- **h** Do you use floor cleaning materials anywhere? Are the right methods and materials being used?

Slips and trips

The most common cause of injuries at work is the slip or trip. They happen in all kinds of businesses, but sectors such as food and catering report higher than average numbers. It's a particularly important subject if members of the public use your premises. The estimated cost to employers of all these injuries is over £500 million a year, and insurance only covers a small part of this. Effective solutions are often simple, cheap and lead to other benefits.

- Do you have floors which are, or can become, slippery, eg when wet?
- Does spillage occur and is it dealt with quickly?

…¹ (paths)
…² (cables)
…³ (floor)

Electricity

How safe is electricity in your workplace?
Electricity can kill. Most deaths are caused by contact with overhead or underground power cables. Even non-fatal shocks can cause severe and permanent injury. Shocks from faulty equipment may lead to falls from ladders, scaffolds or other work platforms. Those using electricity may not be the only ones at risk. Poor electrical installations and faulty electrical appliances can lead to fires which can also result in death or injury to others.

- Does anyone do electrical work in your business? Only those with appropriate technical knowledge and experience should be allowed to do this.
- Is your electrical equipment in good working order?

…⁴ (waterproof)
…⁵ (power)
…⁶ (dig)

Falls from a height

Do you perform work at height and if so is it done safely?
Falls from height at work account for around 60 deaths and just under 4000 major injuries each year. One of the main causes is falls from ladders. To help prevent falls from height, make sure you consider the risks to all your workers, the work is planned, organized and carried out by competent people and you follow the hierarchy for managing risks. Make sure workers are properly trained and supervised, have the right equipment and know how to use it safely.

- Do you carry out simple maintenance or cleaning tasks that require working where you could hurt yourself if you fell?
- Is the equipment you have well maintained and do your employees know how to use it safely?

…⁷ (ladder)
…⁸ (tools)

Recycling

UNIT 8

- Identifying recyclable materials
- Describing a recycling process
- Discussing the pros and cons of recycling

1 Warm-up

A What things (a – n) are the mechanics (1 – 14) checking?

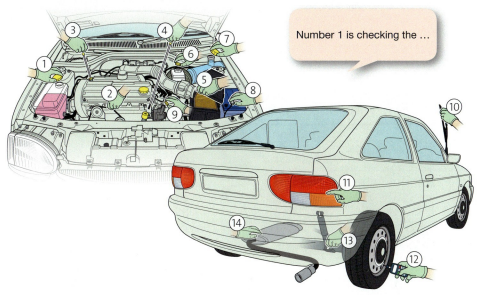

Number 1 is checking the …

a	exhaust	h	oil
b	air filter	i	power steering fluid
c	battery	j	reservoir
d	brake fluid	k	shock absorbers
e	brake lights / indicators	l	transmission fluid
f	anti-freeze	m	tyre pressure
g	fan belt	n	windscreen wipers

B Work with a partner. Discuss which materials can be found in each part of a car.

Bumpers	are made of	aluminium.
Wheel rims		platinum.
Engines	contain	gold.
Catalytic converters		steel.
Windscreens		rubber.
Seats		foam.
Car bodies		steel.
Wires		plastic.
Computer chips		copper.
…		fabric.

Bumpers are made of steel.

Only on old cars. They're usually made of plastic or polymer nowadays.

87

RECYCLING

2 Morrison Vehicle Recycling Ltd

A group of German car mechanics are visiting an ELV (end-of-life vehicle) recycling plant in Nottingham. At the start of their tour around the plant, the owner, Vic Morrison, tells them about car waste management in the UK.

A Listen and read Vic's talk. Then read it again and complete it with the phrases (a–j) below.

Around …^{1} were in use within the UK last year. Every year, owners register approximately 2 million new vehicles and …^{2}. The average lifespan

of a car is 13.5 years. In 2000 over 2 million cars and vans reached the end of their useful lives, either …^{3} or due to accident. If the vehicles are not resold, this equals over 2 million tonnes of recoverable or …^{4}.

In the UK 1.85 million cars are recycled every year. Approximately 80% of waste automotive materials (…^{5}) are recycled, with the remainder going to landfill. The composition of a typical car …^{6} in recent years. For example, ferrous metal content has decreased …^{7} such as plastics are incorporated into vehicle design. As …^{8} continues to increase it is important that the proportion of each end-of-life vehicle (ELV) being recycled is maximised, so that the …^{9} is reduced.

The reuse of parts and the reclamation of materials from motor vehicles is not a new industry. Metal parts in particular have always had a value, either in terms of reuse or recycling. Nowadays many more parts can be recycled, from the plastic bumpers …^{10}. When a car reaches the end of its useful life it is usually sold to a vehicle dismantler such as Morrison Vehicle Recycling Ltd.

a	car ownership
b	environmental impact
c	as lighter, more fuel-efficient materials
d	because of old age
e	to the oil and its filter
f	mainly metal
g	scrap a similar number
h	disposable material
i	has changed substantially
j	30 million motor vehicles

B Listen again and check your text.

RECYCLING

C Find one antonym and one synonym in the box for each of the following words from the text. Complete the table in your exercise books.

1 approximately
2 useful
3 important
4 substantially
5 new
6 similar

comparable • contrasting • current • considerably • essential • exactlyl • handy • irrelevant • out-of-date • roughly • slightly • useless

Word from text	Synonym	Antonym
1 approximately		
2 useful		

3 Helping a colleague

KMK

Sie sind einer der deutschen Mechaniker. Einige Kollegen konnten dem Gespräch (Aufgabe 2A) nicht so gut folgen. Sie bitten Sie, ihnen Vics Erklärungen auf Deutsch zusammenzufassen.

4 Stage 1: de-pollution

The mechanics learn about the basic processes involved in car recycling.
Before a car is crushed, it must be de-polluted.

   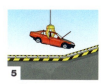

The illustrations (1 – 5) show the stages of de-pollution.
Put the following texts (a – f) into the correct order.

a The vehicle's details (license plate, ownership etc.) are recorded and entered into a database. The ELV is de-registered and a Certificate of Destruction is issued to the owner.

b The vehicle is raised to head-height so trained mechanics can access the underside. They then use purpose-designed equipment to drain off the fluids from the ELV (petrol or diesel, engine or gear box oil, brake fluid, screen wash and engine coolants). This process takes 20 minutes and the fluids are stored in secure tanks.

c The depolluted vehicle is then sent on to the shredder process for the recovery of remaining materials such as metal and plastic.

d ELVs are transported carefully to the facility so no hazardous materials escape en route. They are stored on impermeable surfaces as there are often leakages of pollutants.

e First the battery is removed, followed by wheels, windscreens and other large components, for example plastic bumpers and seat foam. Parts that have a potential for reuse or recycling, such as the catalytic converter, are also removed.

UNIT 8 RECYCLING

5 Stage 2: shredding and sorting

Vic takes the mechanics to the processing plant where the shredder and the sorters operate. Paul, one of the mechanics, is keen to practice his English.

A Read the dialogue between Vic and Paul and then put the illustrations (a – g) below into the correct order.

Vic Here we flatten the depolluted cars to prepare them for shredding. This is also known as size-reduction. Next they're going to be smashed to bits by large hammers on a rotating shaft.

Paul It's really noisy.

Vic The hammers spin at 175 miles per hour. They crush the car into 10mm-sized chunks or even smaller. This makes it easier to separate the different components. We can turn your convertible into confetti in just 45 seconds!

Paul It must create a big mixture of materials. How do you sort them?

Vic First they enter a wind turbine chamber. It sucks all the light materials such as foam and cloth away from the heavy materials, such as metals and plastics.

Paul But you've still got a big mixture there.

Vic We have to do it one step at a time. In the first step we took out the cloth and foam. Now we're going to take out the ferrous materials such as iron and steel. They are pulled out by a magnet separator. For the non-ferrous metals and plastics we use an eddy current separator.

Paul What's that?

Vic Rotating magnets induce an eddy current in good conductors like aluminium and copper. This generates a magnetic field, which causes a repulsion effect. If it's aluminium or copper or something like that, it'll go up. If it's non-metallic material such as plastic and glass, it'll go down.

Paul So you've got three separate groups now. Ferrous metals, non-ferrous metals and non-metals. Where does it all go next?

Vic The non-metallic stream goes for further processing. The ferrous stuff like steel is ready for sale, to steel mills for example. It just needs to be checked by trained workers. Sometimes products such as armatures and non-ferrous items are accidently picked up by the overband magnet.

Paul Who do you sell it to?

Vic We have a lot of UK customers, but we export most of the ferrous material abroad. We just load up the ships and off they go.

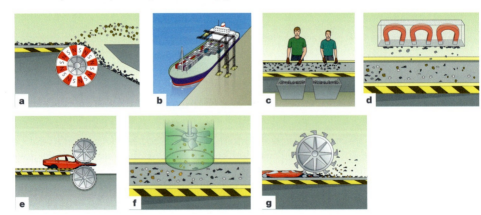

RECYCLING

6 Categories of materials

The mechanics have a go at identifying and sorting some materials by hand.

A Make a list in English of the materials which can be recycled

- from cars
- from household appliances (fridge, TV, etc.)
- from derelict buildings / construction sites
- Compare your list with your classmates' lists and add any new items.

B Draw a table in your exercise book with the following six column headings:

Ferrous metal	Non-ferrous metal	Plastics	Fluids	Fabrics	Other

Fill in the table with your list of materials.

C Work with a partner. One partner thinks of a material. The other partner tries to identify the material by asking Yes / No questions. Use the text box for ideas. Then swap roles.

LANGUAGE

Material Properties

a solid	a liquid
rare	common
a good insulator	a good conductor
an alkaline	an acid
hazardous	safe
ductile	brittle
flammable	non-flammable
soft	hard
transparent	opaque
soluble	insoluble

Is it a solid? — Yes it is.

Is it a metal? — Yes it is.

Is it brittle? — No it isn't.

I think it's … — That's correct. / No, it's …

7 Partner files

Student A: Turn to File 5 on page 129.

Student B: Turn to File 10 on page 132.

8 Steps in recycling

KMK

Ihre Kollegen bitten Sie erneut, die Arbeitsschritte des Recyclings (Aufgaben 4 und 5) kurz auf Deutsch zu notieren.

RECYCLING

9 Pros and cons

The mechanics participate in an online discussion with some British schoolchildren about recycling and reusing. The schoolchildren are well informed, but use some unusual language.

Translate the messages in your exercise books. Change the chat language (1, 3, 5) into standard English, and the standard English (2, 4, 6) into chat language. The language box may help you.

1. uzn 1 thing instead of lots of things u jst throw away lk plastic stuff means nt so mne nd 2B built n th@s gr8 4 t environment.

2. Fine, I agree, but a lot of old things are wonderful, we shouldn't just recycle them all.

3. f u keep uzn smt agn n agn n agn thn it jst gets danjrus, lk hw mne times cn u reuse 1 of those safety seats 4 kids?

4. Reusing often needs cleaning or transportation, which is expensive. But that is still cheaper than recycling at the moment.

5. we've got 2 reuse stuff bc even recycling uses heaps of nrg n releases loads of greenhouse gases, sn it will b 2 l8.

6. Some things that you reuse still need to refurbished like guitars, stereos and mobiles. That creates hi-tech jobs.

LANGUAGE

again	agn	late	l8
and	n	like	lk
at	@	many	mne
because	bc	need	nd
before	b4	not	nt
but	bt	one	1
can	cn	something	smt
creates	cr8s	still	stl
dangerous	danjrus	that(s)	th@(s)
energy	nrg	the	t
expensive	xpensiv	then	thn
fine	5n	to be	2b
for	4	tomorrow	2morow
great	gr8	using	uzn
how	hw	why	y
just	jst	wonderful	1drful
you	u		

RECYCLING

10 Role-play

An online discussion takes place in a chatroom about plastic bag recycling.

Work in groups. Choose a role and have a discussion.

TreeHugger

You hate plastic bags. They should be banned.

4 to 5 trillion are produced worldwide each year.

Thousands of marine animals and one million birds die each year because of plastic bags.

Plastic bags break down slowly, and leave toxic particles that can enter the food chain.

Even recycling plastic bags produces harmful emissions, and 99% of them can't be recycled.

Charging people for bags isn't enough, it's always only a few pence anyway.

PlasticLover

You love plastic bags. Every time you go to the supermarket you use them. You also use them as bin bags.

Most of the animals that eat plastic bags are scavengers like rats and seagulls – the less of them the better!

4 to 5 trillion are made each year, so they're obviously very useful.

They break down in landfill eventually, they're not here forever.

You can recycle them easily.

You don't mind paying for them, as long as they're cheap.

BrightIdea

You don't like plastic bags but you think it's unrealistic to ban them.

You want them to be taxed or sold.

If people have to pay for them, they will use them less.

If they are taxed, the government will get revenue to invest in alternative energy.

Supermarkets have already tried this with great results.

A lot of plastic bags are recycled nowadays anyway.

Plastics are a fact of life, we have to live with them, not without them.

LANGUAGE | Discussion

I agree with …
Yes, I think so, too.
That's a good point.
Yes, another good reason for … is …

I don't agree with …
No, I don't think so.
That's a ridiculous argument!
Well, that's a good point, but …

WEBCODE
TEMU0801

RECYCLING

GRAMMAR

Sentences with *if* and *when*

1 **If** you **add** all the plastic bags together, you **will get** the amazing number of eight billion.
2 **If** plastic bags **are taxed**, the money **can/should/might** be invested in alternative energy.
3 **If** you **haven't bought** a reusable shopping bag yet, **buy** one now!
4 **When** materials are recycled, production costs are reduced.
5 Decide **if** the following statements are true or false.
6 Jane asked me **if** I could look after her cat next week.

- Bedingungssätze bestehen aus einem Nebensatz mit *if* (Bedingung) und einem Hauptsatz (Folge). Wenn der *if*-Nebensatz dem Hauptsatz vorausgeht, werden beide durch Komma getrennt (1, 2, 3).
- Bei Bedingungssätzen (Typ 1):
- Im Nebensatz steht eine Zeit der Gegenwart, d.h. *present* (1, 2), oder *present perfect* (3). Im Hauptsatz steht oft *will-future* (1), ein modales Hilfsverb (2), oder der Imperativ (3).
- **Vorsicht!** Das deutsche „wenn" ist zweideutig:
- „Wenn" in der Bedeutung von „falls, für den Fall, dass…" übersetzt man mit *if*. Aber „wenn" in zeitlicher Bedeutung von „sobald, als, immer wenn" übersetzt man mit *when* (4). Nach einem Imperativ (5) und in der indirekten Frage (6) kann *if* auch die Bedeutung von „ob" haben.

11 Practice

A Complete these sentences with *if* or *when*.

1 … your car reaches the end of its useful life, sell it to a vehicle dismantler.
2 You'll save water … you take shorter showers.
3 … people consume more electricity, the environment will suffer.
4 You should take a canvas bag with you … you go shopping.
5 … you get your first bill, you will see … green electricity is cheaper.

B Make conditional sentences in your exercise book. Add commas if necessary.

1 supermarkets / stop selling plastic bags / consumers refuse to buy them
2 you buy a modern refrigerator / it / use less electricity than the old one
3 attach this meter to your equipment / it / show you how much electricity you use
4 you /save / a lot of electricity / you / not leave / equipment on standby
5 you / reduce your carbon footprint / you follow the above four tips

C What is the German translation for *if* and *when*?

1 Tom will sell you his old microwave oven if you ask him.
2 He will ask you if you are interested in his old fridge as well.
3 If you ask me, I wouldn't buy an old fridge. The electricity bill will be too high.
4 Steel normally sinks when you put it into water.
5 But why did this steel tank not sink when we put it into the water?

KMK exam practice

Sie sind Praktikant in der Presseabteilung von RWE-Umwelt, Deutschlands größten Müllentsorgers. Für die zweisprachige Fassung einer Messebroschüre sollen Sie drei Texte bearbeiten.

12 Mediation

Fassen Sie den Text auf Deutsch in etwa 40 bis 50 Wörtern zusammen.

Ban the bag

On average, everyone in the United Kingdom uses 134 plastic bags every year – that's about eight billion plastic bags. People use them because they're light, strong, waterproof, and very, very cheap – the ideal shopping bag. Americans use 100 billion plastic bags a year, of which 99% go straight into the rubbish after just one use, which helps explain why the entire world is tangled up in the things.

A plastic bag can be a matter of life and death. One state in India banned plastic bags after they had choked the drains. This resulted in floods which caused thousands of deaths. The strength of a plastic bag is also its fatal weakness. It will hold all your shopping all the way home – but it will also take a thousand years to disintegrate. Every time we buy a plastic bag at the supermarket, we are contributing to the pollution of our planet. So it's time to ban the plastic bag. This will encourage manufacturers to provide biodegradable alternatives, supermarkets to offer strong paper sacks, and customers to use traditional reusable shopping bags and baskets.

13 Produktion

A **Ein Text über die Abfallpyramide ist teilweise gelöscht worden. Sie haben den Auftrag, die Grafik zu erklären. Geben Sie Beispiele.**

Specialists have developed a "waste hierarchy" pyramid to help people understand how to work with waste. The concept is based on the "3Rs" – Reduce, Reuse, Recover.

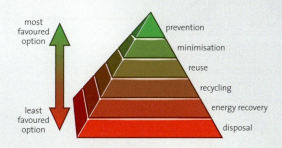

Prevention: Companies should manufacture biodegradable products that produce no waste at all.

Minimisation: …

B Sie sollen einen kurzen Kommentar auf Englisch zu diesen Bildern aus einer Broschüre schreiben. Denken Sie u. a. an die Probleme für die Welternährung, die Fischerei und den Tourismus.

Extra material

14 Plastic bottles

The recyling of plastic bottles is now a big business in the UK. New facilities are being built to service the demand for recycled material.

A Complete the following text with the words in the box.

> between • both • cutting • essential • final • first • into • recycled • running

> On a previously derelict site on the outskirts of Dagenham, sandwiched …[1] the roaring A13 and the Thames, the …[2] components are being placed into giant machines which will soon form the …[3] edge of recycling in Britain.
> The Closed Loop recycling plant claims to be the …[4] in the world to take …[5] milk bottles and clear drinks bottles and turn them back …[6] food-grade plastic.
> Once it is up and …[7], the £13m facility aims to help create a continuous cycle by enabling manufacturers to use …[8] plastic from the UK in their food and drink packaging.

B Use the diagram to put the texts (a – f) into the correct order.

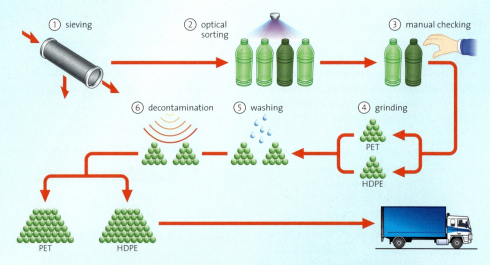

- **a** Optical sorter shines a beam of light at the bottles and sensors determine whether they are HDPE, PET or "other".
- **b** The sorted bottles are ground into flakes and separated into PET (polyethylene terephthalate) and HDPE (high-density polyethylene).
- **c** PET is decontaminated by covering the flakes with caustic soda and then putting them into a kiln where the chemical crystallises and peels away the top layer of the polymer. HDPE is melted, sieved and turned into pellets.
- **d** Bottles are de-baled and then sieved in a trommel which spins them and shakes off dirt and some of the caps. A magnet removes ferrous metals and an electrical current gets rid of other metals such as aluminium.
- **e** Team of manual checkers carries out another sort.
- **f** The flakes are hot washed for an hour.

Situations

It's Open Day at Marie-Bosch-Schule in Weinheim. The English teachers and their students have invited parents and friends to visit a class and see what the students are working on. They have prepared some tasks so that visitors can take part in authentic learning activities.

1 Reporting accidents at work

When there is an accident at school or at work we are required by law to report it to the authorities.

A Listening Comprehension

1. Listen to the text about Sven Olsen's accident (→ page 81, Exercise 8).
2. Write an accident report on a transparency.
3. Present the report to the class using the OHP*.
4. Give the class an oral summary of the accident based on your report.

(* Overhead projector = Tageslichtprojektor)

Accident Report
Place :
Time/Date:
People involved:
Description:

B Reading Comprehension

1. Read the text about a serious accident (page 82, Exercise 9).
2. Write an accident report on a transparency.
3. Present the report to the class using the OHP.
4. Give the class an oral summary of the accident based on your report.

C How could the accidents have been avoided?

2 Preventing accidents at school

Everyone in a school must know what to do (and what not to do!) if a fire breaks out. The safety regulations demand regular fire drills. Prevention is better than cure.

A A fire drill

1. Find out about the safety regulations at your school. Present the alarm plan to the class.
2. Take the class on a guided tour around the school and show them where the fire alarms, the smoke detectors, the sprinklers, the escape routes and the assembly points are.
3. Tell the class what (not) to do in case of a fire alarm.
4. Now simulate a fire drill. Tell your classmates how to leave the classroom, what to take with them and what to leave behind.

Situations

B You might see these signs in any school. What do they mean?

C The first-aid kit

> 1 Bring German-English dictionaries and the school's first aid kit to the class.
> 2 Ask your classmates and visitors what they think the contents the first aid kit are.
> 3 Unpack the items one by one and ask what they are called and what they are used for.
> 4 Ask if any of your classmates or the visitors have done or are doing a first-aid course. If so, ask them to give a demonstration.

3 Rethink your rubbish

For Open Day, the school's Wastebuster Team has created worksheets to make students and visitors aware of how to preserve our resources and to avoid accidents.

A The Six 'Rs' of eco-friendliness

Complete the sentences with one of the 'Six Rs' from the box below.

reduce • recharge • recycle • refill • repair • reuse

1 Printer cartridges can be … 4 Plastic bags and glass bottles should be …
2 Aluminum cans should be …   5 Some broken things can be …
3 Buy batteries that can be … 6 Water and energy use must be…

B Name other things that can be *reduced, recharged, recycled, refilled, repaired* or *reused*.

C Discuss these warning signs.

For example:
What do they warn us against?
What do they advise us to do?
Where can you find them?

> I think sign number one warns against noise. You'll often see them on the door to a workshop.

Providing after-sales service

UNIT 9

- Types of after-sales services
- Understanding difficult technical texts
- Giving and understanding installation instructions

1 Warm-up

A Match the after-sales tasks (1–7) to the descriptions (a–g).

1	Installation	a	This is a series of inspections, cleaning and repair tasks which are carried out at regular intervals by the manufacturer or approved agents.
2	Operator instruction	b	This is a series of routine actions to keep the equipment in working order. It is usually done by the owner of the equipment.
3	Commissioning	c	The equipment is taken to the new owner's premises, assembled and connected to power, etc.
4	Servicing	d	It may be necessary for the supplier to train the owner or his/her employees to operate the equipment.
5	Troubleshooting	e	This is the handover of the equipment from the supplier to the owner. During this process, the supplier checks that the equipment operates correctly, safely and reliably.
6	Repair	f	When a problem occurs with the equipment, a procedure is followed to find the source of the problem.
7	Maintenance	g	If components of the equipment become broken or worn, they must be mended or replaced.

B Which of the tasks above are necessary for these pieces of equipment? Give reasons for your answers.

1
cordless drill

2
light goods vehicle

3
conveyor belt

4
solar panels

5
CNC milling machine

6
computer

7
heating, ventilation and air conditioning system (HVAC)

8
smoke detector

Example: *A cordless drill requires only minimum maintenance and repair is not usually economical.*

99

PROVIDING AFTER-SALES SERVICE

2 A water-heating system

GR Haustechnik installs solar water-heating systems in Germany. The company is preparing to install a system in a holiday house. Installation engineer Werner Gütting asks his new apprentice, Mario Schmidt, to read the owner's manual. The system is made by the Australian company Solahart and the manual is in English.

A Check your knowledge before you read.

- What do you know about solar hot water systems?
- Decide whether the following statements are true or false.
  1. Solar hot water systems use the heat of the sun to produce electricity.
  2. The panels in a solar hot water system are black to help absorb the sun's rays.
  3. Solar hot water systems cannot be used in areas where temperatures fall below 0°C.

B Now read the text below to find out whether you were right.

SOLAHART

Congratulations on choosing a Solahart solar water-heating system. Your Solahart is equipped with the latest technology in solar water heaters. It is one of the most effective and trouble-free systems available today. In addition to reducing your water-heating energy consumption, it will help preserve precious natural resources by using free energy from the sun.

All Solahart solar hot water systems with roof-mounted tanks use the Thermosiphon principle to collect heat from the sun and transfer it to your hot water. The Thermosiphon principle is based on two naturally occurring phenomena:

- Dark-coloured objects absorb more heat than light-coloured objects,
- Hot water rises as it becomes less dense.

All Solahart collector panels are coated with a dark, heat-absorbent surface. This coating absorbs the sun's rays and heats the fluid in the collector panel. As the fluid heats, it rises to the top of the collector panel and into the tank, where it displaces cooler fluid, which flows to the bottom of the collector panel where the process is repeated.

The Closed Circuit Series solar water heaters use collectors which contain a special heat-transfer fluid called Hartgard. Hartgard improves the performance of your Solahart water heater. Hartgard is a special food-grade (non-toxic) solution and is the only fluid which may be used in closed circuit systems. Unlike water, Hartgard fluid resists freezing and protects the solar water heater against frost damage.

In the Closed Circuit Series, heat is absorbed by the collector and passed to the Hartgard heat-transfer liquid inside the collector. As the temperature of the Hartgard increases, the hot fluid rises up through the collector into the heat exchanger jacket which surrounds the potable water storage tank. Here, the heat is transferred to the potable water, cooling the Hartgard fluid. The cooler fluid is then forced back down into the collectors when further hot fluid rises up into the heat exchanger jacket.

The cooler fluid which has been forced down is again heated in the collectors and rises back up to pass the heat to the potable water in the storage tank. This circulation repeats until all water in the storage tank is heated. So that you can enjoy hot water on cloudy days, you can fit your Solahart water heater with an electric or gas booster system.

PROVIDING AFTER-SALES SERVICE

3 Understanding the text

Read the text carefully, then answer the questions below.

1. Why is this system suitable for colder areas?
2. What could happen if you use water instead of Hartgard?
3. List the main components of the system.
4. In this system, is it possible to install the tank at a level lower than the collector, e.g. on the wall of the house? Give reasons for your answer.

TIP

Wie lese ich einen schwierigen Text?

Bevor Sie einen schweren Text lesen, sollten Sie überlegen, welche Informationen Sie benötigen: ein allgemeines Textverständnis oder ein detailliertes Verständnis bestimmter Textabschnitte oder des ganzen Textes. Wählen Sie die Lesetechnik, die Sie am besten ans Ziel bringt.

1. **Vorwissen abklären als Vorbereitung auf das Lesen**
   Vor dem Lesen sollten Sie sich erinnern, was Sie bereits zur Thematik wissen.

2. **Schnelles Lesen zum Erfassen des allgemeinen Textverständnisses**
   Verschaffen Sie sich einen ersten Eindruck vom Text, indem Sie sich zunächst die Überschrift, evtl. auch die Zeichnungen und die Bilder ansehen und dann den Text überfliegen.

3. **Selektives Lesen zum Erfassen wichtiger Textabschnitte**
   Nach dem ersten Lesen merkt man oft, dass nur ein Teil des Textes wichtig ist. Suchen Sie den Text nur auf die Gesichtspunkte oder Fakten ab, die Sie interessieren.

4. **Genaues Lesen zum Erfassen des Detailverständnisses**
   Wollen Sie bei einem Fachtext den Zusammenhang, Fakten oder einzelne Wörter genau verstehen, müssen Sie den Text oder die entsprechenden Textabschnitte langsam, Satz für Satz lesen. Ein Wörter- oder Fachwörterbuch sollte auch hier nur dann zu Rate gezogen werden, wenn Sie alle sprachlichen Differenzierungen verstehen wollen.

5. **Den Text strukturieren und grafisch veranschaulichen**
   Wenn Sie sich den Textinhalt effektiv einprägen wollen, sollten Sie ihn strukturieren (z. B. indem Sie wesentliche Textstellen durch Markierung hervorheben) und grafisch veranschaulichen (z. B. indem Sie die wichtigsten Aussagen in einer Mind Map festhalten).

6. **Umgang mit unbekannten Wörtern**
   Schlagen Sie unbekannte Wörter nur dann im Wörterbuch nach, wenn Sie das Wort aus dem Satzzusammenhang nicht erschließen können und es für das Textverständnis notwendig ist.

PROVIDING AFTER-SALES SERVICE

4 Reading for detail

Mario assistiert Herrn Gütting bei der Installation der Solaranlage. Um sicher zu gehen, dass Mario alles verstanden hat, stellt er ihm Fragen.

Antworte an Marios Stelle mithilfe des nachfolgenden Textes.

1. Was ist bei der Montage von Solaranlagen in Gebieten mit starken Schneefall zu beachten? Begründen Sie ihre Antwort.
2. Wie kann man die Kaltwasserventile gegen Frostschaden schützen? (2 Möglichkeiten!)
3. Im Extremfall kann es hier Tiefsttemperaturen um -15°C geben. Welche zusätzliche Schutzmaßnahme sollten wir einbauen?
4. Wie wird Hartgard in diesem System verwendet? (2 Punkte)
5. Warum müssen wir den Warmwasserhahn aufdrehen?
6. Was machen wir nach Inbetriebnahme des Wasserspeichers?

INSTALLATION IN COLD CLIMATES

In areas which have heavy snow, ensure that snow cannot build up behind the tank. In this case install the tank as close as possible to the roof ridge.

Note that valves can be permanently damaged if water freezes inside them. Install the valves on the cold water supply line indoors if possible. If these valves are outside the building they must be insulated with at least 19 mm of insulation.

In locations which often have temperatures below -10°C, even hot and cold pipes and valves which are insulated may freeze. In these locations, the cold pipes and valves to the Solahart storage tank and the hot pipe from the tank should have electric heater tape under the insulation. The electric heater tape should have a heat output of between 10 and 20 W/m. It should be controlled by a thermostat set at 0°C.

The solar collectors and tank heat exchanger jacket are connected together to create a sealed, closed circuit which is entirely separate from the drinking water in the storage cylinder. The circuit is filled with 'Hartgard' fluid. Under no circumstances can any fluids other than 'Hartgard' be used as the heat transfer fluid. Only drinking water can be used in conjunction with 'Hartgard'.

Filling and commissioning the storage tank

Turn on at least one hot water tap. Turn on the mains water supply tap and allow the water to fill the storage cylinder. It will push air out of the top of the cylinder through the open hot water tap. As soon as water flows freely (without air bursts) from the tap, turn off the tap and allow the cylinder to pressurize. Check that all the joints are watertight.

Having ensured that the power or gas is correctly connected to the electric/gas booster element, turn on the booster element.

Operate both pressure relief valves to ensure that the valves are functional. The storage tank is now filled and ready for use as an electric or gas water heater. For use as a solar water heater, the closed circuit must be commissioned by the authorised Solahart technician who installed it or by another authorised Solahart service contractor. (Refer to the separate Closed Circuit Commissioning Procedure.)

You must fill the storage tank with water before you fill the closed circuit.

> **!** Achtung falscher Freund!
> insulate – *isolieren*
> isolate – *absperren*

PROVIDING AFTER-SALES SERVICE

5 Flow diagram

Copy and complete the flow diagram to show the main stages in commissioning the water tank. Your diagram should have 10–11 stages in total.

Filling and commissioning the water tank

6 Working with words

Complete the instruction below each illustration using eight verbs from the box. (There are more verbs than you need.)

check • connect • fill • freeze • install • insulate • operate
turn off • turn on • use

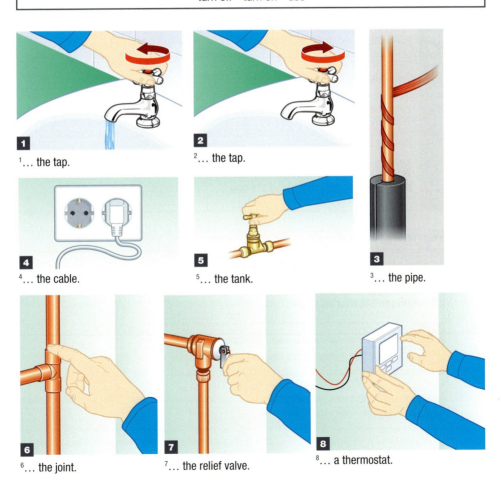

1 ... the tap.

2 ... the tap.

4 ... the cable.

5 ... the tank.

3 ... the pipe.

6 ... the joint.

7 ... the relief valve.

8 ... a thermostat.

103

PROVIDING AFTER-SALES SERVICE

7 | Role-play dialogue

Matt Davies is installing a solar hot water system on a roof in Wales. Unfortunately his instructions have blown away in the wind. He phones the office and asks another installer to give him step-by-step instructions over the phone.

Work with a partner. Complete the following dialogue with your own ideas. Your flow diagram from exercise 5 and the Language box below will help you. Record your dialogue and play it back to the class.

Matt   Hello, is that you, Jack? It's me, Matt. You won't believe this, but I'm on the roof and I've just lost my instructions. Can you talk me through installing the tank, please?.
Jack   Matt, I worry about you sometimes, honestly! … OK, how far have you got?
Mike   I've turned on the hot water tap and the mains supply tap. What do I do now?
Jack   …
Mike   OK, I've done that. What next?
(etc.)

LANGUAGE

Giving instructions

How far have you got?

Right. You need to (fill the tank) next.

First you (turn on the hot water), then you (turn on the mains supply).

Have you (filled the tank) yet?

Good. / Do it now, then.

Has the (tank filled)?

When the (tank fills), (turn off the tap).

Yes, that's fine. No, something's wrong.

I've already (installed the tank), but I haven't (commissioned it) yet.

How do I do that?

OK, I've got that. What next?

Yes, I have. No, I haven't.

OK, I've done that. What do I do now?

Yes, it has. No, it hasn't.

The (valve is leaking). Is that right?

---

8 | Warning signs   `KMK`

Beim Lesen des Handbuchs findet Mario einige wichtige Hinweise auf Gefahren. Herr Gütting bittet Mario, diese dem Besitzer auf Deutsch zu erklären.

Übernehmen Sie Marios Rolle.

> **TIP** Don't try to translate the texts into German word-for-word. The message is important, not the words.

> ⚠ **Warning – electrical hazard**
> This water heater uses 230V power for its electrically operated components. The removal of the front cover will expose 230V wiring. It must only be removed by a qualified electrician.

PROVIDING AFTER-SALES SERVICE

 Hot water!

Your Solahart water heater will generate hot water quickly and efficiently. Under normal family use, it will operate between 60°C and 70°C. However, the temperature can exceed this and may be as high as 95°C. This can occur during prolonged periods of direct sunlight (particularly in summer).

Check the water temperature when you turn on the shower or fill a bath or basin, to ensure that it is safe to use.

Do not touch the pipes which connect the solar storage tank to the solar collectors. The fluid which flows through these pipes may be very hot.

 Period of Reduced Usage or Holidays

If the water heater is left unused for two weeks or more, hydrogen gas may accumulate in the water cylinder. A danger of fire or explosion may occur. To remove this gas safely, turn on a sink hot tap for several minutes. During this procedure there must be no smoking, open flames or any electrical appliance operating nearby. If there is hydrogen in the tank, it will make an unusual sound like air escaping.

 Hartgard Solution

If the water from your water heater appears blue, then this may indicate a leak of Hartgard from the heat exchange jacket into the potable water.

Hartgard is of food-grade quality and will not harm you. However, the blue colour in the water indicates a fault. Contact your Solahart dealer to inspect the system.

9 Writing down some details

18

GR Haustechnik hat die neue Solaranlage installiert und in Betrieb genommen. Doch nach einigen Tagen ruft die Kundin Herrn Gütting an, weil aus dem Überdruckventil Flüssigkeit austritt. Da dies neu für ihn ist, ruft Herr Gütting Solaharts European Service Centre an, um zu fragen, ob dies normal sei.

Hören Sie das Telefongespräch und ergänzen Sie Herrn Güttings Notizen.

Solahart Closed Circuit Series Solar Water Heater

PR ...¹ Sicherheitsventil
Soll Überdruck entlasten, der durch ...² oder ...³ entsteht.
In der ersten Betriebssaison - ...⁴, bis ...⁵.
Entlässt das Ventil nach der ersten Betriebssaison weiterhin Flüssigkeit, ...⁶
Der Kunde soll das Sicherheitsventil ...⁷ und unter keinen Umständen versuchen, ...⁸ - hohe Verletzungsgefahr!
Das Ventil kann nicht entfernt werden, ...⁹.

WEBCODE
TEMU0901

PROVIDING AFTER-SALES SERVICE

GRAMMAR

Relative clauses

Relativpronomen verbinden zwei Hauptsätze zu einem Satz aus Haupt- und Relativsatz. Das Relativpronomen steht gewöhnlich nach seinem vorausgehenden Bezugswort.

1 Mr Bell is a carpenter. **He** creates frames for windows.
Mr Bell is a carpenter **who** creates frames for windows.
2 Smoke detectors are simple devices. **They** need regular servicing.
Smoke detectors are simple devices **which/that** need regular servicing.
3 Mr Gütting is a good employer. **His** employees like working for him.
Mr Gütting is a good employer **whose** employees like working for him.
4 The price of the Solar EcoWarm heater is not **what** was agreed.

- Für Personen steht im Relativsatz ohne Komma vorzugsweise *who* oder weniger häufig *that*. (1)
- Für Tiere und Dinge steht *which* oder *that*. (2)
- Um Besitz oder Zugehörigkeit auszudrücken verwendet man *whose*. (3)
- (Vorsicht! Nicht mit *who's (who is)* verwechseln.)
- Fehlt im Hauptsatz ein Bezugswort, verbindet man die Sätze mit *what*. (4)

10 Practice

A Rewrite these sentence pairs using relative clauses.

Example: *The company supplies EcoWarm heaters. It had a problem recently.*
The company which supplies EcoWarm heaters had a problem recently.

1 The customer phoned them about the problem. She was angry.
2 She couldn't use the heater. It had just been installed.
3 The fluid leaked from the heater. It was coloured blue.
4 The apprentice filled the tank. He didn't read the instructions.
5 The tap supplied hot water. It was turned off.
6 The air was in the tank. It damaged the pipes.
7 The technician had installed the heater. He phoned the manufacturer.
8 The heater was damaged. It had to be replaced.

B Decide which relative pronoun is correct.

1 Solar panels are devices who/which/what are usually maintenance free.
2 Mr Gütting is the installation engineer who/which/who owns GR Haustechnik.
3 Hartgard is a special fluid who/which/who will not freeze at 0°C.
4 The heater that/which/whose/what valve is defect has to be replaced.
5 The Solahart water heater was exactly that/which/whose/what the customer needed.
6 This is a heating system which/whose/what requires a professional installation.
7 Do not touch the pipes who/which/whose/what connect the storage tank to the collectors.
8 The fluid whose/what/which flows through the pipes may be very hot.
9 Solahart is the company that/which/whose/what water-heating system uses a special heat-transfer fluid called Hartgard.
10 Hartgard is that/which/whose/what makes their solar collectors so efficient.

KMK exam practice

Interview with Professor Bornholm about Germany's energy policy

Hören Sie die beiden Teile des Interviews jeweils zweimal. Lesen Sie die betreffenden Aufgabenstellungen vor dem Hören genau durch. Beantworten Sie die Fragen in Ihrem Heft.

11 Hörverstehen (Teil 1)

Entscheiden Sie, ob die folgenden Aussagen richtig oder falsch sind.

1. Professor Bornholm is a prominent member of the German government.
2. Developing alternative energy is the only solution that can slow down climate change.
3. Germany plans to increase the percentage of renewable energy by 35 percent by the year 2015.
4. China and the USA have made binding commitments to reduce greenhouse gases.
5. The government has decided to close down all nuclear plants by 2022.

12 Hörverstehen

Hören Sie das Interview (Teil 1) erneut und beantworten Sie die Fragen auf Deutsch.

1. Inwiefern hat Professor Bornholm Einfluss auf die Energiepolitik Deutschlands?
2. Wovon hängt seiner Meinung nach die Zukunft unseres Planeten ab?
3. Wie hoch ist der Anteil erneuerbarer Energien an der deutschen Energiebilanz zur Zeit des Interviews?
4. Um wieviel Prozent soll dieser Anteil bis 2020 gesteigert werden?
5. Um welchen Prozentsatz soll der Ausstoß von Treibhausgasen bis 2020 im Vergleich zu 1990 verringert werden?

13 Hörverstehen (Teil 2)

Machen Sie sich kurze Notizen auf Englisch zu den folgenden fünf Punkten des Themas.

The turning point in Germany's energy production:
1. The vote in the German parliament
2. The future of nuclear power plants
3. The future of coal-fired power plants
4. Reduction of greenhouse gases
5. Italy and Switzerland

14 Produktion

Schreiben Sie einem englischen Brieffreund Ihre Meinung über die neue deutsche Energiepolitik.

Extra material

15 Heat pumps

Read the text below and find the best place (1 – 5) for the following headings. Two headings are not needed.

a Air source or ground source – which is better?
b Fit and forget
c How do heat pumps work?
d Integration
e Low cost
f Versatility
g What are the key benefits of heat pumps?

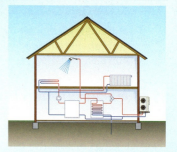

The intelligent heating solution

Heat pumps extract available heat from a natural source and release it in another location at a higher temperature. Heat pumps can be used to heat your home or hot water. There are different types of heat pumps that can take heat from the ground, the air or from water – known as ground source, air source and water source respectively. Heat pumps have some impact on the environment as they need electricity to run (just like your fridge requires electricity to operate) but the heat they extract is from a renewable source.

[1]

Heat naturally flows from a warmer place to a cooler place. However, heat pumps use a special fluid that constantly evaporates and condenses in a closed circuit controlled by valves and a compressor in order to reverse this natural process. In heating applications, heat is removed from ambient air or from water, soil or bedrock using a heat 'collection loop' and delivered to where it is needed, usually into the heating and hot water systems of the house.

[2]

Although heat pumps need electricity to run, they use less electrical energy than the heat energy they generate. This makes them much more efficient than other electrical heating options. Typically you only need one unit of electricity to deliver two to three units of heat with a heat pump. Because heat pumps need electricity to run there will still be some resulting CO_2 emissions, although these can be lower than for other heating systems.

[3]

One of the advantages of heat pumps is that they can be incorporated into many homes. They are more suited to newer highly insulated properties and are not always suitable for flats. Once installed and connected to the heating and hot water circuits they are fully automatic. Heat pumps are also easily integrated with solar hot water systems to provide a comprehensive heating and hot water system.

[4]

The collection loop for ground source heat pumps can be installed horizontally or vertically into the ground. Water source heat pumps need a source of water such as a lake, river or stream and air source heat pumps simply need the outside air. There is, therefore, a type of heat pump suitable for almost every type of house.

[5]

Very little maintenance is required if a well designed heat pump system is installed properly. Equipment should operate automatically with very little noise. Heat pump system components have long life expectancies and high reliability. Life expectancy for the pump is around 20 years, while a ground loop could last around 40 years if designed and installed properly.

16 Your opinion

Should heat pumps be installed in all new and renovated homes? Give reasons for your answer.

Applying for a job

UNIT 10

- Writing a CV
- Applying for a job
- Preparing for an interview

1 Warm-up

A Here are some opinions about jobs. Match them with the summaries below.

1 I really want to work for a famous company. Something that will look impressive on my CV.

2 For me the pension is the most important thing. I need to know I will be OK when I retire.

3 There ought to be good opportunities for training.

9 I'd love to be self-employed or work freelance.

4 I want to have responsibility over other people.

5 I need generous holidays and flexi-time as I need to spend time with my children.

8 I'd expect a company car. You don't have to worry about insurance, petrol, MOT, anything.

7 I don't want to lose my job after six months. So it needs to be a strong company.

6 Obviously the salary has to come first. Who wants to work for nothing?

a job security
b the perks
c an impressive reference
d work–life balance
e a good income
f developing my ability
g independence
h an investment for the future
i being the boss

B Put the summaries in order of their importance to you. Then compare your list with a partner.

APPLYING FOR A JOB

2 | Looking for a job

Sandra Behringer is an HGV (heavy goods vehicle) mechanic. She has recently moved to the UK and is interested in this job.

VEHICLE TECHNICIAN

We are urgently looking for an experienced and motivated HGV mechanic. You will be working in a busy workshop, looking after the company's fleet of vehicles, ranging from light commercial vehicles through to Class 1 and 2 HGVs. Your day-to-day duties will include servicing, repair, fault-finding and diagnostics.

This is a permanent position, working full time for a large national company who offer an extensive range of benefits including a generous tool allowance and ongoing career progression. The basic salary of £35,000 is very competitive and regular overtime is available. Other benefits include sickness pay and 30 days holiday. We also offer a company pension and a private medical insurance after 5 years of employment.

This is an urgent appointment, so interviews can be held at short notice for suitable candidates. Interested? Then send your CV with a covering letter to the address below.

Requirements:
- an accredited qualification in heavy vehicle mechanics
- a good knowledge of English
- the ability to prioritize workloads
- strong communication skills
- one year's experience (minimum) in a similar position
- education to GCE 'O' level or equivalent GCSE level is essential.
- must be a hard worker, and able to work accurately under pressure.
- must possess strong numeracy and literacy skills.

A licence for Heavy Goods Vehicles is essential.

We are an equal opportunities employer. We select candidates according to their skills and experience regardless of gender, ethnicity, sexual orientation, religion or age.

A Read the advertisement and complete the sentences below in your own words.

1. The company are looking for …
2. They will pay …
3. The type of employment contract they are offering is …
4. Their recruitment policy states that …

B Read the advert again and organize the information into three lists.

Skills and Experience	Personal Qualities	Salary / Benefits
one year in a similar position	motivated	£35,000
…	…	…

C Sie sind Sandra Behringer. Da die Firma mehrere KFZ-Mechaniker sucht, schicken Sie Ihrem arbeitsuchenden Freund Thorsten das Stellenangebot nach Deutschland. Sie fassen die Annonce auf Deutsch zusammen, da Thorsten Probleme mit Englisch hat.

APPLYING FOR A JOB

3 Writing a CV

A Read the following advice about creating a German CV and then connect the sentence halves below to summarize the information.

> **DER LEBENSLAUF**
>
> Ein Lebenslauf enthält die wichtigsten persönlichen Daten des Bewerbers oder der Bewerberin. Er soll klar gegliedert sein, damit man einen schnellen Überblick über den Bewerber und dessen Fähigkeiten erhält. Heute wird der Lebenslauf in tabellarischer Form dargestellt und nur noch in bestimmten Ausnahmen in Textform erstellt. Der Lebenslauf ist sicherlich der wichtigste Teil der Bewerbung und wird vom Arbeitgeber am genauestens gelesen. Es ist heute üblich, den Lebenslauf chronologisch zu ordnen, wobei die aktuellsten Daten an erste Stelle stehen sollten ("amerikanischer Lebenslauf").
>
> In Deutschland ist ein Bewerbungsfoto im Lebenslauf zwar keine Pflicht, bietet aber bereits die erste Möglichkeit, positiv auf sich aufmerksam zu machen. In der Regel wird hiervon auch Gebrauch gemacht. Lebensläufe ohne ein Foto sind mittlerweile eher die Ausnahme. Ein vollständiger Lebenslauf umfasst demnach folgende Teile: Bewerbungsfoto, persönliche Daten, Informationen zum Bildungsweg, berufliche Qualifikationen, bisherige Berufe, Berufserfahrungen oder Praktika sowie sonstige Fertigkeiten und Kenntnisse. Vergessen Sie nicht Ort, Datum und Ihre Unterschrift.

1 The CV should present personal information
2 It should offer a rapid overview
3 We recommend organizing the contents in chronological
4 The cover letter should be signed
5 A photo is not mandatory
6 Qualifications and experience should be listed

a order, starting with the most recent.
b but it offers you a chance to make a positive first impression.
c in a form which is concise and clearly structured.
d along with where and when they were achieved.
e of the applicant and his or her abilities.
f as well as the CV.

> **TIP** **Wohnort**
>
> Mit der Ausnahme von Bayern (*Bavaria*), sind die englischen Bezeichnungen für deutsche Bundesländer im alltäglichen Sprachgebrauch fast total unbekannt – also bedeutungslos. Die nächste Großstadt reicht als geografische Referenz aus.
>
> Bekannte englische Namen für deutsche Städte sind: München (*Munich*), Köln (*Cologne*), Hannover (*Hanover*), Nürnberg (*Nuremberg*), Braunschweig (*Brunswick*).

B Download a CV in German from the Internet (search under "Lebenslauf Beispiel"). Compare it with Sandra's British CV on the next page. What differences do you notice?

APPLYING FOR A JOB

C Look at Sandra's English CV and decide where these phrases belong.

a   Career History
b   References
c   Flat 2/3, 39 Clarence Drive, Birmingham, B13 9XJ
d   Volunteer with local girls sports group (football & hockey)
e   Ensure all work is completed on time & within service schedules.
f   Experience and knowledge of the latest IT technologies used in fault diagnosis.
g   First-aid certificate
h   Quick to learn new skills and disciplines with an exemplary time keeping and attendance record

---

Sandra Behringer
...[1]
Tel: +44 7775 837233
Email: Sandrab@cynis.com

Profile
"A multi-skilled mechanic with good all-round technical and mechanical expertise. Dependable, adaptable and flexible with a positive attitude. ...[2]"

Key Skills
- Aware of safety regulations when lifting heavy tools and parts.
- Experience of servicing large vehicles such as 7.5-tonne lorries and above.
- Ability to identify and diagnose vehicle faults.
- HGV license (EU)
- ...[3]
- Experience of mechanical work at a car dealer franchise, petrol stations and auto supply store.

...[4]
WW Möbel-Transport GmbH, Hamburg   MECHANIC   June 2008 - Present

Responsible for carrying out warranty repairs to manufacturer's guidelines, including replacing brakes and suspensions, and servicing of vehicles. ...[5]

Education
Friedrich-Ebert-Grundschule, Sandgasse 14, 69117 Heidelberg (4 years)
Johannes-Kepler-Realschule, 24 Mönchhofstraße, 69120 Heidelberg (6 years)
Carl-Bosch-Schule, Mannheimer Straße 23, 69115 Heidelberg (3 years)

Other Skills
Full driving license (EU)
English B2 (CEFR)
...[6]

Hobbies and Interests
Kit cars, gaming, climbing, ...[7]

...[8]
Fritz Fels GmbH, 108 Hardtstraße, 69124 Heidelberg
Gold Key Logistics GmbH, 1 Mannheimer Straße, 69123 Heidelberg

APPLYING FOR A JOB

4 A letter of application

Sandra writes the letter of application to send with the CV.

A Complete her letter with the words from the box below.

> advertised • ambitious • apply • available • challenge • currently •
> job • responsible • sincerely • vacancy

Dear Ms Carr

...¹ for the position of HGV mechanic

I am writing to ...² for the above position, which I saw ...³ on your company website. Please find enclosed a copy of my curriculum vitae. *(paragraph 1)*

...⁴ I am working as a repairs mechanic for a haulage company in Heidelberg. Here I am ...⁵ for carrying out diagnostics and repairs on our fleet of HGVs. There is also some work involved on lighter vehicles such as cars and vans. As I am recently qualified it is my first ...⁶, however I have risen to the position of assistant workshop supervisor, and for two months running I was voted Employee of the Month. *(paragraph 2)*

Your advert caught my eye because I am looking for a new ...⁷ in the same field. I am ...⁸ and I was attracted by your company's commitment to training and career development. I am also a fast learner and I adapt quickly to new environments. I am able to take responsibility for my own workload, but I also enjoy the experience of working with a team. *(paragraph 3)*

I am ...⁹ for work immediately, as I am moving to the UK, near your firm. I would be delighted if you invited me to an interview. *(paragraph 4)*

I look forward to hearing from you in the near future. *(paragraph 5)*

Yours ...¹⁰

Sandra Behringer

**B Sandra adds the following sentences to her letter.
Which paragraphs does she add them to?**

1. However, I think it's time for a change.
2. If you require any further information, please do not hesitate to contact me.
3. I can also send copies of my certificates if they are required.
4. I am available from the 16th of June.
5. Furthermore, I am flexible and do not mind working long hours or shifts.

C Discuss a job you would like to have with a partner. Think about:

1. The type of company.
2. The position you would like to apply for.
3. The skills you could bring to the job.
4. Why you want the job.

APPLYING FOR A JOB

D Use Sandra's letter and the language box below to write a letter of application for the job.

TIP

Letter of Application

1st paragraph: Explain why you are writing
2nd paragraph: Describe your work and training history
3rd paragraph: Describe your personal qualities
4th paragraph: Say when you are ready to start work / come for an interview

LANGUAGE

Formal applications

Dear Ms/Mr/Mrs …,
Dear Sir or Madam,

I wish to apply for the above post, advertised in …
I read/saw your advert in (name of newspaper) / on (name of website) and I would like to apply for the above position.

I am currently working in a small company called …
Since I have started here I have learned …
I have a very wide range of responsibilities which include …
My main task at present is the maintenance / installation / repair of …

I am seeking a new position that …
- offers responsibility for the full range of …
- provides me with the opportunity to meet and work with a wide range of people.

I like to think that I bring enthusiasm and adaptability to my work.

I am interested in finding a position
- which offers me greater responsibility / a greater challenge.
- where I can apply and expand my skills as a …

I would welcome an opportunity to discuss …
I am available for an interview at any time.
I look forward to hearing from you.

Yours sincerely / faithfully

TIP

CV Language

Use action verbs to talk about duties and achievements.

assisted	built	cleaned	organize
controlled	developed	diagnosed	supervise
enabled	fixed	maintained	be responsible for
operated	repaired	supervised	be in charge of

APPLYING FOR A JOB

5 The interview

A Work with a partner. Write a list of questions you might expect at an interview.

B Listen to Tom's interview with Sandra Behringer. Take notes and answer Tom's questions.

1. Why did she decide to leave her job?
2. What were her responsibilities?
3. What does she like most about mechanics?
4. What are her strengths / weaknesses?
5. What attracts her to the new job?

6 Role-play

Interview each other for the ideal job you talked about in exercise 4C.

Interviewer/in (A)

Fragen Sie B was er/sie zur Zeit macht.

Bewerber/in (B)

Sie haben vor kurzem Ihre Ausbildung abgeschlossen und sind auf Stellensuche.

Bitten Sie ihn/sie, von seiner / ihrer Ausbildung zu erzählen.

Nennen Sie Schule, Firma, Berufsausbildung und Schulabschluss. Erläutern Sie, was Sie gelernt haben.

Fragen Sie ihn/sie, warum er/sie den Beruf gewählt hat.

Nennen Sie drei Gründe für Ihre Berufswahl (z.B. Aufgaben, Berufsaussichten …)

Bitten Sie B persönliche Stärken und Schwächen zu nennen.

Nennen Sie eine persönliche Schwäche und zwei persönliche Stärken.

Fragen Sie, warum die Firma ihn/sie einstellen sollte.

Nennen Sie persönliche Eigenschaften oder Fertigkeiten, die für Ihre Einstellung sprechen.

Laden Sie ihn/sie ein, Fragen zur Firma und dem Stellenangebot zu stellen.

Erkundigen Sie sich über die Ausbildung und Ihre Zukunftsperspektiven in der Firma.

Sagen Sie, dass ein Mentor die Ausbildung begleiten würde. Über Beförderung würde das Management entscheiden.

Sagen Sie, dass Sie hoch motiviert sind und die Stelle mit viel Engagement antreten würden.

Beenden Sie das Interview. Sagen Sie, dass B von Ihnen hören würde.

Sie bedanken und verabschieden sich.

WEBCODE
TEMU1001

UNIT 10 — APPLYING FOR A JOB

> ## GRAMMAR: Adjectives and adverbs
>
> 1. Sandra is a **hard** worker.
> 2. She's **good** at maths.
> 3. We are **highly competent** specialists.
> 4. Applicants must be able to **think logically**.
> 5. Sandra has adapted **extremely well** to her new position.
> 6. But she expects a **bigger** challenge.
> 7. She was the **youngest** of the applicants.
> 8. She answered the questions **more logically** than the boys.
> 9. She was **the most suitable** applicant.
>
> - Adjektive bestimmen Nomen (1) und Pronomen (2).
> - Adverbien bestimmen Adjektive (3), Verben (4) und andere Adverbien (5).
> - Einsilbige Adjektive werden mit *-(e)r* (6) und *-(e)st* (7) gesteigert.
> - Mehrsilbige Adverbien und Adjektive werden mit *more* (8) und *most* (9) gesteigert. Vergleiche bildet man mit *… than* oder *as … as*.
>
> **Merke**: Unregelmäßige Steigerungsformen:
> *good – better – best; bad – worse – worst; little* (wenig) *– less – least;*
> *much/many – more – most; far, farther farthest*

7 Practice

A Complete the sentences with either an adjective or an adverb from the box.

> calm/calmly • good/well • immediate/immediately •
> successful/successfully • urgent/urgently

1. AB Logistics was in … need of mechanics. They needed them … .
2. They advertized the jobs … and they got an … response from Tom.
3. Tom stayed … during the interview and he answered all the questions … .
4. Tom is very … at tests. He always does … under pressure.
5. Ellen … completed the training course, her first step towards a … career.

B Which company would you like to work for? Make comparisons.

	Company A	Company B
1 Salary	£27,000	£35,000
2 Holiday	35 days	35 days
3 Employees	1960	150
4 Size	multi-national	medium-sized
5 Location	20 miles from home	60 miles from home
6 Turnover	500 million	50 million

KMK exam practice

8 Interaktion

Petra, Jean und Manuel bewerben sich im Rahmen des Leonardo-Programms bei der Saturn Corporation Ltd in Crawley, England. John Merrick, Personalchef von Saturn hat sie zu einem Gruppeninterview in sein Büro eingeladen.

Bilden Sie Gruppen von je vier Teilnehmern (3 Bewerber, 1 Interviewer). Wechseln Sie die Rollen innerhalb der Gruppe. Präsentieren Sie das Gruppeninterview der Klasse. Beantworten Sie anschließend Fragen der Klasse.

Partner A:
Als Personalchef fragen Sie die Bewerber,
1. wie sie angereist sind.
2. ob sie Schwierigkeiten hatten, die Firma zu finden.
3. wo sie geboren sind.
4. welche Schulbildung sie haben.
5. nach ihren bisherigen beruflichen Erfahrungen.
6. ob sie lieber eine Teilzeit- oder Ganztagsstelle suchen.
7. nach ihren persönlichen Stärken.
8. nach ihren Fertigkeiten,
9. nach ihren Berufszielen und …
10. was sie in ihrer Freizeit machen.

Bewerber	Partner B: Jean	Partner C: Petra	Partner D: Manuel
Anreise	mit dem Auto	mit der Bahn	mit dem Motorrad
Probleme, die Firma zu finden	keine; besitzt ein Navigationssystem	keine, nahm Taxi vom Bahnhof	Probleme; musste oft Karte zuhilfe nehmen
Geburtsort	Lyon an der Rhone	Köln am Rhein	Barcelona
Schulbildung	Berufsfachschule	Wirtschaftsgymnasium	Realschule
Arbeitserfahrung	arbeitete in einem Computershop, behob Softwarefehler, installierte Netzwerke	arbeitete bei H&M in der Damenabteilung; beriet Kundinnen	arbeitete in einem Mediamarkt, verkaufte Kameras und Handys
Arbeitszeit	Vollzeit	Teilzeit oder Vollzeit	Teilzeit
Fertigkeiten	vertraut mit Software und Hardware, PowerPoint, Excel etc.	gut in Mathematik; gut im Umgang mit Menschen	Amateurfotograf; kann Motorräder reparieren
Persönliche Stärken	fleißig; kreativ; Interesse für neue Technologien	schnelle Auffassungs-gabe; freundlich, geduldig	motiviert, ehrgeizig; guter Teamarbeiter
Berufsziele	Stelle im IT-Bereich, bei der man durch Praxis hinzulernt	Stelle in der Verkaufs- oder Personalabteilung	praktische Arbeit in einer Werkstatt
Freizeitaktivitäten	im Internet surfen Computerspiele	leitet Pfadfindergruppe Freunde treffen	Touren mit dem Motorrad; Musik hören

Extra material

9 Writing your CV

A CV is designed to get you an interview. If you get the key components of your CV right, you will have an advantage over your competition.

…¹

This is your first opportunity to make an impression. Employers need to have a reason to continue reading the rest of your CV. They want to know what you will do for them. Most CVs fall into the trap of being too self-orientated.

…²

Employers spend more time looking at this section than any other part of your CV. Consequently, this section needs to convince a potential employer that you are suitable for the job. Your most recent positions need the most attention because it is your skills and experiences gained in these roles that will determine your suitability for the role. Show your start and finish dates in years only – it looks better and helps hide any gaps when you may have been in-between jobs.

…³

Job hunting is a buyers' and sellers' marketplace. You are the seller and employers are the buyers. If you graduated from a relevant course, obtained excellent results or are currently studying towards a professional qualification relating to your chosen career, then position this section near the top of your CV. However, if your career history is your strongest selling point then place the Education section towards the end of your CV.

…⁴

This section highlights your unique selling points as a prospective employee. Make it easy for employers to spot your talents and be clear about what you are offering. Employers refer to this section to determine what they will get in return on their investment in you. Therefore, you need to sell yourself and demonstrate your abilities achievements. Show how you are going to be a positive addition to their workforce. Keep your list short and tailored to the position that you are applying for – a targeted list will be more effective than one that's overlong.

A Read the advice about CVs and match the titles to the paragraphs. There are two you do not need.

> Education • Employment history • Hobbies and interests •
> Personal statement • References • Skills

B Produce a copy of your CV in a similar format to Sandra Behringer's on Page 112. Include sections in the following order:

- name / contact details
- personal statement
- education history (training / school)
- career history
- other skills
- hobbies and interests
- references

Situations

You are a friend of Lena Bauriedel. Lena has bought a second-hand tablet computer from Fred Norton in England. She wants to connect the tablet computer to the Internet when she's at school or travelling around. Her English isn't good so she asks you to write an email to Fred Norton for her.

1 An Internet connection

A Read Lena's email to you and then write an email to Fred Norton.

> Hallo …,
>
> Zuhause bekomme ich leicht eine Internetverbindung. Aber ich möchte auch unterwegs oder in der Schule im Internet surfen. Ich habe gehört, es gibt so etwas wie ein Dongle oder Surfstick und damit kommt man überall ins Internet. Könntest du für mich bei Fred Norton anfragen, ob er mir so ein Gerät verkaufen kann – neu oder gebraucht. Frage auch nach dem Preis, der Lieferzeit und den Zahlungsbedingungen. Hier seine E-Mail Adresse: webshop@norton.co.uk.
>
> Gruß und vielen, vielen Dank
> Lena

> Dear Mr Norton,
>
> My friend Lena Bauriedel recently bought a second-hand …

B Read Fred Norton's reply and then write an email to Lena and tell her what he says.

> Hi …
>
> Please tell your friend Lena that a surfstick or a dongle won't work with her tablet for the simple reason that her tablet doesn't have a USB port. This surprises many people and I get lots of emails like yours. The solution is simple. There are providers like Simyo, O₂, Telecom on the German market that sell sim cards which can connect her tablet to the Internet. If she buys a sim card, she can insert into the tiny slot on the edge of her tablet.
>
> Best wishes
>
> Fred Norton
> Norton's Webshop

> Hallo Lena,
>
> Fred schreibt, dass …

Situations

2 A CV in German

Help your English friend.

> Hi …,
>
> I told you about my new girlfriend Susan in my last mail, didn't I? She wants to apply for a job in Essen and she needs to write her CV in German. I've attached her CV in English. Could you write it in German and adapt it to German standards?
>
> It would be super if you could help us!
>
> Best wishes
> Fred

CURRICULUM VITÆ

Personal Details:	Susan Alice Haywood
	Date of birth: 03.04.1987
	Place of birth: Bangor, Wales
	Address: 7, Earl Street, Cambridge
	Telephone: 01424 772385
	Mobile: 0775182426
Work experience:	2009 – present
	Employed at Norton's Webshop in Cambridge. Duties include general office work, buying and selling, after-sales service.
	2007 – 2008
	Worked on a part-time basis at Abbot Printmedia, Trumpington, prepared print jobs, flyer design.
Formal qualifications:	2012
	At present I am attending an evening course in Business German at the University of Cambridge.
	2006 – 2007
	Attended courses in business studies and computer science at Anglia Ruskin Technical College.
	2005 – 2006
	I attended a course at the University of Brighton. Subjects: Media and Advertising. Obtained Diploma with distinction.
	2004
	I obtained General Certificate of Education at Advanced Level in English Language and Literature and Business Studies.
Other skills:	Obtained Diploma of Office Management on an evening course at Anglia Ruskin Technical College.
Personal interests:	I like jogging, swimming, theatre and writing stories.
Referees:	Mr J. Doorbar, 58 Albert Road, Derby (manager of Abbot Printmedia)
	Mr Fred Norton, 2 Queen's Road, Hastings (owner of Norton's Webshop)

KMK mock exam (Stufe II)
Zertifikatsprüfung Englisch für gewerblich-technische Berufe

Niveau II (Threshold)

Zugelassene Hilfsmittel: zweisprachiges allgemeinsprachliches Wörterbuch
nur für die schriftliche Prüfung

Datum: _____

Name, Vorname: _____

Geburtsdatum: _____

Ausbildungsberuf/Klasse: _____

Ergebnisse:

	Höchst-punktzahl	Erreichte Punkte

Schriftliche Prüfung:

Teil 1	Rezeption		
	Aufgabe 1	20	
	Aufgabe 2	20	
	gesamt:	40	
Teil 2	Produktion		
	Aufgabe 3	30	
Teil 3	Mediation		
	Aufgabe 4	30	

| **gesamt:** | 100 | | = % |

Mündliche Prüfung:

| Teil 4 | Interaktion/ Mediation | 30 | | = % |

Bestanden: ☐ ja ☐ nein

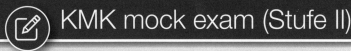

KMK mock exam (Stufe II)

Zertifikatsprüfung Englisch für gewerblich-technische Berufe

1 Mediation — 30 Punkte

Sie sind Praktikant bei FUNSPORTS in Bradford. Die Firma produziert elektrische Skateboards und vertreibt Segway Personal Transporters. Ihr Vorgesetzter bittet Sie, die Pressemitteilung einer deutschen Niederlassung auf Englisch zusammenzufassen.

Schreiben Sie die englische Zusammenfassung in Ihr Heft.

FUNSPORTS bietet demnächst einen innovativen Funsportartikel für Jung und Alt an. Unsere E-Skateboards sind mit batteriebetriebenen Elektromotoren von 150 bis 800 Watt ausgestattet. Zwar werden Sie mit dem 15 bis 20 Kilo schweren E-Board keine akrobatischen Heelflips und Boardslides vollbringen, dafür können Sie nicht nur auf Asphalt carven, sondern auch auf Grasflächen und Waldwegen bequem und sportlich cruisen. Sportlich, denn auch das E-Skateboarding verlangt Körpereinsatz. Sie trainieren sowohl Körperbeherrschung, Halten des Gleichgewichts als auch Bauch-, Bein- und Gesäßmuskeln.
Je nach Alter, Gewicht und Können haben Sie die Wahl zwischen mehreren Modellen. Das 400 W/24 V Senior E-Board für den älteren Einsteiger beschleunigt schnell auf 20 Stundenkilometer. Die Batterie reicht für eine Strecke von etwa 18 Kilometern.
Der sportliche Skater wird sich für das 850 W/36 V Offroad E-Board entscheiden. Es hat eine Reichweite von 26 Kilometern und erreicht eine Geschwindigkeit bis zu 32 Stundenkilometern. Dank seiner rutschfesten Bereifung lässt es den Skater auch im unwegsamen Gelände nicht im Stich und überwindet sogar leichte Steigungen.
Im Gegensatz zu einem normalen Skateboard lässt sich ein E-Board mit der handlichen Fernbedienung beschleunigen und wieder sanft und sicher abbremsen. …

2 Rezeption: Leseverstehen — 20 Punkte

Ihr Freund Kevin ist Praktikant bei SPORTARENA in Berlin. Die Firma plant Segways anzubieten. Kevin soll einen Flyer erstellen, hat aber Probleme mit dem englischen Text. Er bittet Sie um Hilfe und mailt Ihnen den Text zusammen mit seinen Fragen.

The Segway Personal Transporter is kept upright by motors, five gyroscopes and a collection of tilt sensors which function like our inner-ear balancing system. Although only three gyroscopes are needed the extra two sensors are included as a safety precaution. The additional weight sensor tells the computer when a rider has stepped on. The ten onboard microprocessors have about three times the power of a typical PC.
The user commands the Segway to go forward by shifting his weight forward on the platform and backward by shifting his weight backward. When he straightens up it will stop.
The sensors in the Segway register changes to its centre of mass and make corresponding adjustments to maintain both balance and speed – either forwards or backwards. The rider uses the handlebars to turn left or right.

Beantworten Sie Kevins Fragen entweder mit 'Ja' oder 'Nein'.

1. Erfolgt die Richtungsänderung durch Gewichtsverlagerung?
2. Arbeiten Gyroskop und Neigungssensor nach dem gleichen Prinzip?
3. Beschleunigt das Gerät durch Gewichtsverlagerung nach hinten?
4. Sind Neigungssensoren mit unserem Gleichgewichtsorgan vergleichbar?
5. Erfolgt die Richtungsänderung ebenfalls durch Gewichtsverlagerung?
6. Bremst man durch aufrechtes Stehen in Mittelposition?

KMK mock exam (Stufe II)

Zertifikatsprüfung Englisch für gewerblich-technische Berufe

3 Produktion 30 Punkte

Sie haben eine Stelle bei SPORTARENA in Berlin gefunden. Sie sollen per E-Mail bei Ihrer ehemaligen Firma FUNSPORTS folgende Teile für E-Boards bestellen.

Beachten Sie die folgenden Vorgaben und schreiben Sie die Bestellung als E-Mail in einem Heft.

Vorgaben:

- Adressat: sales@funsports.com.uk, Herr David Blair, Sales Department
- Betreff: Bestellung: Teile für E-Boards
- Von: info@sportarena.com
- Anrede (mit Komma)
- Bestellung:
16	850 W/36 V Batterien, Katalognummer OEB-065-335-901,	€ 1800,00
12	400 W/24 V Batterien, Katalognummer SEB, 010-200-801,	€ 960,00
10	Neigungssensoren, Katalognummer NS-003-943-001	€ 1600,00
30	Räder für Senior E-Board, Katalognummer SEBW 010-200-000	€ 750,00
- Lieferung so bald wie möglich
- 5% Skonto bei Zahlung innerhalb von 14 Tagen nach Erhalt der Ware wie vereinbart.
- höflicher Abschluss (ohne Komma)
- Absender: SPORTARENA, 10967 Berlin; Fichtestraße 22

4 Rezeption / Hörverstehen 20 Punkte

22

Sie haben die Aufgabe, den Anrufbeantworter der Einkaufs- und Verkaufsabteilung abzuhören und die Mitarbeiter über Intranet zu informieren.

Hören Sie die drei Nachrichten einzeln ab und schreiben Sie für jede Nachricht eine Telefonnotiz.

KMK mock exam (Stufe II)

Zertifikatsprüfung Englisch für gewerblich-technische Berufe

5 Mündliche Prüfung   15 Punkte

Teil A: Interaktion

- **Partner A:** Führen Sie mit Partner B ein Vorstellungsgespräch auf Englisch. Verwenden Sie die Vorschläge und stellen Sie eigene Fragen.
- **Partner B:** Antworten Sie wahrheitsgemäß in ganzen Sätzen oder verwenden Sie die vorgeschlagenen Stichworte.

Partner A / Partner B

Partner A	Partner B
Fragen Sie Partner B, woher er kommt.	Heidelberg, in der Nähe von Mannheim
… ob es ihm dort gefällt.	wegen schöner Altstadt, Schloss, Odenwald
… wieviele Geschwister er hat.	einen älteren Bruder, eine jüngere Schwester
… wie alt diese sind.	Jens 26, Julia 16
… was sein Bruder beruflich macht.	Wirtschaftsinformatiker bei SAP
… wie er in seine Freizeit verbringt.	Musik hören, sich mit Freunden treffen, Fußball in einem Verein spielen
… wie er seinen Urlaub verbringt.	mit Pfadfindergruppe ins Zeltlager gehen, mit Eltern verreisen
… ob er schon einmal in England war.	in London, letzter Herbst 20…, mit Familie
… was er dort besichtigt hat.	Hyde Park, Speakers' Corner, Brit. Museum
… ob Englisch für seinen Berufswunsch wichtig ist.	Berufswunsch – Wirtschaftsinformatiker, Englisch – in Stellenangeboten gefordert
… welche Aufgaben er in seiner Firma hat.	HeidelbergCement, Umweltabteilung; Vorbereitung einer Fachmesse
Sie bedanken sich für das Gespräch und wünschen B viel Glück für die Zukunft.	Bitte sehr. / Gern geschehen.

Tauschen Sie nun die Rollen. Partner B antwortet wahrheitsgemäß oder für eine Person, die er kennt.

KMK mock exam (Stufe II)

Zertifikatsprüfung Englisch für gewerblich-technische Berufe

Teil B: Produktion

Schlüpfen Sie in die Rolle einer bekannten Persönlichkeit aus den Bereichen Wirtschaft und Technik. Stellen Sie sich mit den wichtigsten Daten Ihres Lebenslaufs der Klasse vor. Die Klasse soll erraten, um wen es sich handelt.

Teil C: Interaktion

Ihre Gruppe führt ein Podiumsgespräch vor der Klasse auf Englisch über die abgebildeten Geräte. Begründen Sie jeweils Ihre Stellungnahme.

smart phone   netbook   tablet computer

Die folgenden Fragen sind lediglich als Denkanstöße gedacht:

Fakten:
- Welche Betriebssysteme haben die Geräte?
- Sind sie untereinander und mit Windows kompatibel?
- Was kann man mit den Geräten machen?
- Worin unterscheiden sich die Geräte?
- Welche Funktionen würden Sie am häufigsten nutzen?
- Kann ein Gerät die beiden anderen weitgehend ersetzen?

Meinungen:
- Wie erklären Sie den Erfolg von Tablet-PC, Netbook und Smartphone?
- Welches Gerät ist Ihrer Meinung nach das Nützlichste?
- Welches Gerät würden Sie kaufen? Warum / warum nicht?
- Warum bevorzugen manche Käufer die teureren Geräte von Apple?
- Wozu würden Sie einem Kunden raten, der noch keines der Geräte besitzt?
- Beantworten Sie Fragen der Klassenkameraden.

KMK mock exam (Stufe II)

Zertifikatsprüfung Englisch für gewerblich-technische Berufe

Bewertungsbogen für die mündliche Prüfung

Schule: _____

Name des Kandidaten / der Kandidatin:

_____

Klasse: _____

Datum: _____

Zeit: _____

Vergeben Sie Punkte von 0 (schlechtester Wert) bis 15 (bester Wert) für die folgenden Teilleistungen der Kandidat(Inn)en. Markieren Sie die vergebene Punktzahl eindeutig durch Ankreuzen oder Einkreisen. Zählen Sie die Werte beider Spalten zusammen.

Interaktive Kompetenz und Aufgabenbewältigung	Sprachbeherrschung (accuracy, range, fluency, adequacy, comprehensibility)
15	15
14	14
13	13
12	12
11	11
10	10
9	9
8	8
7	7
6	6
5	5
4	4
3	3
2	2
1	1
0	0

Summe: _____ Punkte

Partner files

File 1: Unit 1, Exercise 11

Student A

1. You have just started an apprenticeship at EADS. Tell your partner about the company. When you have finished, check that your partner has written down the correct numbers.

2. Your partner has just started an apprenticeship at Hochtief. Listen to him/her and take notes. When you have finished, your partner will check that you have written down the correct numbers.

EADS	
Founded in the year	2000
Divisions / Business Units	4
Sales	€45,750,000,000 ('45 point 75 billion')
Profit	€553,000,000
Employees	about 122,000
Training establishments in Germany	22

File 2: Unit 3, Exercise 6

Student A

You are the electrical contractor. You will need at least two hours for the appointment with the customer, including travel time. Your working hours are 8 a.m. – 4 p.m. Make suggestions about suitable days and times.

	Appointments
Monday	9.30–11.30 a.m. customer visit
Tuesday	1.30–5.30 p.m. installation
Wednesday	12.30 p.m. take afternoon off
Thursday	
Friday	8.30 a.m. – 2 p.m. installation

File 3: Unit 4, Exercise 9

Student A

Read the conditions for the new schedule and discuss possible solutions with your partner.

1. You cannot hire more workers or use another team.
2. It will take Team A five days to finish the job on their own.
3. All the jobs should be finished by the end of the week.

Partner files

File 4: Unit 6, Ex 4

Student A:

1. Copy the following table into your exercise book. Ask your partner for the missing information.

> The light inside the fridge doesn't work. What's the cause?

> And how do I fix it?

Refrigerator & Freezer Appliances

Problem / Symptom	Possible Causes	Solution
Unit isn't cold enough	Dirty condenser coil	Clean the coils with a dry cloth or a brush
Inside light doesn't work		
Frost builds up / moisture on shelves		
Loud noises / rattling / vibrating		
Water on floor		

2. Student B is going to ask you some questions. Answer them using the table below.

> It's probably clogged openings.

> You need to soak them in hot water.

Oven Appliances

Problem / Symptom	Possible Causes	Solution
Heating element doesn't work	Burned out heating element	Buy a replacement
Gas units do not burn evenly	Clogged openings	Soak in soap and hot water, and clean with pipe cleaners.
Heat escapes around oven door	Oven door not properly aligned	Loosen / tighten screws
Oven temperature is too hot / too cold	Vent is blocked	Remove grease / other blockages
Oven lamp doesn't work	Burned out bulb	Replace bulb

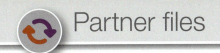

Partner files

File 5: Unit 8, Exercise 7

Student A

A Read the texts and look at the pictures. Answer your partner's questions.

Recycling Car Bumpers

Plastics now account for over 9% of a car's total weight. They are used in bumpers, body panels, interior components (dashboards, steering wheels etc.), seats, carpets and lights. Plastics are extremely versatile. They can be impact resistant and corrosion resistant. They are strong, affordable and lightweight. The use of plastics in the production of new automobiles is vital to meet new emission regulations and minimum fuel efficiency guidelines. Sorting and separating plastics is difficult due to the similarities in the materials, however. Finding markets for some plastics is also difficult because of the specific engineering characteristics of each plastic. It is therefore easier to recycle specific parts for the same use.

A HISTORY OF BUMPER RECYCLING

Year	Details
1992	Began collecting damaged bumpers and recycling them for use as vehicle undercovers.
2001	Implemented mechanical paint removal technology. Increased strength of recycled plastic to the same level as new plastic. Began using recycled plastic to reinforce new bumpers.
2002	Improving the paint removal rate from 98% to 99%. Recycled resin used on many new car models.
2003	Developed an optical selection mechanism and new paint removal technology. Increased the paint removal rate to 99.9%. The resulting recycled plastic achieved the necessary strength and quality for use as replacement bumpers.

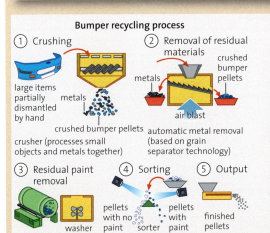

Bumper recycling process

B Your partner has information about the recycling of non-ferrous metals. Ask your partner to tell you about:

1 Common non-ferrous metals used in recycling.
2 Why non-ferrous metals are useful (ask for examples!)
3 How aluminium and copper are used in industry.

129

Partner files

File 6: Unit 1, Exercise 11

Student B

1   Your partner has just started an apprenticeship at EADS. Listen to him/her and take notes. When you have finished, your partner will check that you have written down the correct numbers.

2   You have just started an apprenticeship at Hochtief. Tell your partner about the company. When you have finished, check that your partner has written down the correct numbers.

Hochtief	
Founded in the year	1874
Divisions / Business Units	4
Sales	€20,160,000,000 ('twenty point one six billion')
Profit	€288,000,000
Employees	70,657
Training establishments in Germany	17

File 7: Unit 3, Exercise 6

Student B

You are the customer. You want the electrical contractor to visit you next week, but you have a lot of appointments. Try to help him/her find a suitable day and time.

	Appointments
Monday	12–5 p.m. visit client
Tuesday	9.30–11.00 a.m. meeting with accountant
	11.30–2 p.m. lunch with customer
Wednesday	11 a.m.–12 p.m. see bank manager
Thursday	off work all day
Friday	9.30 a.m.–1 p.m. meeting with architect

File 8: Unit 4, Exercise 9

Student B

Read the conditions for the new schedule and discuss possible solutions with your partner.

1   The jobs on Friday can be moved if necessary.
2   Team B cannot finish the supermarket job on their own by the end of the week.
3   All the jobs need to start on Monday.

Partner files

File 9: Unit 6, Exercise 4

Student B:

1. Student A is going to ask you some questions. Answer them using the table below.

> It's probably a loose bulb connection.

> You should reinsert the bulb or replace it.

Refrigerator & Freezer Appliances

Problem / Symptom	Possible Causes	Solution
Unit isn't cold enough	Dirty condenser coil	Clean the coils with a dry cloth or a brush
Inside light doesn't work	Loose bulb connection / bulb burned out	Reinsert the bulb / replace
Frost builds up / moisture on shelves	Door isn't closing properly	Readjust door, as per manufacturer's instructions
Loud noises / rattling / vibrating	Fridge unstable	Adjust leg levels
Water on floor	Drain pan is out of position	Check position of pan / replace or repair if broken or damaged

2. Copy the following table into your exercise book. Ask your partner for the missing information.

> The gas units don't burn evenly. Do you know why?

> What's the solution then?

Oven Appliances

Problem / Symptom	Possible Causes	Solution
Heating element doesn't work	Burned out heating element	Buy a replacement
Gas units do not burn evenly		
Heat escapes around oven door		
Oven temperature is too hot / too cold		
Oven lamp doesn't work		

Partner files

File 10: Unit 8, Exercise 7

Student B

1. Your partner has information about the recycling of car bumpers. Ask your partner to tell you about:

   1. Why plastics are useful.
   2. The various developments in the technology over the years.
   3. The process of recycling car bumpers.

2. Read the texts and look at the photos. Answer your partners questions in as much detail as possible.

Non-Ferrous Metals

Non-ferrous metals are metals which contain no iron. The most important for recycling are aluminium, copper, lead and tin. Although they have many applications thanks to their ability to resist oxidization, they are susceptible to other forms of corrosion. Copper, for example, builds up a green coating through oxidation with water and air. However, this layer protects the material from further corrosion.

When ferrous metals are required, zinc can be used to slow the process of oxidation dramatically, for example in zinc-coated nails and suspension bridge cables.

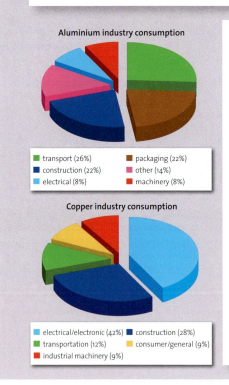

Aluminium

38,108,700 tonnes of aluminium are produced per annum, making it the world's second most used metal. As well as its light weight and high strength to weight ratio, aluminium is very corrosion resistant. These properties make it useful for the food and drinks industry as well as in applications in the aircraft and transportation sectors.

Copper

17,974,300 tonnes are produced per year. Copper is a great conductor of electricity, and of course its use in electric cable and electronics is second to none. Copper is also used extensively in the building industry, in the form of pipes and tubing. This also accounts for a large proportion of the demand for this metal.

Useful phrases

Unit 1, S. 9

Welcoming a visitor	Einen Besucher begrüßen
▪ Introductions	▪ Sich vorstellen
▪ I'm … (Name).	▪ Ich bin … (Name).
▪ I'm a/the … (Stelle).	▪ Ich bin (der/die) … (Stelle).
▪ I work for … (Firmenname).	▪ Ich arbeite für … (Firmenname).
▪ Pleased to meet you.	▪ Schön, Sie kennenzulernen.
▪ Can I introduce you to … (Name)?	▪ Kann ich Ihnen … (Name) vorstellen?

Making the visitor feel welcome	Den Besucher warmherzig willkommen heißen
▪ Welcome to … (Firma).	▪ Willkommen bei … (Firma)
▪ Glad you could make it.	▪ Schön, dass Sie hier sind.
▪ Let me give you a programme/brochure.	▪ Hier haben Sie ein Programm/eine Broschüre.
▪ Let me give you a handout with information about …	▪ Hier haben Sie einen Handzettel mit Informationen zu …
▪ Please help yourself to tea or coffee.	▪ Bitte bedienen Sie sich am Tee oder Kaffee.
▪ Help yourselves to a drink.	▪ Bitte bedienen Sie sich an den Getränken.

Small talk	Smalltalk
▪ Where are you from?	▪ Wo kommen Sie her?
▪ I live / work in …	▪ Ich wohne / arbeite in …
▪ And you?	▪ Und Sie?
▪ Did you have a good journey?	▪ Hatten Sie eine gute Reise?
▪ Yes, thanks.	▪ Ja, danke.
▪ No, the traffic was very heavy.	▪ Nein, es war ziemlich viel Verkehr.
▪ Awful/lovely weather today, isn't it?	▪ Scheußliches/wunderbares Wetter heute, oder?
▪ Yes, it is.	▪ Ja, das stimmt.
▪ What's your room /hotel / hostel like?	▪ Wie ist Ihr Zimmer/Hotel/ Ihre Jugendherberge?
▪ Well, it isn't luxurious, but it's OK for a day or so.	▪ Naja, es nicht luxuriös, aber für einen Tag oder so ist es in Ordnung.
▪ Do you know Germany / this area?	▪ Kennen Sie Deutschland / diese Gegend?
▪ No, I'm afraid not.	▪ Nein, leider nicht.
▪ Yes, a little.	▪ Ja, ein bisschen.

Unit 1, S. 11

Describing your company	Ihr Unternehmen beschreiben
▪ We're a small company in the automotive sector.	▪ Wir sind ein kleines Unternehmen in der Automobilbranche
▪ medium-sized	▪ mittelständisch
▪ global	▪ global, weltweit
▪ We supply components to the automotive industry.	▪ Wir versorgen die Autoindustrie mit Bauelementen.
▪ We provide electrical services to customers in the manufacturing sector.	▪ Wir bieten Elektro-Dienstleistungen für Kunden im verarbeitenden Gewerbe an
▪ plumbing services	▪ Installationsdienstleistungen
▪ We offer repair and maintenance services.	▪ Wir bieten Reparatur- und Instandhaltungsdienstleistungen an.
▪ Our products are used in the renewable energy sector.	▪ Unsere Produkte werden in der Branche der erneuerbaren Energien benutzt.
▪ Our services are used by large multi-nationals.	▪ Unsere Dienstleistungen werden von multinationalen Konzernen benutzt.
▪ We're based in / near / 20 kilometres from …	▪ Wir haben unseren Sitz in / in der Nähe von / 20 km entfernt von …

Useful phrases

Unit 2, S. 22

Jobs, tasks and responsibilities	Berufe, Aufgaben und Zuständigkeitsbereiche
architect	Architekt/in
bricklayer	Maurer/in
plumber	Sanitärinstallateur/in
electrician	Elektriker/in, Elektroinstallateur/in
safety inspector	Sicherheitsbeauftragte/r
site manager	Bauleiter/in
joiner	Schreiner/in, Tischler/in
surveyor	Landvermesser/in, Gutachter/in
decorator	Dekorateur/in, Maler/in
quantity surveyor	Kostenplaner/in
design	entwerfen; Design, Entwurf
mix	mischen, verbinden; Mischung
check	überprüfen; Überprüfung
install	installieren, aufstellen
evaluate	beurteilen, bewerten, berechnen
supervise	beaufsichtigen, überwachen
construct	bauen, entwickeln
measure	(ab)messen; Maß
hang	aufhängen
control	kontrollieren; Kontrolle
buildings	Gebäude, Bauwerke
cement	zementieren: Zement
pipes for leakage	Sickerrohre
plugs and wiring	Steckdosen und elektrische Leitungen
health risks and the use of hazardous materials	Gesundheitsrisiken und die Verwendung gesundheitsschädlicher Materialien
employees and overtime	Arbeitnehmer und Überstunden
timber frames	Fachwerk
precise distances, positions and angles	präzise Distanzen, Plätze und Winkel
wallpaper and paintings	Tapete und Malerarbeiten
costs	Kosten

Unit 3, S. 32

Talking to a customer	Mit einem Kunden sprechen
I'll just take some details.	Ich nehme nur ein paar Einzelheiten auf.
What's the best number to reach you on?	Unter welcher Nummer kann ich Sie am besten erreichen?
Yes, we can do that for you.	Ja, das können wir für Sie erledigen.
I'm afraid that's not our area.	Das fällt leider nicht in unseren Tätigkeitsbereich.
I could come next Thursday.	Ich könnte nächsten Donnerstag kommen.
How does … suit you?	Wie passt Ihnen … ?
Can we make it a bit later/earlier?	Können wir etwas früher/später sagen?
What's the address?	Wie ist die Adresse?
Do you have a fax number?	Haben Sie eine Faxnummer?
That won't be a problem.	Das ist kein Problem.
I recommend that you try … instead.	Ich empfehle Ihnen anstelle dessen … zu versuchen.
How about on / next / the following … ?	Was ist mit dem / nächsten / folgende/n … ?
I can't make that, I'm afraid.	Das schaffe ich leider nicht.
Yes, (Zeit) on (Tag/Datum) will be fine.	Ja, (Zeit) am (Tag/Datum) geht in Ordnung.

Useful phrases

Unit 3, S. 36

Advising a customer	Einen Kunden beraten
■ **Contractor**	■ Vertragspartner/in, Auftragnehmer/in
■ Can I advise you to … ?	■ Kann ich Ihnen … empfehlen?
■ If you only look at the upfront cost, …	■ Wenn Sie sich nur die Vorauszahlungen anschauen, …
■ On the other hand, if you take … into account, then …	■ Auf der anderen Seite, wenn Sie … berücksichtigen, dann …
■ If you compare power usage, you'll find that …	■ Wenn Sie den Stromverbrauch vergleichen, sehen Sie, dass …
■ Over the course of a year, what that means is …	■ Im Verlauf eines Jahres bedeutet das …
■ If we assume an electricity tariff of …, then …	■ Wenn wir von einem Stromtarif von … ausgehen, dann …
■ Looking at the longer term, …	■ Langfristig gesehen …
■ There'll be labour costs, too.	■ Arbeitskosten kommen auch dazu.
■ The … system is more suitable.	■ Das …-system ist besser geeignet.
■ Yes, but it uses less power.	■ Ja, aber es verbraucht weniger Strom.
■ In a year you can save …	■ In einem Jahr können Sie … sparen.
■ Because no further maintenance is required.	■ Weil keine weitere Instandhaltung benötigt wird.
■ **Customer**	■ Kunde
■ I'm not sure about that.	■ Da bin ich mir nicht so sicher.
■ Why do you say that?	■ Warum sagen Sie das?
■ What about … ?	■ Was ist mit …?
■ Will it reduce my electric bill?	■ Wird es meine Stromrechnung senken?
■ What about maintenance?	■ Was ist mit der Instandhaltung?
■ It sounds good in principle, but …	■ Das klingt im Prinzip gut, aber …
■ Really?	■ Wirklich?
■ Please give me an estimate.	■ Machen Sie mir bitte einen Kostenvoranschlag.
■ It's also more expensive.	■ Es ist auch teurer.
■ How much will I save?	■ Wie viel spare ich?
■ How much is that over ten years?	■ Wie viel ist das auf zehn Jahre hochgerechnet?
■ Alright, you've convinced me.	■ In Ordnung, Sie haben mich überzeugt.

Unit 3, S. 37

Making a written complaint	Eine Beschwerde schreiben
■ **Giving background information**	■ Hintergrundinformationen geben
■ We recently ordered … from you.	■ Wir haben kürzlich … von Ihnen bestellt.
■ You recently installed … at our premises.	■ Sie haben kürzlich … auf unserem Firmengelände installiert (eingebaut, verlegt).
■ **Describing the problem**	■ Das Problem beschreiben
■ Our customers complained that …	■ Unsere Kunden haben sich darüber beschwert, dass …
■ Our technician tested the … and found that …	■ Unser Techniker hat … getestet und festgestellt, dass …
■ The … proved to be faulty.	■ Der/die/das … hat sich als defekt herausgestellt.
■ After installation, we found that …	■ Nach der Installation haben wir festgestellt, dass …
■ **Suggesting a solution**	■ Eine Lösung vorschlagen
■ I am returning the … to you for inspection.	■ Ich gebe Ihnen den/die/das … zur Inspektion zurück.
■ Please send us (a) replacement … as soon as possible.	■ Bitte senden Sie uns schnellstmöglich (ein/e/n) Ersatz- …
■ Please refund the cost of the … .	■ Bitte erstatten Sie die Kosten von …
■ Please send your engineer/technician to inspect the … without delay.	■ Bitte senden Sie unverzüglich Ihren Ingenieur/Techniker um den/die/das … zu inspizieren.

Useful phrases

Polite phrases to finish off	*Höfliche Formulierungen zum Abschluss*
Please do not hesitate to contact me if you require further information.	*Zögern Sie bitte nicht, mich zu kontaktieren, wenn Sie weitere Informationen benötigen.*
I look forward to hearing from you.	*Ich freue mich darauf, von Ihnen zu hören.*

Unit 4, S. 46

Discussing plans	**Pläne besprechen**
Why doesn't Team A work with Team B?	*Warum arbeitet Team A nicht mit Team B zusammen?*
We need to finish Amersham Road by the end of the week.	*Wir müssen das Projekt Amersham Road am Ende der Woche fertig haben.*
The supermarket is an urgent job.	*Der Supermarkt ist ein dringender Auftrag.*
That will/won't work.	*Das wird (nicht) funktionieren.*
That's a good/bad idea.	*Das ist eine gute/schlechte Idee.*
Team C and Team B can work together.	*Team C und Team B können zusammenarbeiten.*
Three days is/isn't enough time.	*Drei Tage reichen (nicht) aus.*
I think we'll need more/less time.	*Ich denke, wir brauchen mehr/weniger Zeit.*
How long do you estimate that the job will take?	*Wieviel Zeit schätzen Sie, wird derp Auftrag in Anspruch nehmen?*
Team A could work with Team B.	*Team A könnte mit Team B zusammenarbeiten.*
We must finish the job in four days.	*Wir müssen den Auftrag in vier Tagen fertig bekommen.*
The footpath is not a top priority.	*Der Fußweg hat nicht oberste Priorität.*
How about …?	*Was ist mit …?*
Why don't we …?	*Warum … wir nicht …?*
Has anyone got any good ideas?	*Hat irgendwer gute Ideen?*
Team C can join Team B.	*Team C kann sich mit Team B zusammenschließen.*
Two days is long enough.	*Zwei Tage sind lang genug.*
How can we speed up the work?	*Wie können wir die Arbeit schneller verrichten?*
That's probably long enough/too long.	*Das ist wahrscheinlich lang genug/zu lang.*

Unit 4, S. 47

Describing graphs	**Graphen beschreiben**
to increase; an increase	*zunehmen; eine Zunahme*
to rise; a rise	*(an)steigen; ein Anstieg*
to decrease; a decrease	*abnehmen; eine Abnahme*
to drop; a drop	*fallen, abstürzen; ein Rückgang*
to change; a change	*sich ändern; eine (Ver-)Änderung*
to fluctuate; a fluctuation	*schwanken; eine Schwankung*
sudden, suddenly	*plötzliche/r/s, plötzlich*
dramatic, dramatically	*dramatische/r/s, dramatisch*
drastic, drastically	*drastische/r/s, drastisch*
steady, steadily	*stetige/r/s, stetig*

Unit 5, S. 58

In the workshop	**In der Werkstatt**
Apprentice	*Auszubildender*
What tool should I use for this job?	*Welches Werkzeug soll ich für diese Arbeit benutzen?*
I need to … . What should I use?	*Ich muss … . Was soll ich dafür benutzen?*
Could you show me where the … is/are kept, please?	*Könnten Sie mir bitte zeigen, wo der/die/das … aufbewahrt wird/werden?*
Could you show me how to adjust the speed, please?	*Könnten Sie mir bitte zeigen, wie man die Geschwindigkeit reguliert?*

Useful phrases

- How do I change the depth?
- How do I set the torque?
- I'd like to change the direction.
- Thanks for your help.
- **Supervisor**
- You need to use a …
- You need a … for that.
- The … are kept in this toolstore.
- The … belongs in this cabinet / drawer.
- Of course. Watch carefully: this is how you do it.
- Look it up in the handbook.
- Check the online instruction manual.
- You're welcome.

- Wie kann ich die Breite verstellen?
- Wie stelle ich das Drehmoment ein?
- Ich würde gerne die Richtung ändern.
- Danke für Ihre Hilfe.
- *Abteilungsleiter*
- Sie müssen ein/e … benutzen.
- Dafür benötigen Sie ein/e …
- Die … werden in dieser Werzeugausgabe aufbewahrt.
- Der/die/das … gehört in diesen Kasten / diese Schublade
- Natürlich. Sehen Sie aufmerksam zu: so wird das gemacht.
- Schlagen Sie es im Handbuch nach.
- Sehen Sie in der Online-Gebrauchsanweisung nach.
- Gern geschehen.

Unit 6, S. 68

Asking for and giving help | Um Hilfe bitten und helfen

- I'm afraid I've got a problem with my router.
- Do you know anything about mopeds?
- Can you help me with my laptop?
- It isn't working properly / correctly.
- It's damaging my clothes / CDs / …
- The … is damaged / broken / defective.
- The first thing you must do is …
- Then you must / should …
- Check / look at the …
- Turn the … on / off.
- OK, I've done that.
- What's the next step?
- OK, I think I can manage that.

- Ich habe leider ein Problem mit meinem Router.
- Wissen Sie etwas über Mopeds?
- Können Sie mir mit meinem Laptop helfen?
- Es funktioniert nicht richtig.
- Es macht meine Kleidung / CDs / … kaputt.
- Der/die/das … ist beschädigt / kaputt / defekt.
- Das Erste, was Sie tun müssen, ist …
- Danach müssen / sollten Sie …
- Überprüfen Sie /Schauen Sie sich … an.
- Schalten Sie den/die/das … an/aus.
- Okay, das habe ich gemacht.
- Was ist der nächste Schritt?
- Okay, ich denke, damit komme ich jetzt zurecht.

Unit 7, S. 78

Nouns | Nomen

- The scaffolding is secure.
- Oil is a lubricant.
- Grease is also a lubricant.
- Gravel is a natural product.
- These metal shears are sharp.
- Pliers are useful,
- Goggles protect your eyes.
- Our European headquarters is / are in London.

- Das Baugerüst ist sicher.
- Öl ist ein Schmiermittel.
- Fett ist auch ein Schmiermittel.
- Kies/Schotter ist ein natürliches Produkt.
- Diese Blechschere ist scharf.
- Zangen sind praktisch.
- Eine Schutzbrille schützt die Augen.
- Unser europäischer Hauptsitz ist in London.

Unit 7, S. 80

Preventing accidents | Unfälle vermeiden

- Stacks of bricks shouldn't be too high.
- Stacks of pipes shouldn't be unsecured.
- Stacks of timber shouldn't be too near trenches.
- Drivers of plant machines should obey traffic rules.
- Drivers should be properly qualified.

- Ziegelsteinstapel sollten nicht zu hoch sein.
- Gestapelte Rohre sollten nicht ungesichert sein.
- Holzstapel sollten nicht zu nah an Baugräben sein.
- Fahrer von Baufahrzeugen sollten die Verkehrsregeln beachten.
- Fahrer sollten die entsprechende Fahrerlaubnis haben.

Useful phrases

- Drivers of plant machines should signal when reversing.
- Construction workers must wear protective clothing at all times.
- A safe construction site should have high security fences.
- security gates
- warning signs
- an emergency siren
- a first-aid station
- There should be barriers around excavations and trenches.

- *Fahrer von Baufahrzeugen sollten signalisieren, wenn sie zurücksetzen.*
- *Bauarbeiter müssen zu jeder Zeit Schutzbekleidung tragen.*
- *Eine sichere Baustelle sollte hohe Sicherheitszäune haben.*
- *Sicherheitstüren*
- *Warnschilder*
- *eine Notfallsirene*
- *Eine Erste-Hilfe-Station*
- *Um Erdarbeiten und Baugräben sollte rund herum abgesperrt sein.*

Unit 7, S. 83

What's the problem?

- work accident
- household accident
- long cut
- not deep
- only... stitches
- for at least ... days
- reception
- ask for an appointment
- I'm afraid I've got a ...
- deep wound
- storeroom
- the knife slipped
- Will you have to stitch it?
- Are you going to write me off sick?
- When should I come back for a check-up?
- Thank you, Doctor.
- Goodbye

Was ist das Problem?

- *Arbeitsunfall*
- *Haushaltsunfall*
- *lange Schnittwunde*
- *nicht tief*
- *nur ... Stiche*
- *für mindestens ... Tage*
- *Rezeption/Aufnahme*
- *nach einem Termin fragen*
- *Ich habe unglücklicherweise ein/e/n ...*
- *tiefe Wunde*
- *Lagerraum*
- *das Messer ist ausgerutscht*
- *Muss genäht werden?*
- *Schreiben Sie mich krank?*
- *Wann sollte ich zur Nachuntersuchung kommen?*
- *Vielen Dank, Herr Doktor.*
- *Auf Wiedersehen.*

Unit 8, S. 91

Material Properties

- a solid
- a liquid
- rare
- common
- a good insulator
- a good conductor
- an alkaline
- an acid
- hazardous
- safe
- ductile
- brittle
- flammable
- non-flammable
- soft
- hard
- transparent
- opaque

Materialeigenschaften

- *ein fester Stoff*
- *eine Flüssigkeit*
- *edel, selten*
- *gewöhnlich*
- *ein gutes Isoliermaterial*
- *ein guter Leiter*
- *ein Alkalimetall*
- *eine Säure*
- *gefährlich, gesundheitsschädlich, giftig*
- *sicher, ungefährlich*
- *duktil, verformbar*
- *zerbrechlich, brüchig, spröde*
- *leicht entflammbar*
- *nicht entflammbar*
- *weich, nachgiebig*
- *hart, unnachgiebig*
- *transparent, durchsichtig*
- *trüb, undurchsichtig*

Useful phrases

- soluble
- insoluble

- *löslich, solubel*
- *unlöslich*

Unit 8, S. 93

Discussion	Diskussion

- I agree with …
- I don't agree with …
- Yes, I think so, too.
- No, I don't think so.
- That's a good point.
- Well, that's a good point, but …
- Yes, another good reason for … is …
- That's a ridiculous argument!

- *Ich stimme … zu.*
- *Ich stimme … nicht zu.*
- *Ja, das denke ich auch.*
- *Nein, das denke ich nicht.*
- *Das ist ein guter Punkt.*
- *Ja, das ist ein guter Punkt, aber …*
- *Ja, ein weiterer guter Grund für … ist …*
- *Das ist ein lächerliches Argument!*

Unit 9, S. 104

Giving instructions	Anweisungen geben

- How far have you got?
- I've already installed the tank, but I haven't commissioned it yet.
- Right. You need to fill the tank next.
- How do I do that?
- First you turn on the hot water, then you turn on the mains supply.
- OK, I've got that. What next?

- *Wie weit sind Sie gekommen?*
- *Ich habe den Behälter installiert, ihn aber noch nicht in Betrieb genommen.*
- *Gut. Sie müssen den Behälter als nächstes befüllen.*
- *Wie mache ich das?*
- *Zuerst stellen Sie das heiße Wasser an, dann schalten Sie das Stromnetz an.*
- *Okay, das habe ich gemacht. Was kommt als nächstes?*

- Have you filled the tank yet?
- Yes, I have.
- No, I haven't.
- Do it now, then.
- OK, I've done that. What do I do now?
- Has the tank filled?
- Yes, it has.
- No, it hasn't.
- When the tank fills, turn off the tap.

- *Haben Sie den Behälter bereits befüllt?*
- *Ja, habe ich.*
- *Nein, habe ich noch nicht.*
- *Dann machen Sie es jetzt.*
- *Okay, das ich habe gemacht. Was mache ich jetzt?*
- *Ist der Behälter voll?*
- *Ja, ist er.*
- *Nein, ist er nicht.*
- *Wenn der Behälter sich füllt, drehen Sie das Wasser ab.*

- The valve is leaking.
- Is that right?
- Yes, that's fine.
- No, something's wrong.

- *Das Ventil ist undicht.*
- *Ist das richtig?*
- *Ja, das ist in Ordnung.*
- *Nein, etwas stimmt nicht.*

Unit 10, S. 114

Applying for a job	Sich um eine Stelle bewerben

- Dear Ms/Mr/Mrs …,
- Dear Sir or Madam,
- I wish to apply for the above post, advertised in …
- I read your advert in the … (name of newspaper) and I would like to apply for the above position.
- I saw your advert on (name of website) and I would like to apply for the position.
- I am currently working in a small company called …

- *Sehr geehrte/r Frau/Herr …*
- *Sehr geehrte Damen und Herren,*
- *Ich möchte mich gerne um die obengenannte Stelle bewerben, die in … ausgeschrieben wurde.*
- *Ich habe Ihre Anzeige in der … (Name der Zeitung) gelesen und möchte mich nun auf die obengenannte Stelle bewerben.*
- *Ich habe die Anzeige auf … (Name der Homepage) gesehen und möchte mich gerne auf die Stelle bewerben.*
- *Ich arbeite momentan für ein kleines Unternehmen namens …*

Useful phrases

- Since I have started here I have learned …
- I have a very wide range of responsibilities which include …
- My main task at present is the maintenance and repair of …
- I am responsible for the installation of …
- I am seeking a new position that offers responsibility for the full range of …
- My present position provides me with the opportunity to meet and work with a wide range of people.
- I like to think that I bring enthusiasm and adaptability to my work.
- I am interested in finding a position which offers me greater responsibility.
- I am looking for a greater challenge.
- I am interested in finding a position where I can apply and expand my skills as a …
- I would welcome an opportunity to discuss …
- I am available for an interview at any time.
- I look forward to hearing from you.
- Yours sincerely
- Yours faithfully

- *Seit ich hier angefangen habe, habe ich gelernt …*
- *Ich habe eine breite Spanne von Zuständigkeitsbereichen, welche … beinhalten.*
- *Meine Hauptaufgabe ist im Moment die Wartung und Reparatur von …*
- *Ich bin zuständig für die Installation von …*
- *Ich suche eine neue Stelle, die Verantwortung für ein breites Spektrum von … bietet.*
- *Meine gegenwärtige Stelle ermöglicht es mir, viele unterschiedliche Menschen zu treffen und mit ihnen zu arbeiten.*
- *Ich denke, ich kann von mir sagen, dass ich Enthusiasmus und Anpassungsfähigkeit zu meiner Arbeit mitbringe.*
- *Ich bin an einer Stelle interessiert, bei der ich eine größere Verantwortung habe.*
- *Ich suche nach einer größeren Herausforderung.*
- *Ich interessiere für eine Position, bei der ich meine Fertigkeiten als … anwenden und ausbauen kann.*
- *Ich würde mich über die Möglichkeit, … mit Ihnen zu besprechen, freuen.*
- *Ich stehe jederzeit zu einem Vorstellungsgespräch zur Verfügung.*
- *Ich freue mich darauf, von Ihnen zu hören.*
- *Mit freundlichen Grüßen*
- *Mit freundlichen Grüßen / Hochachtungsvoll*

Basic word list

Diese Liste enthält ca. 900 Grundwörter, die in *Technical Matters* als bekannt vorausgesetzt werden. Nicht aufgeführt, jedoch vorausgesetzt, sind einige elementare Wörter, wie Pronomen, Zahlen, Wochentage sowie Wörter, die im Englischen und Deutschen die gleiche Bedeutung haben, wie z. B. *monitor*, *restaurant* und *hotel*.

A

able, to be ~ können, in der Lage sein
about über, etwa
above über, oben(stehend)
absolutely absolut, völlig
accept annehmen, akzeptieren
access Zugang, Zugriff
accident Zufall, Unfall
accompany begleiten
according to zufolge, laut, nach
account Bericht, Konto
across (quer) über
active aktiv(iert)
activity Tätigkeit, Aktivität
add zusammenzählen, hinzufügen
addition, in ~ to zusätzlich zu
address Adresse; adressieren
advantage Vorteil
advice Ratschlag, (guter) Rat
affect betreffen, beeinflussen
afraid, I'm ~ leider
after (all) schließlich (doch)
afternoon Nachmittag
again wieder
age Alter
agree zustimmen, vereinbaren
aim Ziel, Absicht
air Luft
airport Flughafen
all alle(s)
allow erlauben, gestatten, (zu)lassen
almost fast, beinahe
alone allein(e)
along entlang
already schon, bereits
also auch, außerdem
alternatively alternativ
although obwohl
altogether insgesamt
always immer
a.m. vormittags
among zwischen, unter
amount Menge, Betrag
angry wütend, verärgert
another noch eine/r/s
answer Antwort, Lösung; (be)antworten
any irgendetwas, -welche, jede
anybody jemand, jede/r
anyone jemand, jede/r
anything etwas, alles
anyway jedenfalls, sowieso
anywhere irgendwo(hin)

apart from abgesehen von, außer
appear erscheinen, auftauchen
appointment Termin, Verabredung
approximately ungefähr, etwa
area Gebiet, Bereich
arrange arrangieren, vereinbaren
arrival Ankunft
arrive ankommen
ask fragen, bitten
assistant Assistent/in
away weg, entfernt

B

back zurück; Rückseite, Rücken
bad schlecht, schlimm
badly sehr
bag Tasche, Tüte, Beutel
basic grundsätzlich, einfach
battery Batterie
because weil
become werden
before vor(her)
begin anfangen, beginnen
beginning Anfang
behind hinter, hinten
believe glauben
belong gehören
below unter, unten(stehend)
best beste, am besten
best wishes Viele Grüße
better besser
between zwischen
big groß
birth Geburt
blame sb jm die Schuld geben
blue blau
board Brett, Tafel, Platine
body Körper
book Buch; buchen, bestellen
boss Chef/in
both beide
bottom Unterseite, Unterteil, Boden
box Kasten, Kästchen
bracket Klammer
break Pause
brilliant großartig, glänzend
bring bringen, holen
broken kaputt
build bauen, aufbauen
building Gebäude
business Geschäft, Firma, Sache, Angelegenheit
business card (Visiten-)Karte

busy beschäftigt, besetzt
button Taste, Knopf
buy kaufen
buyer Käufer/in
bye tschüs

C

call Anruf; (an)rufen
caller Anrufer/in
can dürfen, können
cannot nicht können
canteen Kantine
car Auto
case Fall, Kiste
cash Bargeld
cause Ursache, Grund; verursachen
certain sicher, gewiss, bestimmt
challenge Herausforderung
change (Ver-)Änderung; (aus)wechseln, (sich) ändern
cheap billig, günstig
check überprüfen, kontrollieren
choice Wahl, Auswahl
choose (aus)wählen
cinema Kino
city (Groß-)Stadt
class Klasse
classmate Klassenkamerad/in
clean sauber; reinigen, säubern
clear klar, deutlich
clever klug, intelligent
close schließen, zumachen
close (to) nahe
clothes Kleidung, Kleider
clue Hinweis, Tip
coffee Kaffee
collection Sammlung
college Fachhochschule
color (AE)/colour (BE) Farbe
combine verbinden, kombinieren
come kommen, geliefert werden
command Befehl
common üblich, gemeinsam; weit verbreitet
commonly häufig, gewöhnlich, üblicherweise
complain sich beklagen, sich beschweren, reklamieren
complete vollständig; vervollständigen
completely völlig
computing Computerwissenschaft
conflict Konflikt

Basic word list

connect (miteinander) verbinden, anschließen
construct bauen, konstruieren
contact Kontakt, Verbindung
contain enthalten
content zufrieden; Inhalt
control Kontrolle; kontrollieren, regeln, steuern, überwachen
copy Exemplar, Kopie; abschreiben, kopieren
corner Ecke
correct richtig, genau; korrigieren
corridor Gang, Flur
cost Kosten; kosten
could konnte/n, könnte/n
count zählen
counter Theke; Ladentisch
country Land, Staat
couple Paar
course Kurs, Lehrgang, Gang
create (er)schaffen, erstellen
creative kreativ, schöpferisch
cross (an)kreuzen
culture Kultur
cup Tasse
current gegenwärtig, aktuell

D

danger Gefahr
dangerous gefährlich
dark Dunkelheit, dunkel
date Datum, Termin
date of birth Geburtsdatum
day Tag
dear liebe/r
decide entscheiden, beschließen
decision Entscheidung
definite(ly) (ganz) sicher, bestimmt
delay Verzögerung; verzögern
delete löschen
deliver (aus)liefern
delivery Zustellung, Lieferung
demand Forderung; (an)fordern
depend abhängen (von)
describe beschreiben
description Beschreibung, Schilderung
desk (Schreib-)Tisch, Arbeitsplatz
dialogue Gespräch, Dialog
diary (Termin-)Kalender
dictionary Wörterbuch
differ sich unterscheiden
difference Unterschied
different unterschiedlich, verschieden
difficult schwer, schwierig
difficulty Schwierigkeit
dinner (Abend-)Essen
direct direkt, gerade
direction Richtung
dirty schmutzig
disadvantage Nachteil, Schaden
disappear verschwinden
disaster Katastrophe
discover entdecken, feststellen
dislike nicht mögen
divorced geschieden
do tun, machen
door Tür
doubt Zweifel; (be)zweifeln
drink Getränk; trinken
driver Fahrer/in
during während

E

each jede/r/s
early früh
east Osten
easy, easily leicht, einfach
education Erziehung, (Aus-, Schul-)Bildung
educational Bildungs-
effective effektiv, wirksam
either entweder
electrical elektrisch, Strom-
electricity Elektrizität, Strom
electronic elektronisch
else andere/r/s
employ beschäftigen, einstellen
empty leer
end Ende, Schluss; (be)enden
ending Ende
energy Energie
engineer Ingenieur/in, Techniker/in
enjoy genießen, gefallen, gern tun
enough ausreichend, genug
enquiry (An-)Frage, Untersuchung
enter eintreten, betreten, eingeben
entrance Eingang, Einfahrt
environment Umwelt, Umfeld
environmental Umwelt-
equal gleich
era Ära, Zeitalter
especially besonders
essential (absolut) notwendig
even sogar (noch)
evening Abend
ever je(mals)
every jede/r/s
everybody jede/r
everyone jede/r/s, alle
everything alles
exactly exakt, genau
example Beispiel
excellent hervorragend, ausgezeichnet
excited aufgeregt, begeistert
exciting aufregend, spannend
exclude ausschließen
exercise Übung
exercise book (Schul-)Heft
expect erwarten, annehmen
expensive teuer
experience Erfahrung
expert Fachmann/frau
express ausdrücken
extra zusätzlich
extreme äußerst
eye Auge

F

fact Tatsache
factory Fabrik
fairly ziemlich
false falsch
familiar vertraut, bekannt
family Familie
far weit (entfernt)
fast schnell
feel (sich) fühlen, meinen, glauben
feeling Gefühl
female weiblich, Frauen-
(a) few ein paar, wenig/e
file Ordner, Datei
final letzte/r/s
finally schließlich, endlich
financial finanziell
find finden, suchen
find out herausfinden
fine gut, schön
finish (be)enden, abschließen, fertig werden
firm Firma
first(ly) erst; zuerst
fix festlegen, reparieren
flat Wohnung; flach
flight Flug
floor Etage, (Fuß-)Boden
fly fliegen
follow (be)folgen
(the) following der/die/das Folgende
food Essen, Nahrung
football Fußball
foreign ausländisch, Auslands-, fremd
forget vergessen
form Form, Formular
formal(ly) förmlich, formell
forward nach vorne
free frei; gratis, kostenlos
frequently oft, häufig
friend Freund/in
friendly freund(schaft)lich
friendship Freundschaft
front Vorderseite
full voll
fully völlig
funny komisch, merkwürdig
further weitere
future Zukunft; (zu)künftig

Basic word list

G
gap Lücke
general allgemein, generell, normal
generally im Allgemeinen, normalerweise
get holen, bekommen, werden
get rid of sb/sth jn/etwas loswerden
give geben
glad froh
go gehen, fahren
go ahead anfangen, weitermachen
go for sth sich bemühen um, gefallen
go on weitermachen, fortfahren
go out ausgehen
good gut
good luck viel Glück
goodbye auf Wiedersehen
goods Ware(n), Güter
government Regierung
great groß(artig)
greatly in großem Maße
green grün
greet (be)grüßen
greeting Gruß(formel), Begrüßung
ground Boden, Grund
group Gruppe; gruppieren
grow wachsen, werden
guess Annahme; raten, schätzen
guest Gast

H
half Hälfte; halb
hall Diele, Saal, Halle
handle umgehen mit, bearbeiten, fertigwerden mit
happen passieren, geschehen
happy glücklich, zufrieden
health Gesundheit
hear hören
heart Herz
heavy schwer
height Höhe, Größe
help Hilfe; helfen
helpful hilfreich, nützlich
her ihr
here hier
herself sie selbst, sich (selbst)
high; highly hoch; äußerst
him ihn, ihm
himself er selbst, sich (selbst)
history Geschichte
holiday Ferien, Urlaub, Feiertag
home Zuhause, Heim; nach Hause
honest ehrlich, anständig
hope Hoffnung; hoffen
hopefully hoffentlich

hot heiß
hour Stunde
house Haus
household Haushalt
how wie
however doch, jedoch
huge riesig
human menschlich
husband (Ehe-)Mann

I
idea Vorstellung, Idee
ideally ideal, im Idealfall
identity Identität
if wenn, falls, ob
illness Krankheit
image Bild
immediately sofort, unverzüglich
importance Wichtigkeit, Bedeutung
important wichtig
impossible unmöglich
impressive beeindruckend
improve verbessern, sich bessern
include enthalten, umfassen
individual einzeln, individuell
informal ungezwungen, inoffiziell, informell
information Auskunft, Information(en), Angaben
inside innerhalb, drinnen
instant sofortig, augenblicklich
instead stattdessen
interest Interesse, Zins(en); interessieren
interested interessiert
interesting interessant
introduce (sich) vorstellen, (miteinander) bekannt machen, einführen
introduction Einleitung, Einführung, Vorstellung
invitation Einladung
invite einladen
ironic ironisch
itself sich (selbst)

J
job Arbeit(sstelle), Aufgabe
join beitreten, verbinden
just einfach, nur, genau

K
keep (be)halten
key Schlüssel, Taste, Haupt-
kind freundlich; Art, Sorte
knife Messer
know kennen, wissen
knowledge Wissen, Kenntnis(se)

L
language Sprache
large groß
last dauern; letzte/r/s
late spät
later später
latest neueste/r/s
law Gesetz
lead führen
learn lernen, erfahren
least, at ~ wenigstens
leave lassen, verlassen, ab-/wegfahren
left links; übrig
length Länge
less weniger, abzüglich
let erlauben, (zu)lassen
letter Buchstabe, Brief
level Ebene, Niveau
lie Lüge; (be)lügen
life Leben
lift Fahrstuhl, Aufzug
light Licht, Leuchte; hell, leicht
like mögen; (ähnlich) wie
likely wahrscheinlich
line Linie, Leitung, Zeile
list Liste; auflisten, notieren
listen zuhören
little klein, wenig
live wohnen, leben
load laden
local örtlich, lokal
located gelegen, mit Sitz in
location (Stand-)Ort, Lage
log in/on einloggen
log off/out ausloggen
long lang
look Blick, Aussehen; (aus)sehen, blicken
look after sich kümmern um
look for suchen nach
look forward to sth sich auf etw freuen
lose verlieren
lots of / a lot of viel, viele
love Liebe; lieben, sehr gern mögen
lovely schön, hübsch, reizend
low niedrig
lunch Mittagessen

M
machine Gerät, Maschine
magazine Zeitschrift
main Haupt-, wichtigste/r/s
make machen
male männlich
manage leiten, verwalten, regeln, (es) schaffen
many viele
married verheiratet
match zuordnen, (zusammen) passen

Basic word list

maximum Maximum; maximal
may dürfen, können, mögen
maybe vielleicht
mean bedeuten, meinen, heißen
media Medien
medium mittlere; Medium, Mittel
meet (zusammen)treffen, begegnen
meeting Sitzung, Besprechung, Treffen
memory Gedächtnis, Speicher
message Meldung, Nachricht, Mitteilung, Botschaft
metal Metall
method Methode, Verfahren
middle Mitte
might könnte(n) (vielleicht)
minimum Minimum; minimal
miss verpassen, vermissen
missing fehlende/r/s
misspell falsch schreiben
mistake Fehler, Irrtum
mobile mobil
mobile (phone) Mobiltelefon, Handy
money Geld
month Monat
monthly monatlich
more mehr
morning Morgen
most der/die/das meiste, die meisten
mountain Berg
mouse Maus
move (sich) bewegen, umziehen
movement Bewegung
much viel
must müssen
myself selbst

N
name Name; nennen, benennen
national national, staatlich
nationality Staatsangehörigkeit
near in der Nähe von
nearly beinahe, fast
neatly ordentlich
necessary nötig, notwendig, erforderlich
need Bedarf, Bedürfnis; brauchen, benötigen
neither ... nor weder ... noch
never nie(mals)
new neu
news Neuigkeit(en), Nachricht(en)
next nächste/r/s; danach
night Nacht
normal(ly) normal(erweise)
north Norden
note Notiz; beachten, notieren
nothing nichts
now nun, jetzt
nowadays heutzutage
number Nummer, Zahl

O
object Gegenstand
obviously offensichtlich, selbstverständlich
of course natürlich, selbstverständlich
offer Angebot; anbieten, bieten
office Büro
often oft, häufig
old alt
once einmal, einst; sobald
only nur, einzig
open öffnen; offen, geöffnet
opinion Meinung, Ansicht
opposite Gegenteil; gegensätzlich, gegenüber
option Möglichkeit, Option
or oder
order bestellen
ordinary gewöhnlich, normal
organization Organisation
organize organisieren
original original, ursprünglich, Original(-)
other andere/r/s
otherwise sonst
our unser/e
outside außerhalb (von)
over über
own eigene/r/s; besitzen

P
page Seite
pain Schmerz
pair Paar
paper Papier, Zeitung
part Teil, Bauteil
particular besondere/r/s, spezielle/r/s
particularly insbesondere
passport Pass
password Passwort
path Weg, Pfad
pay Lohn, Bezahlung; zahlen, bezahlen
per cent Prozent
perfect vollkommen, perfekt
perfectly völlig
perhaps vielleicht, eventuell
period Zeit(raum)
personal persönlich
petrol Benzin
philosophy Philosophie
phone Telefon; anrufen
photo Foto
phrase Redewendung, Satz(teil)
picture Bild
piece Stück, Teil
place Stelle, Platz; setzen, stellen
plain einfach
plan Plan; planen
plastic Plastik, Kunststoff
pleasant angenehm, nett
plenty viel, reichlich
p.m. nachmittags
point Punkt; Komma
poor arm, schlecht, mangelhaft
popular beliebt, populär
position Stellung, Lage, Position
positive positiv, bejahend
possibility Möglichkeit
possible möglich
possibly möglicherweise
power Kraft, Strom; antreiben
powerful mächtig, stark
practical praktisch
practice Praxis, Training
practise (ein)üben
prefer vorziehen, bevorzugen, lieber mögen
preference Vorliebe
preparation Vorbereitung
prepare (sich) vorbereiten, zubereiten, erstellen
present Gegenwart; gegenwärtig; vorstellen, präsentieren
press drücken
previous vorherige/r/s, frühere/r/s
price Preis
primary school Grundschule
print Druck; drucken, ausdrucken
printer Drucker/in
printout (Computer-)Ausdruck
priority Vorrang
private privat, persönlich
probably wahrscheinlich
produce Produkt(e); produzieren, herstellen
product Produkt, Erzeugnis
production Produktion, Herstellung
promise versprechen
properly richtig
protect (be)schützen
protection Schutz
proud stolz
provide liefern, bieten
public öffentlich; Öffentlichkeit
publish veröffentlichen
push schieben, drücken
put setzen, stellen, legen

Q
quality Eigenschaft, Qualität
quarter past/to Viertel nach/vor
queen Königin
question Frage
quick(ly) schnell
quite ziemlich, ganz

R
rapid schnell, rasch
rarely selten
rather ziemlich, lieber
reach erreichen, greifen

Basic word list

read lesen
reader Leser/in, Lektüre
ready bereit, fertig
real echt, wirklich
really wirklich, eigentlich, tatsächlich
reason Vernunft, Grund
receive erhalten, empfangen, bekommen
recent aktuell, neu
recently neulich, kürzlich
recommend empfehlen
record Aufzeichnung, Beleg
regular(ly) regelmäßig
relation Verwandte/r, Verhältnis
relationship Beziehung, Verhältnis
relative Verwandte/r; relativ
relatively relativ, verhältnismäßig
remain (ver)bleiben
remember sich erinnern, daran denken
remove entfernen
repair reparieren
repeat wiederholen
replace ersetzen, austauschen
require benötigen, erfordern
reservation Reservierung, Buchung
reserve reservieren
respect Respekt, Achtung; (be)achten, respektieren
response Reaktion, Antwort
responsible verantwortlich, zuständig
restart neu starten
result Resultat, Ergebnis; folgen, resultieren
return zurückkehren, zurückgeben
rich reich
right rechts, richtig
risk Risiko; riskieren
road (Land-)Straße
role-play Rollenspiel
room Zimmer, Raum
round Runde; rund
rude unhöflich
rule Regel, Vorschrift
run betreiben, laufen (lassen)

S
sad traurig
safe(ly) sicher
sales Verkauf, Vertrieb, Umsatz
same gleiche/r/s, der-, die-, dasselbe
satisfied zufrieden
save retten, sichern
say sagen
school Schule
science Naturwissenschaft
score Ergebnis, Punkt(estand)
screen Bildschirm
search Suche; (durch)suchen
second zweite(r,s); Sekunde
secondary school weiterführende Schule
secondly zweitens
secretary Sekretär/in
see sehen, besuchen, verstehen
seem (er)scheinen
sell (sich) verkaufen
send senden, schicken
sentence Satz
serious ernst, ernsthaft
service Dienst, Dienstleistung, Service
set setzen, stellen
several etliche, einige, mehrere
shall sollen, werden
share teilen, gemeinsam (be)nutzen
shelf Regal
shop Laden, Geschäft; einkaufen
short kurz, klein, knapp
shorten kürzen
should solle/n, sollte/n
shoulder Schulter
show zeigen
shut schließen
side Seite
sign Zeichen, Anzeichen, Schild
similar ähnlich
simple einfach
since da, weil, seit
single einzig, einzeln
sit sitzen, sich hinsetzen
site Website
size Größe
skill Fähigkeit, Fertigkeit
slow langsam
small klein
so also, damit, deshalb, so
solution Lösung
some einige, etwas
someone jemand
something etwas
sometimes manchmal
somewhere irgendwo(hin)
soon bald
sorry traurig; Verzeihung
sound Klang, Geräusch; klingen, sich anhören
south Süden
space Raum, Platz, Abstand
speak sprechen, reden
special besondere/r/s
specially speziell, extra, besonders
speed Geschwindigkeit
spell buchstabieren, schreiben
spelling Rechtschreibung, Schreibweise
spend (Geld) ausgeben, (Zeit) verbringen
stand stehen, aushalten
standard Standard; normal, üblich
start Beginn; anfangen, starten
statement Aussage, Feststellung, Erklärung
stay Aufenthalt; bleiben
step Schritt, Stufe
still still, trotzdem, (immer) noch
stop (an)halten, aufhören (mit)
street Straße
strength Kraft, Stärke
strong stark, heftig
student Student/in, Lernende/r
study lernen, studieren, untersuchen, betrachten
stuff Material, Stoff
subject (Schul-)Fach, Thema
success Erfolg
successful erfolgreich
such as wie zum Beispiel
suggest vorschlagen, andeuten
suggestion Vorschlag
sure sicher
surname Nachname, Familienname
surprise Überraschung; überraschen

T
table Tisch, Tabelle
take nehmen, bringen, dauern
take off ausziehen, abnehmen, abheben
take part teilnehmen, mitmachen
talk Gespräch, Vortrag; sprechen, reden
task Aufgabe
tax Steuer
teach unterrichten, lehren
teacher Lehrer/in
team Mannschaft
technology Technik, Technologie
telephone (call) Telefon(anruf)
television Fernsehen, Fernseher
tell sagen, erzählen
test untersuchen, prüfen
than als
thank danken
thank you danke
thanks Dank; danke
their ihr/e
them ihnen, sie
themselves sich selbst
then dann
there da, dort(hin)
these diese
they sie
thin dünn
thing Sache, Ding, Gegenstand
think denken, meinen, finden, glauben

Basic word list

thorough(ly) gründlich
those jene
though obwohl
through durch
throughout überall (in), die ganze Zeit hindurch
throw werfen
ticket Karte, Fahrschein
tidy aufgeräumt, ordentlich; aufräumen
time Zeit, Mal
timetable Fahr-, Stundenplan
tiny winzig, klein
tip Hinweis, Tipp
today heute
together zusammen
tomorrow morgen
tonight heute Abend/Nacht
too zu, auch
tool Werkzeug
top Spitze, Gipfel; Spitzen-
topic Thema
total (Gesamt-)Summe; gesamte/r/s, Gesamt-
touch anfassen, berühren
town Stadt
traffic Verkehr
trainee Auszubildende/r, Praktikant/in
translate übersetzen
translation Übersetzung
travel Reisen; reisen, fahren
trip Ausflug, Reise, Besuch
trouble Mühe, Umstände, Problem(e)
true wahr, richtig
try versuchen, probieren
turn (sich) drehen, wenden, werden
twice zweimal
type Art, Sorte, Typ; tippen
typical typisch

U
unable unfähig
under unter
understand verstehen, begreifen
understanding Verständnis
unfortunately leider
unfriendly unfreundlich
university Universität
unless es sei denn, außer wenn
unlike anders als, im Gegensatz zu
until bis
urgent dringend, eilig
use Gebrauch; gebrauchen, benutzen, verwenden
useful nützlich
useless nutzlos, unbrauchbar
user Anwender/in, Benutzer/in
usual gewöhnlich, normal, üblich
usually gewöhnlich, normalerweise, meistens

V
vary variieren, schwanken
visit Besuch; besuchen, besichtigen
visitor Besucher/in, Gast
voice Stimme

W
wait warten
wall Wand, Mauer
want wollen
watch Armbanduhr
water Wasser
way Weg, Methode, Art (und Weise)
weather Wetter
week Woche
weekend Wochenende
weekly wöchentlich
welcome Willkommen; willkommen heißen
well gesund, gut; also
whatever was auch immer
when wenn, als, wann
whenever immer wenn
where wo(hin)
whether ob
which welche
while während
white weiß
who(m) wen, wem
whole ganz
why warum
wide breit, weit
wife (Ehe-)Frau
will Wille; werde(n), wollen
window Fenster
wish Wunsch; wünschen
with mit, bei
within innerhalb (von), in
without ohne
woman Frau
wonderful wunderbar
wood Holz
word Wort
work Arbeit; funktionieren, arbeiten
worker Arbeiter/in
workplace Arbeitsplatz
world Welt
worldwide weltweit
worried besorgt, beunruhigt
worse schlechter, schlimmer
worst schlechteste/r/s, schlimmste/r/s
would würde/n
write schreiben
wrong falsch

Y
year Jahr
yesterday gestern
young jung
your dein, Ihr, euer
Yours sincerely Mit freundlichen Grüßen
yourself du/Sie selbst, sich

Chronological word list

Die neuen Wörter sind in der Reihenfolge ihres Vorkommens im Text verzeichnet. Nicht aufgeführt sind die Wörter aus der Liste des Grundwortschatzes (Basic word list).
T = das Wort befindet sich in den *Transcripts* (Hörverständnistexte in der HRU).
P = das Wort befindet sich in den *Partner files*.

Abkürzungen	AE = amerikanisches Englisch	jdm = jemandem	pl = plural noun
	BE = britisches Englisch	jdn = jemanden	sb = somebody
	etw = etwas	jds = jemandes	sth = something

UNIT 1

7
- **aerospace** ['eərəʊspeɪs] — Raumfahrt-
- **automotive** [ˌɔːtə'məʊtɪv] — Auto(mobil)-
- **chemical engineering** [ˌkemɪkl ˌendʒɪ'nɪərɪŋ] — Verfahrenstechnik
- **construction industry** [kən'strʌkʃn 'ɪndəstri] — Bauindustrie
- **consumer electronics** [kənˌsjuːmər ˌɪlek'trɒnɪks] — Unterhaltungselektronik
- **beverage** ['bevərɪdʒ] — Getränk
- **machine tool** [mə'ʃiːn tuːl] — Werkzeugmaschine
- **power generation** [ˌpaʊə ˌdʒenə'reɪʃn] — Stromerzeugung
- **textile** ['tekstaɪl] — Textilie, Gewebe

8
- **global** ['gləʊbl] — global, weltweit
- **subsidiary** [səb'sɪdiəri] — Tochter(gesellschaft)
- **polymer** ['pɒlɪmə] — Polymer(e)
- **vehicle** ['viːəkl] — Fahrzeug
- **range** [reɪndʒ] — Reihe, Auswahl, Palette
- **to train** [treɪn] — ausbilden, schulen
- **advanced plastics** [ədˌvɑːnst 'plæstɪks] — fortgeschrittene Kunststoffe
- **Pleased to meet you.** [ˌpliːzd tə 'miːt ju] — Es freut mich, Sie kennen zu lernen.
- **co-ordinator** [kəʊ 'ɔːdɪneɪtə] — Koordinator/in
- **to introduce sb to sb** [ˌɪntrə'djuːs tə] — jdn jdm vorstellen, jdn mit jdm bekanntmachen
- **colleague** ['kɒliːg] — Kollege/Kollegin
- **field engineer** [ˌfiːld ˌendʒɪ'nɪə] — Ingenieur/in im Außendienst
- **instructor** [ɪn'strʌktə] — Dozent/in, Ausbilder/in
- **(I'm) glad** [aɪm 'glæd] — ich freue mich
- **to make it** ['meɪk ɪt] — es schaffen
- **training course** ['treɪnɪŋ kɔːs] — Lehrgang, Schulung
- **to convert** [kən'vɜːt] — umbauen
- **small production** [smɔːl prə'dʌkʃn] — Kleinproduktion
- **to run on (electricity)** [ˌrʌn 'ɒn] — durch (Strom) angetrieben werden, mit (Strom) fahren
- **lightweight** ['laɪtweɪt] — Leicht-
- **component** [kəm'pəʊnənt] — (Bau-)Teil
- **badge** [bædʒ] — Namensschild
- **handout** ['hændaʊt] — Merkblatt
- **to help yourself to** ['help jəself tə] — sich bedienen mit

9
- **participant** [pɑː'tɪsɪpənt] — Teilnehmer/in
- **automotive technician** [ˌɔːtə'məʊtɪv tek'nɪʃn] — Kfz-Techniker/in
- **production supervisor** [prə'dʌkʃn 'suːpəvaɪzə] — Produktionsleiter/in
- **industrial tools** [ɪn'dʌstriəl tuːlz] — Industriemaschinen
- **aerospace engineer** [ˌeərəʊspeɪs ˌendʒɪ'nɪə] — Raumfahrtingenieur/in
- **site manager** ['saɪt mænɪdʒə] — Bauleiter/in
- **heating system** [ˌhiːtɪŋ 'sɪstəm] — Heizungsanlage
- **brochure** ['brəʊʃə] — Prospekt
- **heavy (traffic)** ['hevi] — stark, dicht (Verkehr)
- **luxurious** [lʌg'ʒʊəriəs] — luxuriös

10
- **staff** [stɑːf] — Mitarbeiter(stab)
- **to develop** [dɪ'veləp] — entwickeln
- **to supply** [sə'plaɪ] — liefern, bereitstellen, versorgen (mit)
- **polymer-based** ['pɒlɪmə beɪst] — aus Polymeren bestehend
- **development** [dɪ'veləpmənt] — Entwicklung
- **concept** ['kɒnsept] — Konzept
- **raw material** [ˌrɔː mə'tɪəriəl] — Rohstoff(e)
- **construction** [kən'strʌkʃn] — Konstruktion
- **to comprise** [kəm'praɪz] — umfassen
- **window frame** ['wɪndəʊ freɪm] — Fensterrahmen

Chronological word list

specification [ˌspesɪfɪ'keɪʃn]	Angabe	
to meet standards [miːt 'stændədz]	Ansprüche erfüllen	
flexible ['fleksəbl]	flexibel, biegbar	
plumbing ['plʌmɪŋ]	Rohrleitungen, Installationen	
insulated ['ɪnsjuleɪtɪd]	isoliert	
renewable [rɪ'njuːəbl]	erneuerbar	
biogas ['baɪəʊgæs]	Biogas	
heat pump ['hiːt pʌmp]	Wärmepumpe	
heavy-duty [ˌhevi 'djuːti]	Hochleistungs-	
civil engineering [ˌsɪvl endʒɪ'nɪərɪŋ]	Tiefbau, Bauingenieurwesen	
conduit ['kɒndjuɪt]	Kabelrohr	
data ['deɪtə]	Daten	
luxury ['lʌkʃəri]	Luxus	
exterior [ɪk'stɪəriə]	Außen-	
bumper ['bʌmpə]	Stoßstange	
seal [siːl]	Dichtung	
internal [ɪn'tɜːnl]	Innen-	
hose [həʊz]	Schlauch	
headlight ['hedlaɪt]	Scheinwerfer	
washer ['wɒʃə]	Waschanlage	
reservoir ['rezəvwɑː]	Behälter	
virtually ['vɜːtʃuəli]	praktisch, nahezu	
branch [brɑːntʃ]	Zweig, Branche, Bereich	
diverse [daɪ'vɜːs]	unterschiedlich	
appliance [ə'plaɪəns]	Gerät	
commercial [kə'mɜːʃl]	gewerblich	
refrigerator [rɪ'frɪdʒəreɪtə]	Kühlschrank	
freezer ['friːzə]	Gefrierschrank, -truhe	
dryer ['draɪə]	(Wäsche-)Trockner	
research [rɪ'sɜːtʃ]	Forschung	
effort ['efət]	Bemühung	
to optimise ['ɒptɪmaɪz]	optimieren	
value ['væljuː]	Wert, Nutzen	
requirement [rɪ'kwaɪəmənt]	Anforderung	
alloy ['ælɔɪ]	Legierung	
hemp [hemp]	Hanf	
jute [dʒuːt]	Jute	
combination [ˌkɒmbɪ'neɪʃn]	Verbindung	

11
medium-sized ['miːdiəm saɪzd]	mittelgroß	
manufacturing sector [ˌmænjuˈfæktʃərɪŋ sektə]	produzierender Bereich	
maintenance ['meɪntənəns]	Wartung	

to be based in [bi beɪst ɪn]	seinen Hauptsitz haben in	
T construction company [kən'strʌkʃn kʌmpəni]	Bauunternehmen, -firma	
residential building [ˌrezɪˌdenʃl 'bɪldɪŋ]	Wohngebäude	
commercial building [kəˌmɜːʃl 'bɪldɪŋ]	Geschäftsgebäude	
airliner ['eəlaɪnə]	Verkehrsflugzeug	
aircraft ['eəkrɑːft]	Flugzeug	
satellite ['sætəlaɪt]	Satellit	
manufacturer [ˌmænju'fæktʃərə]	Hersteller/in	
family-owned business [ˌfæməli əʊnd 'bɪznəs]	Familienunternehmen	

12
employee [ɪm'plɔɪiː]	Mitarbeiter/in	
region ['riːdʒən]	Gebiet, Bereich	
sales office ['seɪlz ɒfɪs]	Verkaufsbüro	
plant [plɑːnt]	Werk, Betrieb	
administrative [əd'mɪnɪstrətɪv]	Verwaltungs-	
logistics [lə'dʒɪstɪks]	Auslieferung	
apprentice [ə'prentɪs]	Auszubildende/r	
total ['təʊtl]	(ins)gesamt	
distribution [ˌdɪstrɪ'bjuːʃn]	Vertrieb, (Aus-)Lieferung	
headquarters [ˌhed'kwɔːtəz]	Zentrale, Firmensitz	
technical development [ˌteknɪkl dɪ'veləpmənt]	technische Entwicklung	
to operate ['ɒpəreɪt]	betreiben	
technique [tek'niːk]	Methode	
properly ['prɒpəli]	richtig, korrekt	
T to bore [bɔː]	langweilen	
site [saɪt]	Standort	
head office [ˌhed 'ɒfɪs]	Zentrale	
procurement [prə'kjʊəmənt]	Beschaffung	
geographical [ˌdʒiːə'græfɪkl]	geographisch	
manufacture [ˌmænju'fæktʃə]	herstellen, produzieren	

13
one point four (1.4) [ˌwʌn pɔɪnt 'fɔː]	eins Komma vier	
billion ['bɪliən]	Milliarde	
division [dɪ'vɪʒn]	(Betriebs-)Sparte, Abteilung	
department [dɪ'pɑːtmənt]	Ressort, Abteilung	
relevant ['reləvənt]	wesentlich	
statistics [stə'tɪstɪks]	statistische Angaben	
to illustrate ['ɪləstreɪt]	illustrieren, veranschaulichen	

Chronological word list

	sample ['sɑːmpl]	Muster, (Kost-)Probe
P	profit ['prɒfɪt]	Profit, Gewinn
	establishment [ɪˈstæblɪʃmənt]	Einrichtung

14	to found [faʊnd]	gründen
	to invent [ɪnˈvent]	erfinden
	balloon [bəˈluːn]	Ballon
	bracket ['brækɪt]	(runde) Klammer
	trainee [treɪˈniː]	Auszubildende/r, Praktikant/in
	conversion [kənˈvɜːʃn]	Umwandlung, -stellung

15	inventor [ɪnˈventə]	Erfinder/in
	visionary ['vɪʒənri]	Visionär/in
	Bavarian [bəˈveəriən]	bayerisch
	outbreak ['aʊtbreɪk]	Ausbruch
	to force sb to do sth [fɔːs]	jdn zwingen, etw zu tun
	mechanical engineer [mɪˌkænɪkl ˌendʒɪˈnɪə]	Maschinen(bau)- ingenieur/in
	scholarship ['skɒləʃɪp]	Stipendium
	polytechnic [ˌpɒliˈteknɪk]	Fachhochschule
	various ['veəriəs]	verschiedene
	solar-powered [ˌsəʊlə ˈpaʊəd]	mit Solarantrieb
	steam engine ['stiːm endʒɪn]	Dampfmaschine
	ammonia vapour [əˈməʊniə veɪpə]	Ammoniakdampf
	to explode [ɪkˈspləʊd]	explodieren
	World Fair ['wɜːld feə]	Weltausstellung
	to fuel ['fjuːəl]	antreiben
	aboard [əˈbɔːd]	an Bord
	steamer ['stiːmə]	Dampfer
	voyage ['vɔɪɪdʒ]	(See-)Reise
	to attend [əˈtend]	teilnehmen (an)
	to retire [rɪˈtaɪə]	sich zurückziehen
	fisherman, pl fishermen ['fɪʃəmən, -mən]	Fischer
	to recover [rɪˈkʌvə]	bergen
	to float [fləʊt]	(im Wasser) treiben
	belongings [bɪˈlɒŋɪŋz]	Sachen, Habseligkeiten
	to identify [aɪˈdentɪfaɪ]	identifizieren
	suicide ['suːɪsaɪd]	Selbstmord
	to commit suicide [kəˌmɪt ˈsuːɪsaɪd]	Selbstmord begehen
	difficulty ['dɪfɪkəlti]	Schwierigkeit
	theory ['θɪəri]	Theorie
	killer ['kɪlə]	Killer/in, Mörder/in
	to hire ['haɪə]	(an)heuern
	to fear [fɪə]	(be)fürchten
	to advance (a theory) [ədˈvɑːns]	aufstellen, vorbringen

	accidentally [ˌæksɪˈdentəli]	aus Versehen
	overboard ['əʊvəbɔːd]	über Bord
	compression [kəmˈpreʃn]	Kompression, Druck
	piston ['pɪstən]	Kolben
	to inject [ɪnˈdʒekt]	(ein)spritzen
	to ignite [ɪɡˈnaɪt]	(sich) entzünden
	compressed [kəmˈprest]	komprimiert
	spark plug ['spɑːk plʌɡ]	Zündkerze
	ignition [ɪɡˈnɪʃn]	Zündung
	to consume [kənˈsjuːm]	verbrauchen
	friction ['frɪkʃn]	Reibung
	heat radiation [hiːt ˌreɪdiˈeɪʃn]	Wärme(ab)strahlung
	exhaust gas [ɪɡˈzɔːst ɡæs]	Abgas(e), Auspuffgas(e)
	efficient [ɪˈfɪʃnt]	effizient, leistungsfähig
	starter motor ['stɑːtə məʊtə]	Anlasser

16	unusual-looking [ʌnˈjuːʒuəl lʊkɪŋ]	ungewöhnlich aussehend
	fuel-efficient [ˌfjuːəl ɪˈfɪʃnt]	Treibstoff sparend, mit geringem Treibstoffverbrauch
	high-strength [ˌhaɪ ˈstreŋθ]	extrem stabil
	carbon-fibre-reinforced plastic [ˌkɑːbən ˌfaɪbə ˌriːɪnˌfɔːst ˈplæstɪk]	kohlefaserverstärkter Kunststoff
	bonnet ['bɒnɪt]	Motorhaube
	chassis ['ʃæsi]	Fahrgestell
	support frame [səˈpɔːt freɪm]	Fahrzeugrahmen
	transmission [trænsˈmɪʃn]	Getriebe, Gangschaltung
	CEO (Chief Executive Officer) [ˌsiː iː ˈəʊ]	Vorstandsvorsitzende/r, Generaldirektor/in
	reinforced [ˌriːɪnˈfɔːst]	verstärkt
	bold [bəʊld]	stark, kräftig
	to mould [məʊld]	formen
	complicated ['kɒmplɪkeɪtɪd]	kompliziert
	shape [ʃeɪp]	Form
	significantly [sɪɡˈnɪfɪkəntli]	erheblich, deutlich
	weight [weɪt]	Gewicht
	fuel efficiency [ˌfjuːəl ɪˈfɪʃnsi]	Kraftstoffwirkungsgrad
	roughly ['rʌfli]	ungefähr, etwa
	carmaker ['kɑː meɪkə]	Autohersteller
	ergonomic [ˌɜːɡəˈnɒmɪk]	ergonomisch
	feature ['fiːtʃə]	Eigenschaft

Chronological word list

	aerodynamic [ˌeərəʊdaɪˈnæmɪk]	aerodynamisch		electrician [ɪˌlekˈtrɪʃn]	Elektriker/in, Elektrotechniker/in
	durability [ˌdjʊərəˈbɪləti]	(Lebens-)Dauer, Haltbarkeit	18	machinist [məˈʃiːnɪst]	Maschinist/in, Maschinenschlosser/in
	to result in [rɪˈzʌlt ɪn]	ergeben, zur Folge haben		workforce [ˈwɜːkfɔːs]	Belegschaft
	lifetime [ˈlaɪftaɪm]	Lebenszeit		to troubleshoot [ˈtrʌblʃuːt]	Störungen beseitigen
	high-end [ˌhaɪ ˈend]	im gehobenen Marktsegment		molten [ˈməʊltən]	flüssig, geschmolzen
	cost effective [ˌkɒst ɪˈfektɪv]	kostengünstig		frame [freɪm]	Rahmen
	affordable [əˈfɔːdəbl]	erschwinglich		timber [ˈtɪmbə]	Holz(balken)
	consumer vehicle [kənˌsjuːmə ˈviːəkl]	Fahrzeug für den Normalverbraucher		load [ləʊd]	Ladung, Last
	to claim [kleɪm]	behaupten, erklären		machinery [məˈʃiːnəri]	Maschinen(park), Geräte
	inexpensive [ˌɪnɪkˈspensɪv]	preiswert		researcher [rɪˈsɜːtʃə]	Forscher/in
	impressive [ɪmˈpresɪv]	beeindruckend, eindrucksvoll		to dig [dɪg]	graben, ausheben
				foundation [faʊnˈdeɪʃn]	Fundament
	technological [ˌteknəˈlɒdʒɪkl]	technologisch		ceiling [ˈsiːlɪŋ]	(Zimmer-)Decke
	standpoint [ˈstændpɔɪnt]	Standpunkt		to erect [ɪˈrekt]	errichten, (auf)bauen
				wiring [ˈwaɪərɪŋ]	Verkabelung, Leitungen
	performance [pəˈfɔːməns]	Leistung		to perform [pəˈfɔːm]	aus-, durchführen
	conventional [kənˈvenʃnl]	herkömmlich, konventionell		manufacturing process [ˌmænjufæktʃərɪŋ ˈprəʊses]	Herstellung, Produktionsprozess
				guided tour [ˌgaɪdɪd ˈtʊə]	Führung, Besichtigung

UNIT 2

				budget [ˈbʌdʒɪt]	Etat, Budget
				progress [ˈprəʊgres]	Fortschritt(e)
17	foundry [ˈfaʊndri]	Gießerei	T	state-of-the-art [ˌsteɪt əv ði ˈɑːt]	letzter Stand der Technik
	laboratory [ləˈbɒrətri]	Labor(atorium)		composite [ˈkɒmpəzɪt]	Bauteile
	warehouse [ˈweəhaʊs]	Lager(halle)		canteen [kænˈtiːn]	Kantine, Cafeteria
	building site [ˈbɪldɪŋ saɪt]	Baustelle		seat [siːt]	(Sitz-)Platz
	forklift [ˈfɔːklɪft]	Gabelstapler		to treat sb to sth [ˈtriːt tə]	jdm etw anbieten
	forklift operator [ˈfɔːklɪft ɒpəreɪtə]	Gabelstaplerfahrer/in		ahead of schedule [əˌhed əv ˈʃedjuːl]	vor dem Zeitplan
	joiner [ˈdʒɔɪnə]	Tischler/in, Schreiner/in		administration [ədˌmɪnɪˈstreɪʃn]	Verwaltung
	IT (Information Technology) [ˌaɪ ˈtiː]	Informationstechnologie		fully-equipped [ˌfʊli ɪˈkwɪpt]	vollständig eingerichtet
	specialist [ˈspeʃəlɪst]	Spezialist/in, Fachmann/frau		facility [fəˈsɪləti]	Einrichtung
				recreation [ˌrekriˈeɪʃn]	Erholung
	steelworker [ˈstiːlwɜːkə]	Stahlarbeiter/in		crèche [kreʃ]	Kindertagesstätte
	supervisor [ˈsuːpəvaɪzə]	Aufseher/in, Leiter/in, Ausbilder/in	19	portacabin [ˌpɔːtəˈkæbɪn]	(Bau-)Container
	scaffolder [ˈskæfəldə]	Gerüstbauer/in		surveyor [səˈveɪə]	Landmesser/in
	builder [ˈbɪldə]	Bauarbeiter/in		levelling instrument [ˌlevlɪŋ ˈɪnstrəmənt]	Vermessungsgerät, Theodolit
	assembly line [əˈsembli laɪn]	Montage-, Fließband		surface [ˈsɜːfɪs]	(Ober-)Fläche, (Straßen-)Belag
	bricklayer [ˈbrɪkleɪə]	Maurer/in			
	mechanic [mɪˈkænɪk]	Mechaniker/in		cement mixer [sɪˈment mɪksə]	Betonmischmaschine
	fitter [ˈfɪtə]	Monteur/in, Installateur/in		crane [kreɪn]	Kran
	welder [ˈweldə]	Schweißer/in			

Chronological word list

lorry (**AE:** truck) ['lɒri]	Lastwagen, Lkw
to lay (the foundations) [leɪ ðə faʊn'deɪʃnz]	(die Fundamente) legen
assembly [ə'sembli]	Montage(halle)
to house [haʊz]	unterbringen, enthalten
clean room ['kli:n ru:m]	Waschraum
paint shop ['peɪnt ʃɒp]	Lackiererei
trim shop ['trɪm ʃɒp]	Werkstatt für die Innenausstattung
autoclave ['ɔ:təkleɪv]	Autoklav, Druckbehälter, -kammer
to consist of [kən'sɪst əv]	bestehen aus
delivery bay [dɪ'lɪvəri beɪ]	Lieferzone
for obvious reasons [fər ˌɒbviəs 'ri:znz]	aus naheliegenden Gründen
storage facility [ˌstɔ:rɪdʒ fə'sɪləti]	Lagerhalle
a.s.a.p. [ˌeɪ es eɪ 'pi:]	so bald/schnell wie möglich
reception area [rɪ'sepʃn eəriə]	Empfang(sbereich)
a suite of [ə 'swi:t əv]	eine Reihe von
HR (human resources) [ˌeɪtʃ 'ɑ:]	Personalwesen, -abteilung
finance ['faɪnæns]	Finanzabteilung
accounts department [ə'kaʊnts dɪpɑ:tmənt]	Buchhaltung
marketing ['mɑ:kɪtɪŋ]	Werbung, Vertrieb
fancy furniture [ˌfænsi 'fɜ:nɪtʃə]	schicke Möbel
executive office [ɪg'zekjətɪv ɒfɪs]	Managerbüro

20
ground floor (BE) [ˌgraʊnd 'flɔ:]	Erdgeschoss
first floor (AE) [ˌfɜ:st 'flɔ:]	Erdgeschoss
storey (AE) ['stɔ:ri]	Stock(werk), Etage
story (BE) ['stɔ:ri]	Stock(werk), Etage
rest room (AE) ['rest ru:m]	Toilette
day nursery (AE) ['deɪ nɜ:səri]	Kindertagesstätte

21
extractor fan [ɪk'stræktə fæn]	Entlüfter, Abzugshaube
vapour ['veɪpə]	Dampf, Dunst
to extend [ɪk'stend]	vergrößern, erweitern
parking bay ['pɑ:kɪŋ beɪ]	Parkbucht
concrete ['kɒŋkri:t]	Beton
workbench ['wɜ:kbentʃ]	Werkbank
custom-made ['kʌstəm meɪd]	maßgeschneidert
counter ['kaʊntə]	Schalter, Tresen
to run [rʌn]	verlegen
electricity supply [ɪlekˌtrɪsəti sə'plaɪ]	Netz-, Stromanschluss
to wipe [waɪp]	(ab)wischen
dust [dʌst]	Staub
to weld [weld]	schweißen
security bars [sɪ'kjʊərəti bɑ:z]	Sicherheitsgitter
to tile [taɪl]	kacheln, fliesen
job title ['dʒɒb taɪtl]	Berufsbezeichnung
pipefitter ['paɪpfɪtə]	Rohrleger/in
health and safety manager [ˌhelθ ən 'seɪfti mænɪdʒə ŋr]	Arbeitsschutzbeauftragte
plumber ['plʌmə]	Installateur/in, Klempner/in

T
wooden ['wʊdn]	aus Holz, Holz-
to prefabricate [ˌpri:'fæbrɪkeɪt]	vorfabrizieren
high-pressure [ˌhaɪ 'preʃə]	Hochdruck-
migrant ['maɪgrənt]	Gastarbeiter/in
day-glo jacket [ˌdeɪ gləʊ 'dʒækɪt]	leuchtende Schutzjacke
nasty ['nɑ:sti]	schlimm
to injure ['ɪndʒə]	verletzen
to get injured [get 'ɪndʒəd]	verletzt werden
paperwork ['peɪpəwɜ:k]	Papierkram
to electrocute [ɪ'lektrəkju:t]	durch Stromschlag verletzen/töten

22
responsibility [rɪˌspɒnsə'bɪləti]	Verantwortung
safety inspector [ˌseɪfti ɪn'spektə]	Sicherheitsbeauftragte/r
decorator ['dekəreɪtə]	Maler/in, Tapezierer/in
quantity surveyor [ˌkwɒntəti sə'veɪə]	Bauwirtschaftler/in
to evaluate [ɪ'væljueɪt]	bewerten
to supervise ['su:pəvaɪz]	beaufsichtigen
to measure ['meʒə]	(ver)messen
cement [sɪ'ment]	Zement
leakage ['li:kɪdʒ]	Leck(stelle)
health risk ['helθ rɪsk]	Gesundheitsrisiko
hazardous ['hæzədəs]	gefährlich, schädlich
overtime ['əʊvətaɪm]	Überstunden
precise [prɪ'saɪs]	genau, präzise
distance ['dɪstəns]	Entfernung, Abstand
angle ['æŋgl]	Winkel
wallpaper ['wɔ:lpeɪpə]	Tapete
fully-qualified [ˌfʊli 'kwɒlɪfaɪd]	vollständig ausgebildet
hourly rate [ˌaʊəli 'reɪt]	Stundenlohn, -satz

Chronological word list

salary ['sæləri]	Gehalt	
logistical support officer [lə‚dʒɪstɪkl sə‚pɔːt 'ɒfɪsə]	Angestellter in der Auslieferung	
logistics clerk [lə'dʒɪstɪks klɑːk]	Logistik-Mitarbeiter/in	
materials section [mə'tɪərɪəlz sekʃn]	Materialabteilung	
certification [‚sɜːtɪfɪ'keɪʃn]	Zertifikat, Anerkennung	
trial period [‚traɪəl 'pɪərɪəd]	Probezeit	
well equipped [‚wel ɪ'kwɪpt]	gut ausgestattet	
to draw sth up [‚drɔː 'ʌp]	etw ausfertigen	
bulk order [‚bʌlk 'ɔːdə]	Großauftrag, -bestellung	
cabling ['keɪblɪŋ]	Verkabelung	
foam [fəʊm]	Schaum(stoff)	

23
operations boss [‚ɒpə'reɪʃnz bɒs]	Bauleiter/in	
to report to [rɪ'pɔːt tə]	unterstehen	
contracts manager ['kɒntrækts mænɪdʒə]	Projektleiter/in	
unauthorized [‚ʌn'ɔːθəraɪzd]	unbefugt	
to sort sth out [‚sɔːt 'aʊt]	sich um etw kümmern	
boss sb around [‚bɒs ə'raʊnd]	jdn herumkommandieren	
conference ['kɒnfərəns]	Konferenz, Tagung	
skilled labourer [skɪld 'leɪbərə]	Facharbeiter/in	
lever ['liːvə]	Hebel	
to pull a lever [‚pʊl ə 'liːvə]	einen Hebel betätigen	
calculator ['kælkjuleɪtə]	(Taschen-)Rechner	
operating director [‚ɒpəreɪtɪŋ də'rektə]	Bauleiter/in	
contract ['kɒntrækt]	Vertrag	
bookkeeper ['bʊkkiːpə]	Buchhalter/in	

24
to go ahead [‚gəʊ ə'hed]	anfangen	
tiler ['taɪlə]	Fliesenleger/in	
security measures [sɪ'kjʊərəti meʒəz]	Sicherheitsvorkehrungen	
brick [brɪk]	Ziegel(stein)	
to maintain [meɪn'teɪn]	warten	
protective clothing [prə‚tektɪv 'kləʊðɪŋ]	Schutz(be)kleidung	
gloves [glʌvz]	Handschuhe	
hard hat (AE) [‚hɑːd 'hæt]	Schutzhelm	
safety helmet [‚seɪfti 'helmɪt]	Schutzhelm	
cup mask ['kʌp mɑːsk]	Atem(schutz)maske, Mundschutz	
ear protectors [ɪə prə'tektəz]	Ohrenschützer	
to avoid [ə'vɔɪd]	(ver)meiden, verhüten	
sharp [ʃɑːp]	scharf, spitz	
splinter ['splɪntə]	Splitter	
to breathe in [‚briːð 'ɪn]	einatmen	
harmful ['hɑːmfl]	schädlich	
injury ['ɪndʒəri]	Verletzung	

25
to expand [ɪk'spænd]	wachsen	
to contract [kən'trækt]	schrumpfen	
to specialize in ['speʃəlaɪz ɪn]	sich spezialisieren auf	
healthcare ['helθkeə]	Gesundheitsfürsorge, medizinische Versorgung	
educational building [edʒu‚keɪʃənl 'bɪldɪŋ]	Schulgebäude	
telecommunications [‚telɪkə‚mjuːnɪ'keɪʃnz]	Fernmeldewesen	
infrastructure ['ɪnfrəstrʌktʃə]	Infrastruktur	
waste-water treatment plant [‚weɪst 'wɔːtə 'triːtmənt plɑːnt]	Kläranlage	
car manufacturing plant [‚kɑː ‚mænjuˈfæktʃərɪŋ plɑːnt]	Automobilwerk	
advanced facilities [əd‚vɑːnst fə'sɪlɪtiz]	moderne Einrichtungen	
client ['klaɪənt]	Kunde/Kundin	
corporate client [‚kɔːpərət 'klaɪənt]	Firmenkunde, -kundin	
institutional client [‚ɪnstɪ‚tjuːʃənl 'klaɪənt]	institutionelle/r Kunde/Kundin	
innovative ['ɪnəveɪtɪv]	innovativ, aufgeschlossen	
management ['mænɪdʒmənt]	Geschäftsführung, Verwaltung	
techniques [tek'niːks]	Methoden, (Arbeits-)Technik	
personnel [‚pɜːsə'nel]	Personal, Mitarbeiter	
on schedule [ɒn 'ʃedjuːl]	planmäßig, pünktlich	
within budget [wɪ‚ðɪn 'bʌdʒɪt]	innerhalb des Finanzplans	
inception [ɪn'sepʃn]	Beginn	
operational facility [‚ɒpə‚reɪʃənl fə'sɪləti]	funktionsfähige Einrichtung	
effectiveness [ɪ'fektɪvnəs]	Effektivität	
despite [dɪ'spaɪt]	trotz	
shrinking ['ʃrɪŋkɪŋ]	schrumpfen d	
demand [dɪ'mɑːnd]	Nachfrage, Bedarf	
tender ['tendə]	Angebot	
major ['meɪdʒə]	bedeutend, größer	

Chronological word list

26	set the pace [set ðə 'peɪs]	wegweisend sein
	draftsman, pl draftsmen ['drɑːftsmən, -mən] ŋin	Zeichner
	to commute [kə'mjuːt]	pendeln, zum Arbeitsplatz fahren
	fluency ['fluːənsi]	fließende Sprachkenntnisse
	vocational [vəʊ'keɪʃənl]	beruflich, Berufs-
	work experience [ˌwɜːk ɪk'spɪəriəns]	Berufs-, Arbeitserfahrung
	proficiency [prə'fɪʃnsi]	Kompetenz, Leistungsfähigkeit
	architectural [ˌɑːkɪ'tektʃərəl]	Architektur-
	to assist [ə'sɪst]	assistieren, unterstützen
	rough [rʌf]	Roh(skizze)
	scale [skeɪl]	Maß(stab)
	to scale [tə 'skeɪl]	maßstabgerecht, nach Maß
	precision [prɪ'sɪʒn]	Präzision
	to generate ['dʒenəreɪt]	herstellen
	supplier [sə'plaɪə]	Lieferant/in, Zulieferer
	competitive [kəm'petətɪv]	konkurrenzfähig
	generous ['dʒenərəs]	großzügig
	benefits package ['benɪfɪts pækɪdʒ]	Zusatzleistungen
	to consider [kən'sɪdə]	berücksichtigen
	résumé ['rezjumeɪ]	Lebenslauf
27	to sweep up, swept, swept [ˌswiːp 'ʌp, swept]	Angestellter in der Auslieferung zusammenfegen
	plaster ['plɑːstə]	Gips
	to last [lɑːst]	ausreichen
	complex of offices [ˌkɒmpleks əv 'ɒfɪsɪz]	Bürokomplex
	redecoration [ˌriːdekə'reɪʃn]	Renovierung
	on time [ɒn 'taɪm]	pünktlich, rechtzeitig
	to guarantee [ˌgærən'tiː]	garantieren
	to compromise on ['kɒmprəmaɪz ɒn]	Kompromisse eingehen bei
	shoddy ['ʃɒdi]	schludrig, minderwertig
	vocational college [vəʊˌkeɪʃənl 'kɒlɪdʒ]	Berufsschule
	plumbing firm ['plʌmɪŋ fɜːm]	Sanitärfirma
	to unscrew [ˌʌn'skruː]	abschrauben
	P-trap ['piː træp]	Siphon
	long-term [ˌlɒŋ 'tɜːm]	langfristig, Langzeit-

	pressure ['preʃə]	Druck
	deadline ['dedlaɪn]	Liefertermin, Frist
	to get off sb's back [ˌget 'ɒf]	jdn in Ruhe lassen
	challenge ['tʃælɪndʒ]	Herausforderung
	water supply ['wɔːtə səplaɪ]	Wasseranschluss, -versorgung
	to irrigate ['ɪrɪgeɪt]	bewässern
	premises ['premɪsɪz]	(Betriebs-)Gelände
	rainwater ['reɪnwɔːtə]	Regenwasser
	to flush the toilet [ˌflʌʃ ðə 'tɔɪlət]	die Toilettenspülung betätigen
	mains [meɪnz]	(Wasser-)Leitung
	external [ɪk'stɜːnl]	äußer(lich)
	domestic building [dəˌmestɪk 'bɪldɪŋ]	Wohngebäude
	to compete with [kəm'piːt wɪð]	konkurrieren mit
28	managing director [ˌmænɪdʒɪŋ də'rektə]	Geschäftsführer/in
	high volume [ˌhaɪ 'vɒljuːm]	umfangreich
	turn around copy [ˌtɜːn ə'raʊnd kɒpi]	doppelseitige Kopie
	capable of ['keɪpəbl əv]	in der Lage sein
	stock [stɒk]	Vorrat, Lager
	refreshment [rɪ'freʃmənt]	Erfrischung
	to apologize for [ə'pɒlədʒaɪz fə]	sich entschuldigen für
	digital imaging technology [ˌdɪdʒɪtl ˌɪmɪdʒɪŋ tek'nɒlədʒi]	digitale bildgebende Technologie
	inauguration [ɪnˌɔːgjə'reɪʃn]	Eröffnung
	turnover ['tɜːnəʊvə]	Umsatz
	steady ['stedi]	stetig
	increase ['ɪŋkriːs]	Steigerung, Erhöhung
	recession [rɪ'seʃn]	Rezession, Wirtschaftsflaute
29	to deal with ['diːl wɪð]	bearbeiten, erledigen
	complaint [kəm'pleɪnt]	Beanstandung, Reklamation
	illustration [ˌɪlə'streɪʃn]	Abbildung
	to bind [baɪnd]	binden
	to calculate ['kælkjuleɪt]	kalkulieren
	data bank ['deɪtə bæŋk]	Datenbank

UNIT 3

30	agricultural [ˌægrɪ'kʌltʃərəl]	landwirtschaftlich
	heavy industrial [ˌhevi ɪn'dʌstriəl]	Schwerindustrie-

Chronological word list

light industrial [ˌlaɪt ɪnˈdʌstrɪəl]	Leichtindustrie-	
professional [prəˈfeʃənl]	professionell	
residential [ˌrezɪˈdenʃl]	Wohn-	
purchase [ˈpɜːtʃəs]	(Ein-)Kauf, Anschaffung	
potential [pəˈtenʃl]	möglich, potenziell	

31
- retail [ˈriːteɪl] — Einzelhandel
- domestic [dəˈmestɪk] — häuslich, privat
- to set up a business [ˌset ʌp ə ˈbɪznəs] — ein Geschäft eröffnen
- to put a call through to sb [ˌpʊt ə kɔːl ˈθruː tə] — einen Anruf zu jdm durchstellen
- studio [ˈstjuːdiəʊ] — Studio, Atelier
- to lease [liːs] — leasen, mieten
- fluorescent tube lighting [flɔːˌresnt tjuːb ˈlaɪtɪŋ] — Neonlicht
- ugly [ˈʌgli] — hässlich
- to intend to do sth [ɪnˈtend] — beabsichtigen etw zu tun
- to run a business [ˌrʌn ə ˈbɪznəs] — ein Geschäft führen
- to display [dɪˈspleɪ] — zeigen, ausstellen
- structural [ˈstrʌktʃərəl] — baulich
- audio-visual [ˌɔːdiəʊ ˈvɪʒuəl] — audiovisuell

32
- contractor [kənˈtræktə] — Bauunternehmer/in
- to suit [suːt] — passen

33
- wire [ˈwaɪə] — Draht
- inefficient [ˌɪnɪˈfɪʃnt] — unwirtschaftlich
- gas-filled [ˈgæs fɪld] — mit Gas gefüllt
- tube [tjuːb] — Röhre, Rohr
- bulb [bʌlb] — Glühbirne, -lampe
- tungsten wire [ˈtʌŋstən waɪə] — Wolframdraht
- solid [ˈsɒlɪd] — fest
- semiconductor [ˌsemikənˈdʌktə] — Halbleiter

34
- spotlight [ˈspɒtlaɪt] — Scheinwerfer
- directional lighting [dəˌrekʃnəl ˈlaɪtɪŋ] — bewegliche Leuchten
- to discuss [dɪˈskʌs] — besprechen
- lighting level [ˈlaɪtɪŋ levl] — Helligkeitsstufe
- exhibition [ˌeksɪˈbɪʃn] — Ausstellung
- dimmer switch [ˈdɪmə swɪtʃ] — Dimmerschalter
- precisely [prɪˈsaɪsli] — genau, präzise

- environmentally friendly [ɪnˌvaɪrənˌmentəli ˈfrendli] — umweltfreundlich
- energy efficient [ˌenədʒi ɪˈfɪʃnt] — energiesparend
- to draw up a plan [ˌdrɔː ˈʌp ə plæn] — einen Plan aufstellen
- lighting plan [ˈlaɪtɪŋ plæn] — Beleuchtungsplan
- rather [ˈrɑːðə] — ziemlich, recht
- harsh [hɑːʃ] — hat, grell
- versatile [ˈvɜːsətaɪl] — vielseitig
- by [baɪ] — mal
- parallel [ˈpærəlel] — parallel
- row [rəʊ] — Reihe
- recessed [rɪˈsest] — eingelassen
- downlight [ˈdaʊnlaɪt] — Deckenstrahler
- ambient [ˈæmbiənt] — Umgebungs-, Raum-
- to adjust [əˈdʒʌst] — anpassen, einstellen
- to achieve [əˈtʃiːv] — erreichen, erzielen
- principle [ˈprɪnsəpl] — Prinzip

35
- key to symbols [kiː tə ˈsɪmblz] — Zeichenerklärung
- track light [ˈtræk laɪt] — Systemleuchte
- sconce [skɒns] — Wandleuchte
- search phrase [ˈsɜːtʃ freɪz] — Suchbegriff
- fixture [ˈfɪkstʃə] — (Elektro-)Installation

36
- alternative [ɔːlˈtɜːnətɪv] — Alternative
- concerned [kənˈsɜːnd] — besorgt
- to convince [kənˈvɪns] — überzeugen
- ballast power [ˈbæləst paʊə] — Ballastleistung
- to disconnect [ˌdɪskəˈnekt] — abklemmen, entfernen
- ongoing [ˈɒngəʊɪŋ] — (fort)laufend, andauernd
- upfront cost [ˌʌpˈfrʌnt kɒst] — Vorauskosten
- to take into account [ˌteɪk ɪntu əˈkaʊnt] — berücksichtigen
- usage [ˈjuːsɪdʒ] — Verbrauch
- to assume [əˈsjuːm] — annehmen
- tariff [ˈtærɪf] — Tarif, Gebühr
- estimate [ˈestɪmət] — (Kosten-)Voranschlag

37
- to prove [pruːv] — sich herausstellen als
- faulty [ˈfɔːlti] — fehlerhaft, defekt
- inspection [ɪnˈspekʃn] — Untersuchung
- replacement [rɪˈpleɪsmənt] — Ersatz(teil)
- to refund [rɪˈfʌnd] — erstatten
- to inspect [ɪnˈspekt] — untersuchen

Chronological word list

	to hesitate ['hezɪteɪt]	zögern
38	thunderstorm ['θʌndəstɔːm]	Gewitter
	additional [əˈdɪʃənl]	zusätzlich
	showroom ['ʃəʊruːm]	Ausstellungsraum
39	to fold out [ˌfəʊld 'aʊt]	ausklappen
	pillion seat ['pɪliən siːt]	Soziussitz
	footrest ['fʊtrest]	Fußstütze
	automatically [ˌɔːtəˈmætɪkli]	automatisch
	mount [maʊnt]	Halterung
	handlebars ['hændlbɑːz]	(Fahrrad-)Lenker
	immobilizer [ɪˈməʊbəlaɪzə]	Wegfahrsperre
	anti-theft protection [ˌænti θeft prəˈtekʃn]	Diebstahlsicherung
	to deactivate [ˌdiːˈæktɪveɪt]	deaktivieren
	off we go [ˌɒf wi 'gəʊ]	los geht's
	slight [slaɪt]	gering, leicht
	navigation [ˌnævɪˈgeɪʃn]	Navigation
	speed [spiːd]	Geschwindigkeit
	battery charge level [ˌbætəri 'tʃɑːdʒ levl]	Batterieladezustand
	capacity [kəˈpæsəti]	Kapazität, Leistung
	smart drive kit ['smɑːt draɪv kɪt]	Smart-Drive-Kit
	to park [pɑːk]	parken
	tracking app ['trækɪŋ æp]	Suchfunktion
	scooter ['skuːtə]	(Motor-)Roller
	to equip [ɪˈkwɪp]	ausrüsten, ausstatten
	ultra-modern [ˌʌltrə ˈmɒdn]	ultramodern
	rarely ['reəli]	selten
	motorcycle (auch: motorbike) ['məʊtəsaɪkl]	Motorrad
	anti-lock braking system (ABS) [ˌænti lɒk ˈbreɪkɪŋ sɪstəm]	Antiblockiersystem
	brake [breɪk]	Bremse
	two-wheeler ['tuː wiːlə]	Zweirad
	airbag ['eəbæg]	Airbag
	to integrate ['ɪntɪgreɪt]	einbauen
	panelling ['pænəlɪŋ]	Anzeigetafel
	beneath [bɪˈniːθ]	unter(halb)
	triangle ['traɪæŋgl]	Dreieck
	to flash [flæʃ]	blinken
	rear-view mirror [ˌrɪə vjuː 'mɪrə]	Rückspiegel
	visible ['vɪzəbl]	sichtbar
	blind spot ['blaɪnd spɒt]	toter Winkel
	headlamp ['hedlæmp]	Scheinwerfer
	backlight ['bæklaɪt]	Rücklicht
	brake light ['breɪk laɪt]	Bremslicht
	to suffice [səˈfaɪs]	genügen
	to retard [rɪˈtɑːd]	verlangsamen, verzögern
	rear [rɪə]	Hinter-
	simultaneously [ˌsɪmlˈteɪniəsli]	gleichzeitig
	hub [hʌb]	(Rad-)Nabe
	normally ['nɔːməli]	normalerweise
	to propel [prəˈpel]	(an)treiben
	forwards ['fɔːwədz]	vorwärts
	generator ['dʒenəreɪtə]	Generator
	resistance [rɪˈzɪstəns]	Widerstand
	lithium-ion battery [ˌlɪθiəm ˌaɪɒn 'bætəri]	Lithium-Ionen-Batterie
	unbelievable [ˌʌnbɪˈliːvəbl]	unglaublich
	socket ['sɒkɪt]	Steckdose
40	low-power [ˌləʊ 'paʊə]	mit niedrigem Stromverbrauch
	low-heat [ˌləʊ 'hiːt]	mit geringer Erwärmung
	variety [vəˈraɪəti]	Auswahl
	confusion [kənˈfjuːʒn]	Verwirrung
	surrounding [səˈraʊndɪŋ]	um … herum
	image content [ˌɪmɪdʒ ˈkɒntent]	Bild inhalt
	to label ['leɪbl]	bezeichnen, nennen
	flat panel television [ˌflæt pænl ˈtelɪvɪʒn]	Flachbildfernseher
	method ['meθəd]	Methode, Verfahren
	to place [pleɪs]	platzieren
	edge [edʒ]	Rand, Kante
	to spread [spred]	(sich) verbreiten, verteilen
	deep [diːp]	tief, stark
	several ['sevrəl]	einige, mehrere
	entire [ɪnˈtaɪə]	ganz, vollständig
	brightness ['braɪtnəs]	Helligkeit
	darkness ['dɑːknəs]	Dunkelheit
	thick [θɪk]	dick, stark
	to consider [kənˈsɪdə]	erwägen
	brand [brænd]	Marke, Typ
	arena [əˈriːnə]	Arena, Stadion
	high-resolution [ˌhaɪ ˌrezəˈluːʃn]	mit hoher Auflösung
	billboard ['bɪlbɔːd]	Werbeplakat
	abbreviation [əˌbriːviˈeɪʃn]	Abkürzung

Chronological word list

UNIT 4

41
aggregate	['ægrɪgət]	Zuschlag(stoff)
asphalt	['æsfælt]	Asphalt
clay	[kleɪ]	Ton, Lehm
gravel	['grævl]	Kies, Kieselsteine
limestone	['laɪmstəʊn]	Kalkstein
sand	[sænd]	Sand
blast furnace	['blɑːst fɜːnɪs]	Hochofen
to extract	[ɪk'strækt]	extrahieren, gewinnen
iron	['aɪən]	Eisen
ore	[ɔː]	Erz
drainage	['dreɪnɪdʒ]	Entwässerung, Drainage
sticky	['stɪki]	klebrig
viscous	['vɪskəs]	zähflüssig
particle	['pɑːtɪkl]	Teil(chen)
silt	[sɪlt]	Schlick
to fire	['faɪə]	verbrennen
kiln	[kɪln]	Brennofen
traction	['trækʃn]	Zugkraft
characteristics	[ˌkærəktə'rɪstɪks]	Eigenschaften
properties	['prɒpətiz]	Eigenschaften
ceramic	[sə'ræmɪk]	Keramik
copper	['kɒpə]	Kupfer
polystyrene foam	[ˌpɒli'staɪriːn fəʊm]	Styropor

42
placement	['pleɪsmənt]	Praktikum
time frame	['taɪm freɪm]	Zeitrahmen
binder	['baɪndə]	Bindemittel, Bindeschicht
underneath	[ˌʌndə'niːθ]	(dar)unter
pothole	['pɒthəʊl]	Schlagloch
priority	[praɪ'ɒrəti]	Vorrang, Priorität
wasteland	['weɪstlænd]	Ödland, Brache
weed	[wiːd]	Unkraut
to lay down	[ˌleɪ 'daʊn]	anlegen, aufstellen
paving block	['peɪvɪŋ blɒk]	Bodenplatte
flat bedding	[flæt 'bedɪŋ]	Verfüllung, Lager
footpath	['fʊtpɑːθ]	Fußweg
footbridge	['fʊtbrɪdʒ]	Fußgängerbrücke
tarmac	['tɑːmæk]	Asphalt
flagstone	['flægstəʊn]	Steinplatte
edging	['edʒɪŋ]	Einfassung
uneven	[ʌn'iːvn]	uneben
narrow	['nærəʊ]	eng, schmal
to screed	[skriːd]	glattstreichen, einebnen
duration	[dju'reɪʃn]	Dauer

43
paving material	[ˌpeɪvɪŋ mə'tɪərɪəl]	Pflastermaterial
suitable	['suːtəbl]	geeignet, passend
unsuitable	[ʌn'suːtəbl]	ungeeignet, unpassend
flag	[flæg]	Steinplatte
slab	[slæb]	Platte, Tafel
reasonable	['riːznəbl]	angemessen, günstig
bituminous	[bɪ'tjuːmɪnəs]	bituminös
macadam	[mə'kædəm]	Makadam, Straßenbelag mit Teer oder Bitumen
forecourt	['fɔːkɔːt]	Vorplatz, Vorhof
vulnerable to	['vʌlnərəbl tə]	empfindlich gegen
spillage	['spɪlɪdʒ]	Pfütze, Lache
to dissolve	[dɪ'zɒlv]	auflösen
plain	[pleɪn]	einfach
midprice	[ˌmɪd'praɪs]	im mittleren Preissegment
time-consuming	['taɪm kənsjuːmɪŋ]	zeitaufwendig
patio	['pætiəʊ]	Terrasse
duckstone	['dʌkstəʊn]	großer Kieselstein
to round	[raʊnd]	(ab)runden
pebble	['pebl]	Kieselstein
slippy	['slɪpi]	rutschig, glatt
cutter	['kʌtə]	Schneider
bulldozer	['bʊldəʊzə]	Planierraupe
jib	[dʒɪb]	Kranbalken, Ausleger
planing machine	['pleɪnɪŋ məʃiːn]	Hobelmaschine
theodolite	[θiː'ɒdəlaɪt]	Theodolit, Winkelmessgerät
wheelbarrow	['wiːlbærəʊ]	Schubkarre

44
to establish	[ɪ'stæblɪʃ]	errichten, aufbauen
diversion	[daɪ'vɜːʃn]	Umleitung
to relay	['riːleɪ]	neu verlegen
to melt down	[ˌmelt 'daʊn]	einschmelzen
to mark out	[ˌmɑːk 'aʊt]	abgrenzen
cone	[kəʊn]	Kegel
road marking	[rəʊd 'mɑːkɪŋ]	Straßenmarkierung
to harden	['hɑːdn]	härten, hart werden
herringbone pattern	['herɪŋbəʊn pætn]	Fischgrätmuster
bedding	['bedɪŋ]	Einbettung
mortar	['mɔːtə]	Mörtel
organic matter	[ɔːˌgænɪk 'mætə]	organische(r) Stoff(e)
depth	[depθ]	Tiefe

Chronological word list

sub-base [ˈsʌb beɪs]	Untergrund, Fundament	
lightly [ˈlaɪtli]	leicht	
to compact [kəmˈpækt]	verdichten	
shovel [ˈʃʌvl]	Schaufel	
rake [reɪk]	Harke, Rechen	
to pile [paɪl]	aufschütten	
mound [maʊnd]	Hügel, Haufen	
resident [ˈrezɪdənt]	An-, Einwohner/in	
barrier [ˈbæriə]	Absperrung, Barriere	
playground [ˈpleɪgraʊnd]	Spielplatz	
defect [ˈdiːfekt]	Schaden, Defekt	
damaged [ˈdæmɪdʒd]	beschädigt	
local council [ˌləʊkl ˈkaʊnsl]	Stadtverwaltung	
to carry out [ˌkæri ˈaʊt]	durchführen	
foreman [ˈfɔːmən]	Vorarbeiter, Polier	
urgent [ˈɜːdʒənt]	dringend, eilig	
high priority [haɪ praɪˈɒrəti]	hohe Priorität	
low priority [ˌləʊ praɪˈɒrəti]	geringe Priorität	

45 domestic contract [dəˌmestɪk ˈkɒntrækt] — Wohnungsbauauftrag

46
- to estimate [ˈestɪmeɪt] — schätzen
- to speed up [ˌspiːd ˈʌp] — beschleunigen
- bar chart [ˈbɑː tʃɑːt] — Säulen-, Balkendiagramm
- flow chart [ˈfləʊ tʃɑːt] — Flussdiagramm
- Gantt chart [ˈgænt tʃɑːt] — Gantt-Diagramm
- line graph [ˈlaɪn grɑːf] — (Kurven-, Linien-) Diagramm
- pie chart [ˈpaɪ tʃɑːt] — Torten-, Kreisdiagramm
- proportion [prəˈpɔːʃn] — Proportion, Verhältnis
- **T** to clear up [ˌklɪər ˈʌp] — aufräumen
- minor [ˈmaɪnə] — klein, geringfügig
- domestic job [dəˌmestɪk ˈdʒɒb] — Wohnungsbau
- to cancel [ˈkænsl] — stornieren, streichen
- to move back [ˌmuːv ˈbæk] — (nach hinten) verschieben
- throughout [θruːˈaʊt] — die ganze Zeit hindurch, während

47
- traffic flow [ˈtræfɪk fləʊ] — Verkehrsfluss
- midweek [ˌmɪdˈwiːk] — in der Wochenmitte

48
- worksite [ˈwɜːksaɪt] — Arbeitsplatz
- to fill in [ˌfɪl ˈɪn] — ausfüllen
- questionnaire [ˌkwestʃəˈneə] — Fragebogen

49
- operator [ˈɒpəreɪtə] — Telefonist/in
- **T** initial [ɪˈnɪʃl] — anfänglich
- foolproof [ˈfuːlpruːf] — idiotensicher
- arrangement [əˈreɪndʒmənt] — Vereinbarung, Termin
- sightseeing [ˈsaɪtsiːɪŋ] — Besichtigung (von Sehenswürdigkeiten)
- to be due to [bi ˈdjuː tə] — etw tun sollen
- to fix a date [fɪks ə ˈdeɪt] — einen Termin ausmachen

50
- to suffer damage [ˌsʌfə ˈdæmɪdʒ] — Schaden erleiden
- inclined [ɪnˈklaɪnd] — geneigt, mit Gefälle
- to endure [ɪnˈdjʊə] — aushalten
- stiff [stɪf] — steif
- unable [ʌnˈeɪbl] — unfähig, nicht in der Lage
- to bend [bend] — (sich) (ver)biegen
- rigid [ˈrɪdʒɪd] — starr, steif
- bend [bend] — Kurve
- gradient [ˈgreɪdiənt] — Steigung
- volume [ˈvɒljuːm] — Menge, Umfang
- commercial traffic [kəˌmɜːʃl ˈtræfɪk] — gewerblicher Verkehr
- HGV (= Heavy Goods Vehicles) [ˌeɪtʃ dʒiː ˈviː] — LKW
- to withstand [wɪðˈstænd] — aushalten
- to possess [pəˈzes] — besitzen
- smooth [smuːð] — glatt
- to resist [rɪˈzɪst] — widerstehen
- stretch [stretʃ] — Ausdehnung
- wear [weə] — Abnutzung
- to skid [skɪd] — schleudern
- to shape [ʃeɪp] — formen
- to flatten [ˈflætn] — einebnen, platt machen
- hollow [ˈhɒləʊ] — Senke, Mulde
- to roll [rəʊl] — walzen
- firm [fɜːm] — fest
- to strengthen [ˈstreŋθn] — verstärken
- crushed stone [krʌʃt ˈstəʊn] — Schotter
- basecourse [ˈbeɪskɔːs] — Tragschicht
- thickness [ˈθɪknəs] — Dicke, Stärke
- determined by [dɪˈtɜːmɪnd baɪ] — bestimmt durch
- projected [prəˈdʒektɪd] — vorhergesagt, prognostiziert
- wearing course [ˈweərɪŋ kɔːs] — Deckschicht
- property [ˈprɒpəti] — Eigenschaft
- to stretch [stretʃ] — sich ausdehnen
- to crack [kræk] — brechen, reißen

Chronological word list

	resistant [rɪˈzɪstənt]	widerstandsfähig
	continuous [kənˈtɪnjuəs]	ununterbrochen, durchgehend
	to reinforce [ˌriːɪnˈfɔːs]	verstärken
	joint [dʒɔɪnt]	Naht(stelle), Stoßfuge
	expansion [ɪkˈspænʃn]	Ausdehnung
	contraction [kənˈtrækʃn]	Zusammenziehung
	blacktop [ˈblæktɒp]	Asphalt
	roadbase [ˈrəʊdbeɪs]	Unterbau
	dense [dens]	dicht
	waterbound [ˈwɔːtəbaʊnd]	wassergebunden
	mechanical [mɪˈkænɪkl]	mechanisch
	paver [ˈpeɪvə]	Fertiger
	ten-stage [ˈten steɪdʒ]	zehnstufig
	sequence [ˈsiːkwəns]	Reihenfolge
51	outskirts [ˈaʊtskɜːts]	Außengebiete, Stadtrand
	tenant [ˈtenənt]	Mieter/in
	lease [liːs]	Mietvertrag
	to inform [ɪnˈfɔːm]	informieren, unterrichten
	applicant [ˈæplɪkənt]	Bewerber/in
	to man [mæn]	besetzen
	inhabitant [ɪnˈhæbɪtənt]	Einwohner/in
	availability [əˌveɪləˈbɪləti]	Verfügbarkeit
	condition [kənˈdɪʃn]	Zustand
	business convention [ˌbɪznəs kənˈvenʃn]	Firmenkonferenz
	trade fair [ˈtreɪd feə]	Handelsmesse
	investor [ɪnˈvestə]	Investor/in, Anleger/in
	property developer [ˌprɒpəti dɪˈveləpə]	Bauträger/in
52	income [ˈɪnkʌm]	Einkommen, Einnahmen
	reaction [riˈækʃn]	Reaktion
	wrestling [ˈreslɪŋ]	Ringen
	contest [ˈkɒntest]	Wettbewerb
	investment [ɪnˈvestmənt]	Investition
	no-interest loan [ˌnəʊ ˈɪntrəst ləʊn]	zinsfreies Darlehen
	loan [ləʊn]	Kredit, Darlehen
	critical [ˈkrɪtɪkl]	kritisch
	to sum up [ˌsʌm ˈʌp]	zusammenfassen

UNIT 5

53	mechatronic technician [mekəˌtrɒnɪk tekˈnɪʃn]	Mechatroniker/in
	to diagnose [ˈdaɪəgnəʊz]	diagnostizieren
	pipework [ˈpaɪpwɜːk]	Rohrleitung(en)
54	hand tool [ˈhænd tuːl]	Handwerkzeug
	handsaw [ˈhændsɔː]	Handsäge
	hacksaw [ˈhæksɔː]	Handbügelsäge, Metallsäge
	crosscut saw [ˈkrɒskʌt sɔː]	Fuchsschwanz(säge)
	coping saw [ˈkəʊpɪŋ sɔː]	Handstichsäge
	keyhole saw [ˈkiːhəʊl sɔː]	Stichsäge
	chisel [ˈtʃɪzl]	Meißel, Stemmeisen
	weird [wɪəd]	merkwürdig, seltsam
	cold chisel [kəʊld ˈtʃɪzl]	Flachmeißel
	rather than [ˈrɑːðə ðən]	anstelle von, anstatt
	hammer [ˈhæmə]	Hammer
	claw hammer [ˈklɔː hæmə]	Kugelhammer
	ball-peen hammer [ˌbɔːl piːn ˈhæmə]	Tischlerhammer (mit Kuhfuß)
	rack [ræk]	Ständer, Gestell
	screwdriver [ˈskruːdraɪvə]	Schraubenzieher, -dreher
	Phillips [ˈfɪlɪps]	Kreuzschlitzschraubendreher
	slot-head screwdriver [ˌslɒt hed ˈskruːdraɪvə]	Schlitzschraubendreher
	spanner [ˈspænə]	Schraubenschlüssel
	open spanner [ˌəʊpən ˈspænə]	Maul-, Gabelschlüssel
	ring spanner [ˈrɪŋ spænə]	Ringschlüssel
	socket spanner [ˈsɒkɪt spænə]	Steckschlüssel
	socket [ˈsɒkɪt]	Stecknuss
	torque wrench [ˈtɔːk rentʃ]	Drehmomentschlüssel
	to reserve for [rɪˈzɜːv fə]	reservieren für
	to mistreat [ˌmɪsˈtriːt]	misshandeln
	accurate [ˈækjərət]	genau
	nuisance [ˈnjuːsns]	Ärgernis
	equivalent [ɪˈkwɪvələnt]	Entsprechung, Übersetzung
55	to seek instruction [siːk ɪnˈstrʌkʃn]	Anweisung(en) einholen
	edged tool [edʒd tuːl]	Schneidwerkzeug
	to sharpen [ˈʃɑːpən]	schärfen

Chronological word list

	defective [dɪˈfektɪv]	fehlerhaft	precision-made [prɪˈsɪʒn meɪd]	Präzisions-
	permission [pəˈmɪʃn]	Erlaubnis, Genehmigung	light-duty [ˌlaɪt ˈdjuːti]	Leichtarbeiten, nur leicht belastbar
	securely fixed [sɪˌkjuəli ˈfɪkst]	sicher befestigt	cordless [ˈkɔːdləs]	schnur-, kabellos
	handle [ˈhændl]	(Hand-)Griff	battery-powered [ˈbætəri pauəd]	batteriebetrieben
	ground [graund]	geschliffen	mains voltage [ˌmeɪnz ˈvəultɪdʒ]	Stromnetz
	cutting angle [ˈkʌtɪŋ æŋgl]	Span-, Schnittwinkel	flex [fleks]	Netzkabel
	purpose [ˈpɜːpəs]	Zweck	trip hazard [ˌtrɪp ˈhæzəd]	Stolperrisiko
	unfamiliar [ˌʌnfəˈmɪliə]	unbekannt, ungewohnt	craftsperson [ˈkrɑːftspɜːsn]	Handwerker/in
	mechatronics [ˌmekəˈtrɒnɪks]	Mechatronik	drill [drɪl]	Bohrer, Bohrmaschine
	item [ˈaɪtəm]	Gegenstand, Ding	to bore [bɔː]	bohren
	to smooth [smuːð]	glätten	masonry [ˈmeɪsənri]	Mauerwerk
	pliers [ˈplaɪəz]	(Kombi-)Zange	torque [tɔːk]	Drehmoment, -kraft
	metal shears [ˈmetl ʃɪəz]	Blechschere	reverse drive [rɪˈvɜːs draɪv]	Rückwärtsgang
	scissors [ˈsɪzəz]	Schere	to function [ˈfʌŋkʃn]	funktionieren
	file [faɪl]	Feile	reciprocating saw [rɪˈsɪprəkeɪtɪŋ sɔː]	Gattersäge
	multimeter [ˌmʌltiˈmiːtə]	Vielfachmessinstrument	blade [bleɪd]	Blatt, Klinge
	soldering iron [ˈsəuldərɪŋ aɪən]	Lötkolben	motion [ˈməuʃn]	Bewegung
	vernier calliper [ˈvɜːniə kælɪpə]	Messschieber	jigsaw [ˈdʒɪgsɔː]	Laub-, Stichsäge
	vice [vaɪs]	Schraubstock	circular saw [ˈsɜːkjələ sɔː]	Kreissäge
	to grip [grɪp]	festhalten	high-speed [ˈhaɪspiːd]	Hochgeschwindigkeits-
	to loosen [ˈluːsn]	lockern, lösen	to rest [rest]	aufsetzen
	tighten [ˈtaɪtn]	anziehen, festschrauben	router [ˈruːtə]	Fräsmaschine, Oberfräse
	dimension [dɪˈmenʃn]	Abmessung, Maß	slot [slɒt]	Nut(e), Schlitz
	electrical circuit [ɪˌlektrɪkl ˈsɜːkɪt]	Stromkreis	groove [gruːv]	Rille, Profil
	nut [nʌt]	(Schrauben-)Mutter	varying [ˈveəriɪŋ]	unterschiedlich
	bolt [bəult]	Schraube	bit [bɪt]	Bit, Aufsatz
	screw [skruː]	Schraube	profile [ˈprəufaɪl]	Profil
56 T	incorrectly [ˌɪnkəˈrektli]	falsch, unrichtig	planer [ˈpleɪnə]	Hobelmaschine
	to damage [ˈdæmɪdʒ]	beschädigen	adjustment dial [əˈdʒʌstmənt daɪəl]	Einstellknopf
	to ruin [ˈruːɪn]	ruinieren	fabric [ˈfæbrɪk]	Stoff
	emphasis [ˈemfəsɪs]	Betonung	nail gun [ˈneɪl gʌn]	Nagler, Nagelpistole
	common sense [ˌkɒmən ˈsens]	gesunder Menschenverstand	to drive (nails into) [draɪv]	(Nägel ein)schlagen
57	portable [ˈpɔːtəbl]	transportabel, tragbar	compressed air [kəmˈprest eə]	Druckluft
	DIY [ˌdiː aɪ ˈwaɪ]	Heimwerker-, Do it yourself-	flammable gas [ˌflæməbl gæs]	(leicht) brennbares Gas
	DIY enthusiast [ˌdiː aɪ ˈwaɪ ɪnˈθjuːziæst]	Heimwerker/in	butane [ˈbjuːteɪn]	Butan
	enthusiast [ɪnˈθjuːziæst]	Begeisterte/r	explosive charge [ɪkˌspləusɪv ˈtʃɑːdʒ]	Sprengladung
	professional [prəˈfeʃənl]	Fachmann, Profi	to treat [triːt]	behandeln
	vital [ˈvaɪtl]	wesentlich	58 to shatter [ˈʃætə]	zerbrechen
	toolkit [ˈtuːlkɪt]	Werkzeugkasten	tough [tʌf]	robust, hart
			convenient [kənˈviːniənt]	bequem, praktisch

Chronological word list

	finish ['fɪnɪʃ]	Finish, letzter Schliff
	to be capable of [bi 'keɪpəbl əv]	fähig sein zu, imstande sein zu
	overtightening [ˌəʊvə'taɪtnɪŋ]	Überdrehen
	carpentry ['kɑːpəntri]	Tischlerei
	toolstore ['tuːlstɔː]	Werkzeugkasten
	cabinet ['kæbɪnət]	(Werkzeug-) Schrank
	drawer [drɔː]	Schub(lade)
	handbook ['hændbʊk]	Bedienungsanleitung, Handbuch
	instruction manual [ɪnˌstrʌkʃn 'mænjuəl]	Bedienungsanleitung, Benutzerhandbuch
T	to cut to size [ˌkʌt tə 'saɪz]	zurechtschneiden
	to nail [neɪl]	nageln
	width [wɪdθ]	Breite, Weite
	roof [ruːf]	Dach
	plywood ['plaɪwʊd]	Sperrholz
	to cover ['kʌvə]	(be-, zu-, ab)decken
	waterproof tar paper [ˌwɔːtəpruːf 'tɑː peɪpə]	wasserdichte Dachpappe
	sticky bitumen [ˌstɪki 'bɪtʃəmən]	klebriger Bitumen
	backing ['bækɪŋ]	Rückseite
59	band saw ['bænd sɔː]	Bandsäge
	column drill ['kɒləm drɪl]	Ständerbohrmaschine
	bench grinder ['bentʃ graɪndə]	Schleifbock
	table saw ['teɪbl sɔː]	Tischsäge
	burr [bɜː]	Grat, Naht, raue Kante
	diameter [daɪ'æmɪtə]	Durchmesser
	bronze [brɒnz]	(aus) Bronze
	faceplate ['feɪspleɪt]	Front-, Schutz-, Richtplatte
	to regrind, reground, reground [ˌriː'graɪnd, ˌriː'graʊnd]	abschleifen
	centred ['sentəd]	in der Mitte
	lighted eye shield [ˌlaɪtɪd 'aɪ ʃiːld]	erleuchteter Sichtschutz
	spark arrestor [ˌspɑːk ə'restə]	Funkenfänger
	coarse grinding wheel [ˌkɔːs 'graɪndɪŋ wiːl]	grobe Schleifscheibe
	tool rest ['tuːl rest]	Werkstückauflage
	wheel guard ['wiːl gɑːd]	Radschutz, Schutzhaube
	adjusting nut [ə'dʒʌstɪŋ nʌt]	Einstellschraube
	fine grinding wheel [ˌfaɪn 'graɪndɪŋ wiːl]	feine Schleifscheibe
	to grind, ground, ground [graɪnd, graʊnd, graʊnd]	schleifen
	cutting edge [ˌkʌtɪŋ 'edʒ]	Schnittkante
	accidental [ˌæksɪ'dentl]	zufällig, unbeabsichtigt
60	to pronounce [prə'naʊns]	aussprechen
	nought [nɔːt]	Null
T	speed chart ['spiːd tʃɑːt]	Geschwindigkeitstabelle
	to insert [ɪn'sɜːt]	einsetzen
	quick chuck ['kwɪk tʃʌk]	Schnellspann-Bohrfutter
	workpiece ['wɜːkpiːs]	Werkstück
	scrap [skræp]	Abfall
	to splinter ['splɪntə]	splittern
	point [pɔɪnt]	Spitze
	to clamp [klæmp]	einspannen, festschrauben
	to switch on [ˌswɪtʃ 'ɒn]	an-, einschalten
T	lubricant ['luːbrɪkənt]	Gleit-, Schmiermittel
61	to last [lɑːst]	(durch)halten
62	blade knife ['bleɪd naɪf]	Messerklinge
	clip point knife [ˌklɪp pɔɪnt 'naɪf]	Klipppunktmesser
	serrated knife [səˌreɪtɪd 'naɪf]	Sägemesser, Messer mit Wellschliff
	tweezers ['twiːzəz]	Pinzette
	needlenose pliers [ˌniːdlnəʊz 'plaɪəz]	Spitzzange
	wire cutter ['waɪə kʌtə]	Seitenschneider
	reamer ['riːmə]	(Reib-)Ahle
	sewing eye ['səʊɪŋ aɪ]	Nadelöhr
	hard-wire cutter [ˌhɑːd waɪə 'kʌtə]	Drahtschneider
	magnifying lens ['mægnɪfaɪɪŋ lens]	Lupe
	stranded-wire cutter [ˌstrændɪd ˌwaɪə 'kʌtə]	Litzenschneider
	wire stripper ['waɪə strɪpə]	Abisolierzange
	corkscrew ['kɔːkskruː]	Korkenzieher
	crimper ['krɪmpə]	Quetschzange
	bit driver ['bɪt draɪvə]	Ratsche
	cross-head screwdriver [ˌkrɒs hed 'skruːdraɪvə]	Kreuzschlitz-Schraubendreher
	metal file ['metl faɪl]	Metallfeile
	nail file ['neɪlfaɪl]	Nagelfeile
	diamond-coated file [ˌdaɪəmənd kəʊtɪd 'faɪl]	diamantbeschichtete Feile
	straight pin ['streɪt pɪn]	Zylinderstift
	bottle opener ['bɒtl əʊpnə]	Flaschenöffner

Chronological word list

tin opener ['tɪn əʊpnə]	Dosenöffner	
can opener ['kæn əʊpnə]	Büchsen-, Dosenöffner	
fish scaler ['fɪʃ skeɪlə]	Fischentschupper	
hook disgorger [hʊk dɪs'gɔːdʒə]	(Angel-)Hakenentferner	

63
combination square [ˌkɒmbɪ'neɪʃn skweə]	Universalwinkelmesser
lock bolt ['lɒk bəʊlt]	Feststellschraube
slip [slɪp]	(ver)rutschen
square head ['skweə hed]	Vierkant(kopf)
protractor head [prə'træktə hed]	Winkelmesser(kopf)
handy ['hændi]	praktisch
spirit level ['spɪrɪt levl]	Wasserwaage
mitre face ['maɪtə feɪs]	Gehrungwinkel
to scribe [skraɪb]	anreißen, vorzeichnen
scriber ['skraɪbə]	Reißahle, -nadel
craft knife ['krɑːft naɪf]	Tapezier-, Schneidemesser
depth gauge ['depθ geɪdʒ]	Tiefenmesser
to permit [pə'mɪt]	erlauben
vernier scale ['vɜːniə skeɪl]	Messschieber
centre head ['sentə hed]	Zentrierkopf
to locate [ləʊ'keɪt]	liegen, platzieren
cylindrical [sə'lɪndrɪkl]	zylindrisch
jaw [dʒɔː]	Backe
steel rule ['stiːl ruːl]	Stahllineal
to rotate [rəʊ'teɪt]	drehen
knot [nɒt]	Knoten
bump [bʌmp]	Erhöhung
inaccurate [ɪn'ækjərət]	ungenau, falsch

UNIT 6

64
troubleshooting ['trʌblʃuːtɪŋ]	Fehlersuche
blocked drain [blɒkt 'dreɪn]	verstopfter/s Abfluss(rohr)
burst pipe [bɜːst 'paɪp]	(Wasser-)Rohrbruch
bodywork ['bɒdiwɜːk]	Karosserie
to leak [liːk]	tropfen
tap [tæp]	(Wasser-)Hahn
mould [məʊld]	Schimmel
to sort out [ˌsɔːt 'aʊt]	in Ordnung bringen
to straighten ['streɪtn]	gerade machen, begradigen

65
spare time [ˌspeə 'taɪm]	Freizeit
post [pəʊst]	Internetbeitrag

desktop (computer) ['desktɒp]	Bürocomputer	
peripheral [pə'rɪfərəl]	Peripherie(gerät)	
tumble dryer [ˌtʌmbl 'draɪə]	Trommeltrockner	
amplifier ['æmplɪfaɪə]	Verstärker	
speaker ['spiːkə]	Lautsprecher	
to indicate ['ɪndɪkeɪt]	(an)zeigen	
to vibrate ['vaɪbreɪt]	vibrieren	
to shut down [ˌʃʌt 'daʊn]	ab-, ausschalten	
error ['erə]	Fehler	
symptom ['sɪmptəm]	Symptom	
spin cycle ['spɪn saɪkl]	Schleudern	
drain cycle ['dreɪn saɪkl]	Abpumpen	
obvious ['ɒbviəs]	erkennbar, sichtbar	
buzzing ['bʌzɪŋ]	Summ(ton)	
control panel [kən'trəʊl pænl]	Kontrollpult, Bedienungsfeld	
erratically [ɪ'rætɪkli]	ungleichmäßig	
to depress [dɪ'pres]	(nieder)drücken	
trigger ['trɪgə]	Auslöser	
to respond [rɪ'spɒnd]	reagieren	
connection [kə'nekʃn]	Anschluss	
wirelessly ['waɪələsli]	drahtlos, per Funk	
hard reset [hɑːd 'riːset]	komplette Neuinstallation	
to unplug [ˌʌn'plʌg]	den Stecker herausziehen	
to uninstall [ˌʌnɪn'stɔːl]	deinstallieren	
to reinstall [ˌriːɪn'stɔːl]	neu installieren	
configuration [kənˌfɪgə'reɪʃn]	Konfiguration	
basically ['beɪsɪkli]	im Grunde, eigentlich	
to cool down [ˌkuːl 'daʊn]	(sich) abkühlen	
overheating [ˌəʊvə'hiːtɪŋ]	Überhitzung	
heat sink ['hiːt sɪŋk]	Wärmeableiter, Kühlkörper	
vent [vent]	Lüftungsschlitz	
poster ['pəʊstə]	Poster/in, Absender/in (eines Internetbeitrags)	
built-in [ˌbɪlt 'ɪn]	eingebaut	
be off-balance [bi ˌɒf 'bæləns]	nicht waagerecht stehen	
drum [drʌm]	Trommel
to rebalance [ˌriː'bæləns]	ausbalancieren

66 T
inappropriate [ˌɪnə'prəʊpriət]	falsch, unangemessen
video card ['vɪdiəʊ kɑːd]	Videokarte

161

Chronological word list

culprit ['kʌlprɪt]	Schuldige/r, Übeltäter/in	
memory-hungry [ˌmeməri 'hʌngri]	viel Speicher benötigend	
video-editing [ˌvɪdiəʊ 'edɪtɪŋ]	Video bearbeitung	
fan [fæn]	Lüfter, Ventilator	
to clog [klɒg]	verstopfen	
casing ['keɪsɪŋ]	Gehäuse	
manually ['mænjuəli]	manuell, von Hand	
failure ['feɪljə]	Fehler, Versagen	
to clarify ['klærəfaɪ]	erläutern	
to undo [ʌn'duː]	rückgängig machen, annullieren	
fragmented [fræg'mentɪd]	zerstört	
incompatible [ˌɪnkəm'pætəbl]	nicht (zueinander) passend	
to reset [ˌriː'set]	zurückstellen	
blank [blæŋk]	leer	
poetic [pəʊ'etɪkl]	poetisch	
corrupt [kə'rʌpt]	beschädigt	
defragment [ˌdiː'frægmənt]	(in einzelne Teile) zerlegen	
anti-virus [ˌænti 'vaɪrəs]	Antiviren-	
to cope [kəʊp]	(damit) zurechtkommen	
calculation [ˌkælkju'leɪʃn]	Rechenoperation	
to stall [stɔːl]	ausgehen	
setting ['setɪŋ]	Einstellung	
to update ['ʌpdeɪt]	aktualisieren	

67
interior [ɪn'tɪəriə]	Innen-	
voltage ['vəʊltɪdʒ]	Spannung	
connector [kə'nektə]	Verbindungsstecker	
rear [rɪə]	Hinter-, Rückseite	
dispenser [dɪ'spensə]	Verteiler	
diagnostic [ˌdaɪəg'nɒstɪk]	Diagnose-	
short [ʃɔːt]	Kurzschluss	
fan motorcircuit [fæn ˌməʊtə 'sɜːkɪt]	Stromkreis des Ventilatormotors	
to die [daɪ]	ausgehen	
indicator ['ɪndɪkeɪtə]	Anzeige	
to malfunction [ˌmæl'fʌŋkʃn]	nicht funktionieren	
pin [pɪn]	Kontaktstift	

P
condenser coil [kən'densə kɔɪl]	Kondensatorspule	
cloth [klɒθ]	Tuch, Lappen	
brush [brʌʃ]	Pinsel	
moisture ['mɔɪstʃə]	Feuchtigkeit	
to rattle ['rætl]	klappern, rattern	
oven ['ʌvn]	Ofen, Herd	
evenly ['iːvnli]	gleichmäßig	

opening ['əʊpnɪŋ]	Öffnung	
to soak [səʊk]	einweichen	
to align [ə'laɪn]	ausrichten	
grease [griːs]	Schmiere, Fett	
blockage ['blɒkɪdʒ]	Verstopfung	
loose [luːs]	lose, locker	
to reinsert [ˌriːɪn'sɜːt]	wieder einführen	
to readjust [ˌriːə'dʒʌst]	neu einstellen	
unstable [ʌn'steɪbl]	instabil	
drain pan ['dreɪn pæn]	Abflussbehälter	

68
backup ['bækʌp]	Sicherungskopie	
indication [ˌɪndɪ'keɪʃn]	Anzeichen	
service patch ['sɜːvɪs pætʃ]	Softwareaktualisierung	
to eliminate [ɪ'lɪmɪneɪt]	eliminieren, beseitigen	
to restore [rɪ'stɔː]	wiederherstellen	
moped ['məʊped]	Moped	
crane driver ['kreɪn draɪvə]	Kranfahrer/in	

70
oscilloscope [ə'sɪləskəʊp]	Oszilloskop	
crimping pliers [ˌkrɪmpɪŋ 'plaɪəz]	Kombizange	
current ['kʌrənt]	Strom	
analogue ['ænəlɒg]	analog	
wave shape ['weɪv ʃeɪp]	Wellenform	
unexpected [ˌʌnɪk'spektɪd]	unerwartet	
pattern ['pætn]	Muster	
circuit ['sɜːkɪt]	(Strom-)Kreis	
sellotape ['seləteɪp]	Tesafilm	
staple ['steɪpl]	Heftklammer	
gizmo ['gɪzməʊ]	(elektronisches) Kleingerät	
terminal ['tɜːmɪnl]	Anschluss	

71
to hiss [hɪs]	zischen, fauchen	
steam [stiːm]	Dampf	
to drop [drɒp]	abfallen, sinken	
to ignore [ɪg'nɔː]	ignorieren, nicht beachten	
eventually [ɪ'ventʃuəli]	schließlich, zum Schluss	
brake line ['breɪk laɪn]	Bremsleitung, -schlauch	
fluid ['fluːɪd]	Flüssigkeit	
to accelerate [ək'seləreɪt]	beschleunigen, Gas geben	
whirring ['wɜːrɪŋ]	Surren	
to increase [ɪn'kriːs]	(an)steigen, (sich) erhöhen	
alternator ['ɔːltəneɪtə]	Lichtmaschine	
bearing ['beərɪŋ]	Lager	

Chronological word list

fan belt ['fæn belt]	Keilriemen
to reattach [ˌriːəˈtætʃ]	wieder befestigen
to change gears [tʃeɪndʒ ˈɡɪəz]	(in einen anderen Gang) schalten
grinding [ˈɡraɪndɪŋ]	schleifen d
to be out of [bi ˈaʊt əv]	fehlen
to refill [ˌriːˈfɪl]	neu befüllen
clutch [klʌtʃ]	Kupplung
worn [wɔːn]	verschlissen, abgenutzt
exhaust [ɪɡˈzɔːst]	Auspuff(rohr)
leak [liːk]	undichte Stelle, Leck
to patch up [ˌpætʃ ˈʌp]	notdürftig reparieren, zusammenflicken
coat hanger [ˈkəʊt hæŋə]	Kleiderbügel
valve seal [ˈvælv siːl]	Ventildichtung
ignition box [ɪɡˈnɪʃn bɒks]	Zündung, Anlasser
ignition switch [ɪɡˈnɪʃn swɪtʃ]	Zündschalter
dashboard [ˈdæʃbɔːd]	Armaturenbrett
steering wheel [ˈstɪərɪŋ wiːl]	Lenkrad, Steuer
sweaty [ˈsweti]	verschwitzt, Schweiß-
to apply the brakes [əˈplaɪ ðə breɪks]	die Bremsen betätigen
screeching noise [ˌskriːtʃɪŋ ˈnɔɪz]	kreischen des Geräusch
to take a class [teɪk ə ˈklɑːs]	einen Kurs mitmachen
brake fluid [ˈbreɪk fluːɪd]	Bremsflüssigkeit
brake pad [ˈbreɪk pæd]	Bremsbelag
none [nʌn]	keine/r/s
brake disc [ˈbreɪk dɪsk]	Bremsscheibe
miles per gallon [ˌmaɪlz pə ˈɡælən]	Meilen pro Gallone
flat [flæt]	platt er Reifen
kingdom [ˈkɪŋdəm]	Königreich

72

laundry [ˈlɔːndri]	Wäsche; Wäscherei
water tap [ˈwɔːtə tæp]	Wasserhahn
prototype [ˈprəʊtətaɪp]	Prototyp
seat-mounted [ˈsiːt maʊntɪd]	am Sitz montiert
soundproof [ˈsaʊndpruːf]	schalldicht
to hit the brakes [hɪt ðə ˈbreɪks]	auf die Bremsen treten
to swing [swɪŋ]	drehen, reißen
slippery [ˈslɪpəri]	glatt, glitschig
Thank goodness! [θæŋk ˈɡʊdnəs]	Gott sei Dank!
deer [dɪə]	Reh, Hirsch
to switch off [ˌswɪtʃ ˈɒf]	ab-, ausschalten
radiator [ˈreɪdieɪtə]	Kühler
kettle [ˈketl]	(Wasser-)Kessel
breakdown lorry [ˈbreɪkdaʊn lɒri]	Pannenwagen
to tow [təʊ]	(ab)schleppen
insurance company [ɪnˈʃʊərəns kʌmpəni]	Versicherungsgesellschaft
to occur [əˈkɜː]	geschehen, stattfinden
moderate [ˈmɒdərət]	mäßig
mph [ˌem piː ˈeɪtʃ]	m/h (Meilen pro Stunde)
junction [ˈdʒʌŋkʃn]	(Straßen-)Kreuzung
sideways [ˈsaɪdweɪz]	seitwärts, zur Seite
considerable [kənˈsɪdərəbl]	beträchtlich
damage [ˈdæmɪdʒ]	Schaden, Schäden
Best regards [best rɪˈɡɑːdz]	Freundliche Grüße

73

recall [rɪˈkɔːl]	Rückruf
vehicle identification number (VIN) [ˌviːəkl aɪˌdentɪfɪˈkeɪʃn nʌmbə]	Kfz-Kennzeichen
Dear Sir or Madam [dɪə ˌsɜː ɔː ˈmædəm]	Sehr geehrte Damen und Herren,
rumour [ˈruːmə]	Gerücht
to stick [stɪk]	(fest)klemmen
brake pedal [ˈbreɪk pedl]	Bremspedal
to confirm [kənˈfɜːm]	bestätigen
dealer [ˈdiːlə]	Händler/in
nor [nɔː]	und auch nicht, noch
certain [ˈsɜːtn]	sicher
to request [rɪˈkwest]	bitten (um)
to authorize [ˈɔːθəraɪz]	autorisieren, bevollmächtigen
dealership [ˈdiːləʃɪp]	Vertretung(en)
estimated [ˈestɪmeɪtɪd]	geschätzt
to extend [ɪkˈstend]	sich erstrecken
possession [pəˈzeʃn]	Besitz
inconvenience [ˌɪnkənˈviːniəns]	Unbequemlichkeit, Unannehmlichkeit
precautionary [prɪˈkɔːʃənəri]	Vorsichts-
measure [ˈmeʒə]	Maßnahme
Sincerely [sɪnˈsɪəli]	Mit freundlichen Grüßen

74

to highlight [ˈhaɪlaɪt]	hervorheben, auswählen
advanced users [ədˌvɑːnst ˈjuːzəz]	fortgeschrittene Nutzer
misaligned [ˌmɪsəˈlaɪnd]	verstellt, falsch ausgerichtet
shaft [ʃɑːft]	Welle
to transmit [trænsˈmɪt]	übertragen

Chronological word list

power transmission system [ˌpaʊə trænsˈmɪʃn sɪstəm]	Antriebssystem	plasterboard screw [ˈplɑːstəbɔːd skruː]	Gipskartonschraube
imbalance [ɪmˈbæləns]	Unausgeglichenheit	antenna cable [ænˈtenə keɪbl]	Antennenkabel
alignment [əˈlaɪnmənt]	Ausrichtung	plunger [ˈplʌndʒə]	Ausgussreiniger, Stampfer
load [ləʊd]	Ladung, (Strom-)Spannung	teflon packing tape [ˌteflɒn ˈpækɪŋ teɪp]	Teflonklebeband
tight [taɪt]	fest(sitzend)	pipe wrench [ˈpaɪp rentʃ]	Rohrzange
frozen [ˈfrəʊzn]	eingefroren	antenna connector [ænˌtenə kəˈnektə]	Antennenanschluss
squealing [ˈskwiːlɪŋ]	Quietschen	bucket [ˈbʌkɪt]	Eimer
burnout [ˈbɜːnaʊt]	Ausbrennen, Brennschluss	to unblock [ˌʌnˈblɒk]	Verstopfung beseitigen
to lubricate [ˈluːbrɪkeɪt]	schmieren	cheerful [ˈtʃɪəfl]	fröhlich, vergnügt
scheduled [ˈʃedjuːld]	planmäßig, regelmäßig		
to ensure [ɪnˈʃʊə]	sicherstellen, gewährleisten		

UNIT 7

fitting [ˈfɪtɪŋ]	Teil		
to introduce [ˌɪntrəˈdjuːs]	einbringen	77 to prevent [prɪˈvent]	verhindern, verhüten
excessive [ɪkˈsesɪv]	überflüssig	hazard [ˈhæzəd]	Risiko, Gefahr
deterioration [dɪˌtɪərɪəˈreɪʃn]	Verschleiß	caution [ˈkɔːʃn]	Vorsicht
commutator [ˈkɒmjuteɪtə]	Kollektor, Stromwender	flammable [ˈflæməbl]	(leicht) brennbar, feuergefährlich
to observe [əbˈzɜːv]	beobachten	admittance [ədˈmɪtəns]	Zutritt, Durchgang
sparking [ˈspɑːkɪŋ]	Funken auslösen	unauthorised [ˌʌnˈɔːθəraɪzd]	unbefugt
to chatter [ˈtʃætə]	klappern	protective [prəˈtektɪv]	Schutz-
holder [ˈhəʊldə]	Halterung	footwear [ˈfʊtweə]	Schuhwerk
spring tension [ˈsprɪŋ tenʃn]	Feder spannung	high-visibility jacket [haɪ ˌvɪzəˈbɪləti ˈdʒækɪt]	reflektierende Warn(schutz)weste
polished [ˈpɒlɪʃt]	sauber, poliert	storeroom [ˈstɔːruːm]	Lagerraum
operational [ˌɒpəˈreɪʃənl]	laufend, in Betrieb	aerosol [ˈeərəsɒl]	Sprühdose
		cleaning fluid [ˈkliːnɪŋ fluːɪd]	Reinigungsmittel
75 round-the-clock [ˌraʊnd ðə ˈklɒk]	rund um die Uhr, 24 Stunden	inspection shaft [ɪnˈspekʃn ʃɑːft]	Inspektionsschacht
to lock oneself out [ˌlɒk ˈaʊt]	sich aussperren	scaffolding rig [ˈskæfəldɪŋ rɪg]	(Bau-)Gerüst
flooded [ˈflʌdɪd]	überschwemmt	cleaning agent [ˈkliːnɪŋ ˈeɪdʒənt]	Reinigungsmittel
handyman [ˈhændɪmæn]	Handwerker	high-voltage [ˌhaɪ ˈvəʊltɪdʒ]	Hochspannungs-
PA (= personal assistant) [ˌpiː ˈeɪ]	persönliche/r Assistent/in	grinder [ˈgraɪndə]	Schleifmaschine
involved [ɪnˈvɒlvd]	damit verbunden	storage area [ˈstɔːrɪdʒ eəriə]	Baumateriallager
drain [dreɪn]	Abfluss(rohr)	T to unload [ˌʌnˈləʊd]	abladen
to block [blɒk]	verstopfen	to die for [ˈdaɪ fə]	sterben für
to enquire about [ɪnˈkwaɪər əbaʊt]	sich erkundigen nach, fragen nach	a smoke [ə ˈsməʊk]	eine Zigarette
charges [ˈtʃɑːdʒɪz]	(Un-)Kosten	78 confined space [kənˈfaɪnd]	geschlossener Raum
sat-receiver [ˌsæt rɪˈsiːvə]	Satellitenempfänger	excavation work [ˌekskəˈveɪʃn]	Erdarbeiten
parabolic dish [ˌpærəˈbɒlɪk dɪʃ]	Parabolschüssel	lifting [ˈlɪftɪŋ]	Kranarbeiten
76 van [væn]	(Werkzeug-)Wagen		
torch [tɔːtʃ]	Taschenlampe		
flexible auger [ˌfleksəbl ˈɔːgə]	Rohrreinigungsspirale		

Chronological word list

PPE (= personal protective equipment) [ˌpɜːsənl prəˌtektɪv ɪˈkwɪpmənt]	Schutzkleidung	
powered system [ˌpaʊəd ˈsɪstəm]	Elektrogerät	
appropriate [əˈprəʊpriət]	entsprechend	
operating procedure [ˌɒpəreɪtɪŋ prəˈsiːdʒə]	Bedienungsanleitung	
to obey [əˈbeɪ]	beachten	
regulation [ˌregjuˈleɪʃn]	Vorschrift, Regel	
on-site [ˌɒn ˈsaɪt]	vor Ort, auf der Baustelle	
off-site [ˌɒf ˈsaɪt]	außerhalb der Baustelle	
qualified [ˈkwɒlɪfaɪd]	qualifiziert, ausgebildet	
task-specific [ˌtɑːsk spəˈsɪfɪk]	arbeitsgerecht, der Aufgabe entsprechend	
hydraulic [haɪˈdrɔːlɪk]	hydraulisch	
thermal [ˈθɜːml]	thermisch	
radioactive [ˌreɪdiəʊˈæktɪv]	radioaktiv	
to render inoperative [ˌrendə ɪnˈɒpərətɪv]	stilllegen, abschalten	
vessel [ˈvesl]	Gefäß, Behälter	
verify [ˈverɪfaɪ]	nachprüfen	
properly-equipped [ˌprɒpəli ɪˈkwɪpt]	sachgerecht ausgestattet	
safety attendant [ˌseɪfti əˈtendənt]	Sicherheitsbeauftragte/r	
standby worker [ˈstændbaɪ wɜːkə]	Ersatzarbeiter/in	
nearby [ˌnɪəˈbaɪ]	in der Nähe	
precaution [prɪˈkɔːʃn]	Vorsichtsmaßnahme	
to position [pəˈzɪʃn]	positionieren	
trench wall [ˈtrentʃ wɔːl]	Grabenwand	
to stabilize [ˈsteɪbəlaɪz]	stabilisieren	
scaffolding [ˈskæfəldɪŋ]	(Bau-)Gerüst	
roof [ruːf]	Dach	
safety harness [ˈseɪfti hɑːnɪs]	Sicherheitsgurt	
secure [sɪˈkjʊə]	sicher	
goggles [ˈɡɒɡlz]	Schutzbrille	
79 walkway [ˈwɔːkweɪ]	Laufgang, Fußweg	
to distract [dɪˈstrækt]	ablenken	
emergency [ɪˈmɜːdʒənsi]	Notfall	
first-aid kit [ˌfɜːst ˈeɪd kɪt]	Verbandskasten	
equipment cage [ɪˈkwɪpmənt keɪdʒ]	Maschinen schutzkäfig	
face shield [ˈfeɪs ʃiːld]	Gesichtsschutz	
machine guard [məˈʃiːn ɡɑːd]	Maschinenschutz, -verkleidung	
overall [ˈəʊvərɔːl]	Overall, Arbeitsanzug	
padlock [ˈpædlɒk]	Vorhängeschloss	
reflective jacket [rɪˌflektɪv ˈdʒækɪt]	reflektierende Warn(schutz)weste	
respirator [ˈrespəreɪtə]	Atemschutzmaske	
siren [ˈsaɪrən]	Sirene	
welding visor [ˌweldɪŋ ˈvaɪzə]	(Schutzhelm mit) Visier, Schweißerschutzvisier	
ladder [ˈlædə]	Leiter	
metalworker [ˈmetlwɜːkə]	Metallarbeiter/in	
spark [spɑːk]	Funke	
80 induction [ɪnˈdʌkʃn]	Arbeitseinführung	
stack [stæk]	Stapel	
unsecured [ˌʌnsɪˈkjʊəd]	ungesichert	
to reverse [rɪˈvɜːs]	rückwärts fahren, zurücksetzen	
excavation [ˌekskəˈveɪʃn]	Graben, Ausschachtung	
81 alright [ɔːlˈraɪt]	in Ordnung	
T oil spill [ˈɔɪl spɪl]	Öllache	
toolbox [ˈtuːlbɒks]	Werkzeugkasten	
to fetch [fetʃ]	holen	
to bleed [bliːd]	bluten	
like hell [laɪk ˈhel]	höllisch, teuflisch	
to disinfect [ˌdɪsɪnˈfekt]	desinfizieren	
gauze pad [ˈɡɔːz pæd]	Mullverband	
painful [ˈpeɪnfl]	schmerzhaft	
bruise [bruːz]	Bluterguss, blauer Fleck	
relief [rɪˈliːf]	Hilfe	
to lie down [ˌlaɪ ˈdaʊn]	sich hinlegen	
accident report [ˌæksɪdənt rɪˈpɔːt]	Unfallbericht	
82 licence [ˈlaɪsn]	Lizenz, Führerschein	
platform [ˈplætfɔːm]	Rampe	
wheel loader [ˈwiːl ləʊdə]	Radlader	
witness [ˈwɪtnəs]	Zeuge/Zeugin	
to back into sth [ˈbæk ɪntə]	rückwärts in etw hineinfahren	
no offence intended [ˌnəʊ əˌfens ɪnˈtendɪd]	nimm's mir nicht übel	
lad [læd]	Bursche	
brickie [ˈbrɪki]	Maurer/in	
damn [dæm]	verdammt, verflucht	
silly sod [ˌsɪli ˈsɒd]	Dummkopf	
horse [hɔːs]	Pferd	
sense [sens]	Verstand	
83 wound [wuːnd]	Wunde, Verletzung	
to stitch [stɪtʃ]	nähen; Stich	

Chronological word list

	to write sb off sick [raɪt ˌɒf 'sɪk]	jdn krankschreiben
	check-up ['tʃek ʌp]	(Nach-)Untersuchung
84	argument ['ɑːgjumənt]	Streit
	to mislay [ˌmɪs'leɪ]	verlegen
	biker ['baɪkə]	Radfahrer/in
	thumb [θʌm]	Daumen
	pleased [pliːzd]	zufrieden
	to tolerate ['tɒləreɪt]	tolerieren
	agency ['eɪdʒənsi]	Agentur, Büro
	to persuade [pə'sweɪd]	überreden
	final exam [ˌfaɪnl ɪg'zæm]	Abschlussprüfung
	to make up your mind [meɪk ˌʌp jɔː 'maɪnd]	sich entscheiden
	Yours sincerely [jɔːz sɪn'sɪəli]	Mit freundlichen Grüßen
85	excerpt ['eksɜːpt]	Auszug
	service manual [ˌsɜːvɪs 'mænjuəl]	Wartungshandbuch
	roadworthiness ['rəʊdwɜːðɪnəs]	Verkehrssicherheit
	to make yourself familiar with [ˌmeɪk jɔːself fə'mɪliə wɪð]	sich vertraut machen mit
	speed limit ['spiːd lɪmɪt]	Geschwindigkeitsbegrenzung
	prevailing [prɪ'veɪlɪŋ]	vorherrschend
	road conditions [ˌrəʊd kən'dɪʃnz]	Straßenverhältnisse
	icy ['aɪsi]	vereist
	crash helmet ['kræʃ helmɪt]	Sturzhelm
	intersection [ˌɪntə'sekʃn]	Kreuzung
	(car park) entrance ['entrəns]	(Parkplatz-)Einfahrt
	(car park) exit ['eksɪt]	(Parkplatz-)Ausfahrt
	to rely on [rɪ'laɪ ɒn]	sich verlassen auf
	partial ['pɑːʃl]	teilweise
	optional ['ɒpʃənl]	wahlweise
	luggage carrier ['lʌgɪdʒ kæriə]	Gepäckträger
	to distribute [dɪ'strɪbjuːt]	verteilen
	loads [ləʊdz]	Lasten
	service and maintenance plan [ˌsɜːvɪs ənd 'meɪntənəns plæn]	Inspektions- und Wartungsplan
	to service ['sɜːvɪs]	eine Inspektion durchführen
	insurance cover [ɪnˌʃʊərəns 'kʌvə]	Versicherungsschutz
	breakdown ['breɪkdaʊn]	Panne
86	health and safety executive [ˌhelθ ən 'seɪfti ɪg'zekjətɪv]	Arbeitsschutzbeauftragt/r
	unlit [ˌʌn'lɪt]	unbeleuchtet
	mobile elevating work platform [ˌməʊbaɪl ˌeləveɪtɪŋ wɜːk 'plætfɔːm]	fahrbare Hebebühne
	waterproof ['wɔːtəpruːf]	wasserdicht
	dustproof ['dʌstpruːf]	staubdicht
	temporary ['temprəri]	vorübergehend
	alteration [ˌɔːltə'reɪʃn]	Änderung
	trailing ['treɪlɪŋ]	herabhängend
	overhead power cable [ˌəʊvəhed 'paʊə keɪbl]	Ober-, Freileitung
	long-handled [ˌlɒŋ 'hændld]	mit langem Handgriff
	trip [trɪp]	Stolpern
	food and catering [ˌfuːd ən 'keɪtərɪŋ]	Versorgung mit Speisen und Getränken
	insurance [ɪn'ʃʊərəns]	Versicherung
	to cover ['kʌvə]	(ab)decken
	benefit ['benɪfɪt]	Vorteil, Vorzug
	non-fatal [ˌnɒn 'feɪtl]	nicht lebensgefährlich
	severe [sɪ'vɪə]	ernst, schwer
	permanent ['pɜːmənənt]	dauerhaft
	at risk [ət 'rɪsk]	in Gefahr
	to account for [ə'kaʊnt fə]	ausmachen
	hierarchy ['haɪərɑːki]	Rangfolge

UNIT 8

87	pros and cons [ˌprəʊz ənd 'kɒnz]	Für und Wider
	air filter ['eə fɪltə]	Luftfilter
	anti-freeze ['ænti friːz]	Gefrier(mittel), Frostschutz(mittel)
	power steering fluid [ˌpaʊə stɪərɪŋ 'fluːɪd]	Servolenkungsflüssigkeit
	shock absorber ['ʃɒk əbsɔːbə]	Stoßdämpfer
	transmission fluid [trænsˌmɪʃn 'fluːɪd]	Getriebeöl
	tyre pressure ['taɪə preʃə]	Reifendruck
	windscreen wiper ['wɪndskriːn waɪpə]	Scheibenwischer
	catalytic converter [ˌkætəˌlɪtɪk kən'vɜːtə]	Katalysator
	platinum ['plætɪnəm]	Platin
88	ELV (= end-of-life vehicle) [end əv ˌlaɪf 'viːəkl]	Schrottwagen
	to register ['redʒɪstə]	anmelden

Chronological word list

lifespan	['laɪfspæn]	Lebenszeit, -dauer
due to	['djuː tə]	aufgrund von
to resell	[ˌriːˈsel]	wieder verkaufen
to equal	['iːkwəl]	entsprechen
recoverable	[rɪˈkʌvərəbl]	wieder verwertbar
automotive material	[ˌɔːtəˈməʊtɪv məˈtɪərɪəl]	Autozubehör
remainder	[rɪˈmeɪndə]	Rest
landfill	['lændfɪl]	Mülldeponie
composition	[ˌkɒmpəˈzɪʃn]	Aufbau, Zusammensetzung
ferrous metal	['ferəs metl]	Eisenmetall
to decrease	[dɪˈkriːs]	abnehmen, (sich) verringern
to incorporate	[ɪnˈkɔːpəreɪt]	einsetzen, verwenden
to maximise	['mæksɪmaɪz]	maximieren
reuse	[ˌriːˈjuːs]	Wiederverwendung
reclamation	[ˌrekləˈmeɪʃn]	Wiedergewinnung
dismantler	[dɪsˈmæntlə]	Abwrackbetrieb
ownership	['əʊnəʃɪp]	Besitz, Eigentum
impact	['ɪmpækt]	(Aus-)Wirkung, Effekt
oil filter	['ɔɪl fɪltə]	Ölfilter
mainly	['meɪnli]	hauptsächlich, vor allem
to scrap	[skræp]	verschrotten
disposable	[dɪˈspəʊzəbl]	Einweg-, Wegwerf-
substantially	[səbˈstænʃəli]	wesentlich, erheblich

89

comparable	['kɒmpərəbl]	vergleichbar
contrasting	[kənˈtrɑːstɪŋ]	gegensätzlich
considerably	[kənˈsɪdərəbli]	beträchtlich
irrelevant	[ɪˈreləvənt]	unwesentlich
out-of-date	[ˌaʊt əv ˈdeɪt]	abgelaufen, überholt
slightly	['slaɪtli]	leicht, geringfügig
de-pollution	[ˌdiː pəˈluːʃn]	Säuberung, Schadstoffbeseitigung
to depollute	[ˌdiːpəˈluːt]	entsorgen, reinigen
database	['deɪtəbeɪs]	Datenbank
stage	[steɪdʒ]	Stadium
to de-register	[ˌdiːˈredʒɪstə]	abmelden
destruction	[dɪˈstrʌkʃn]	Zerstörung, Vernichtung
certificate of destruction	[səˌtɪfɪkət əv dɪˈstrʌkʃn]	Abwrackbescheinigung
to issue	['ɪʃuː]	ausstellen, erteilen

to raise	[reɪz]	(hoch)heben
head-height	['hed haɪt]	Kopfhöhe
to access	['ækses]	besichtigen
underside	['ʌndəsaɪd]	Unterseite
purpose-designed	[ˌpɜːpəs dɪˈzaɪnd]	Spezial-
to drain off	[ˌdreɪn ˈɒf]	ablassen
engine oil	['endʒɪn ɔɪl]	Motoröl
gear box oil	['gɪə bɒks ɔɪl]	Getriebeöl
engine coolant	[ˌendʒɪn ˈkuːlənt]	Motorkühlmittel
to store	[stɔː]	aufbewahren
shredder process	[ˌʃredə ˈprəʊses]	Shredderprozess
recovery	[rɪˈkʌvəri]	Wiedergewinnung
en route	[ˌɒn ˈruːt]	unterwegs, auf der Strecke
impermeable	[ɪmˈpɜːmiəbl]	undurchlässig
pollutant	[pəˈluːtənt]	Schadstoff

90

to shred	[ʃred]	shreddern, zerkleinern
to sort	[sɔːt]	(aus)sortieren
shredder	['ʃredə]	Shredder, Reißwolf
sorter	['sɔːtə]	Sortiermaschine
size-reduction	[ˌsaɪz rɪˈdʌkʃn]	Verkleinerung
to smash	[smæʃ]	zerschlagen, zertrümmern
to spin	[spɪn]	(sich) drehen
chunk	[tʃʌŋk]	Klumpen, Brocken
convertible	[kənˈvɜːtəbl]	Kabrio
confetti	[kənˈfeti]	Konfetti
wind turbine chamber	[ˌwɪnd ˌtɜːbaɪn ˈtʃeɪmbə]	Windturbinenkammer
to suck	[sʌk]	saugen
ferrous	['ferəs]	Eisen-
magnet separator	[ˌmægnət ˈsepəreɪtə]	Magnetabscheider
non-ferrous metal	[ˌnɒn ˌferəs ˈmetl]	Nichteisenmetall
eddy current separator	[ˌedi ˌkʌrənt ˈsepəreɪtə]	Wirbelstromabscheider
to induce	[ɪnˈdjuːs]	auslösen
eddy current	[ˌedi ˈkʌrənt]	Wirbelstrom
conductor	[kənˈdʌktə]	Leiter
magnetic field	[mægˌnetɪk ˈfiːld]	Magnetfeld
repulsion	[rɪˈpʌlʃn]	Abstoßung
non-metallic	[ˌnɒn məˈtælɪk]	nichtmetallisch
non-metal	[ˌnɒn ˈmetl]	Nichtmetall

Chronological word list

stream [striːm]	Strom, Anteil	
processing [ˈprəʊsesɪŋ]	Verarbeitung	
steel mill [ˈstiːl mɪl]	Stahlwerk	
armature [ˈɑːmətʃə]	Armatur	
accidently [ˈæksɪdəntli]	versehentlich	
overband magnet [ˌəʊvəbænd ˈmæɡnət]	Überbandmagnet	
to export [ɪkˈspɔːt]	ausführen, exportieren	
to load up [ˌləʊd ˈʌp]	beladen	

91
derelict [ˈderəlɪkt]	verfallen, baufällig
material properties [məˌtɪərɪəl ˈprɒpətɪz]	Materialeigenschaften
solid [ˈsɒlɪd]	fester Körper
liquid [ˈlɪkwɪd]	Flüssigkeit
rare [reə]	selten
insulator [ˈɪnsjuleɪtə]	Isolator, Nichtleiter
alkaline [ˈælkəlaɪn]	Alkali, alkalischer Stoff
ductile [ˈdʌktaɪl]	(ver)formbar
brittle [ˈbrɪtl]	brüchig, spröde
non-flammable [ˌnɒn ˈflæməbl]	nicht brennbar
transparent [trænsˈpærənt]	durchsichtig, transparent
opaque [əʊˈpeɪk]	undurchsichtig, nicht durchscheinend
soluble [ˈsɒljəbl]	löslich
insoluble [ɪnˈsɒljəbl]	unlöslich

P
body panel [ˈbɒdi pænl]	Karosserieteil
carpet [ˈkɑːpɪt]	Teppich (boden)
impact resistant [ˌɪmpækt rɪˈzɪstənt]	stoßfest
corrosion resistant [kəˌrəʊʒn rɪˈzɪstənt]	korrosionsbeständig, rostfrei
emission regulation [ɪˌmɪʃn ˌreɡjuˈleɪʃn]	Abgasregelung
guideline [ˈɡaɪdlaɪn]	Richtlinie
similarity [ˌsɪməˈlærəti]	Ähnlichkeit
engineering characteristics [endʒɪnɪərɪŋ ˌkærəktəˈrɪstɪks]	technische Eigenschaften
therefore [ˈðeəfɔː]	deshalb
residual [rɪˈzɪdjuəl]	Rest-, restlich
to dismantle [dɪsˈmæntl]	zerlegen, auseinander nehmen
pellet [ˈpelɪt]	Kügelchen, Pellet
output [ˈaʊtpʊt]	Ausstoß
air blast [ˈeə blɑːst]	(Luft-)Gebläse
crusher [ˈkrʌʃə]	Presse, Brechwerk(anlage)
separator [ˈsepəreɪtə]	Trenner
undercover [ˌʌndəˈkʌvə]	Bodenverkleidung
to implement [ˈɪmplɪment]	einführen, einsetzen

paint removal [ˌpeɪnt rɪˈmuːvəl]	Farblösung	
resin [ˈrezɪn]	(Kunst-)Harz	
optical [ˈɒptɪkl]	optisch	
selection [sɪˈlekʃn]	Trennung	
mechanism [ˈmekənɪzəm]	Mechanismus	
resulting [rɪˈzʌltɪŋ]	daraus folgend	
lead [led]	Blei	
tin [tɪn]	Zinn	
ability [əˈbɪləti]	Fähigkeit	
oxidization [ˌɒksədaɪˈzeɪʃn]	Oxidierung, Oxidation	
susceptible to [səˈseptəbl tə]	anfällig für	
coating [ˈkəʊtɪŋ]	Beschichtung	
oxidation [ˌɒksɪˈdeɪʃn]	Oxidation, Oxidierung	
zinc [zɪŋk]	Zink	
dramatically [drəˈmætɪkli]	dramatisch, drastisch	
coated [ˈkəʊtɪd]	beschichtet	
zinc-coated [ˈzɪŋk kəʊtɪd]	verzinkt	
suspension bridge [səˈspenʃn brɪdʒ]	Hängebrücke	
transportation [ˌtrænspɔːˈteɪʃn]	Transport	
consumption [kənˈsʌmpʃn]	Verbrauch	
per annum [pər ˈænəm]	jährlich, pro Jahr	
ratio [ˈreɪʃiəʊ]	Verhältnis	
electronics [ˌɪlekˈtrɒnɪks]	Elektronik	
second to none [ˌsekənd tə ˈnʌn]	an erster Stelle	
extensively [ɪkˈstensɪvli]	umfassend, vielfach	
tubing [ˈtjuːbɪŋ]	Röhren	
demand for [dɪˈmɑːnd fə]	Nachfrage nach	

92
to participate in [pɑːˈtɪsɪpeɪt ɪn]	teilnehmen an, sich beteiligen an
unusual [ʌnˈjuːʒuəl]	ungewöhnlich
environment [ɪnˈvaɪrənmənt]	Umwelt
safety seat [ˈseɪfti siːt]	Sicherheitssitz
heaps of [ˈhiːps əv]	Unmengen von
loads of [ˈləʊdz əv]	jede Menge an
greenhouse gas [ˌɡriːnhaʊs ˈɡæs]	Treibhausgas
refurbish [riːˈfɜːbɪʃ]	renovieren, herrichten

93
to ban [bæn]	verbieten
trillion [ˈtrɪljən]	Trillion
marine animal [məˌriːn ˈænɪml]	Meerestier

Chronological word list

to break down [ˌbreɪk ˈdaʊn]	sich zersetzen, zersetzt werden	cutting-edge [ˌkʌtɪŋ ˈedʒ]	Speerspitze
toxic [ˈtɒksɪk]	giftig, toxisch	to claim [kleɪm]	beanspruchen
food chain [ˈfuːd tʃeɪn]	Nahrungskette	food-grade [ˈfuːd greɪd]	lebensmitteltauglich
emission [ɪˈmɪʃn]	Emission, Abgase	to aim [eɪm]	beabsichtigen
bin bag [ˈbɪn bæg]	Müll(eimer)beutel	continuous cycle [kənˌtɪnjuəs ˈsaɪkl]	ununterbrochener Kreislauf
scavenger [ˈskævɪndʒə]	Aasfresser	to enable [ɪˈneɪbl]	ermöglichen
rat [ræt]	Ratte	sieving [ˈsɪvɪŋ]	Sieben
seagull [ˈsiːgʌl]	Möwe	manual [ˈmænjuəl]	manuell, von Hand
unrealistic [ˌʌnriːəˈlɪstɪk]	unrealistisch	decontamination [ˌdiːkənˌtæmɪˈneɪʃn]	Dekontamination, Entgiftung
to tax [tæks]	besteuern	HDPE (high-density polyethylene) [ˌhaɪ ˌdensəti ˌpɒliˈeθəliːn]	hochverdichtetes Polyäthylen
revenue [ˈrevənjuː]	Einkünfte, Einnahmen		
to invest [ɪnˈvest]	investieren	PET (polyethylene terephthalate) [ˌpɒliˈeθəliːn ˌterəˈθælət]	PET
alternative energy [ɔːlˌtɜːnətɪv ˈenədʒi]	alternative Energie		
ridiculous [rɪˈdɪkjələs]	lächerlich	to shine a beam of light at [ˌʃaɪn ə ˌbiːm əv ˈlaɪt ət]	einen Lichtstrahl richten auf
94 re-usable [ˌriːˈjuːzəbl]	wieder verwendbar		
to suffer [ˈsʌfə]	leiden	to determine [dɪˈtɜːmɪn]	bestimmen, feststellen
canvas bag [ˈkænvəs bæg]	Stofftasche	flake [fleɪk]	Flocke
consumer [kənˈsjuːmə]	Verbraucher/in	to separate [ˈsepəreɪt]	trennen
to refuse [rɪˈfjuːz]	sich weigern	high-density [ˌhaɪ ˈdensəti]	Dichte
standby [ˈstændbaɪ]	Standby, Ruhezustand		
carbon footprint [ˈkɑːbən fʊtprɪnt]	ökologischer Fußabdruck, CO2-Bilanz	decontaminated [ˌdiːkənˈtæmɪneɪtɪd]	de kontaminiert, entgiftet
		to cover [ˈkʌvə]	(be)decken
95 tangled up [ˌtæŋgld ˈʌp]	verstrickt in	caustic soda [ˌkɔːstɪk ˈsəʊdə]	Ätznatron
choke the drains [ˌtʃəʊk ðə ˈdreɪnz]	die Abwasserrohre verstopfen	to crystallise [ˈkrɪstəlaɪz]	kristallisieren
flood [flʌd]	Überschwemmung, -flutung	to peel away [ˌpiːl əˈweɪ]	abschmelzen, abtragen
fatal [ˈfeɪtl]	tödlich, fatal	de-bale [ˌdiːˈbeɪl]	entpaketieren
to disintegrate [dɪsˈɪntɪgreɪt]	zerfallen, sich auflösen	trommel [ˈtrɒməl]	Trommel
to contribute [kənˈtrɪbjuːt]	beitragen	checker [ˈtʃekə]	Überprüfer/in
bio-degradable [ˌbaɪəʊ dɪˈgreɪdəbl]	biologisch abbaubar	sort [sɔːt]	Sortierung, Sortiergang
sack [sæk]	Tüte	**97** open day [ˈəʊpən deɪ]	Tag der offenen Tür
to recover [rɪˈkʌvə]	zurück-, wiedergewinnen	authentic [ɔːˈθentɪk]	authentisch, echt
prevention [prɪˈvenʃn]	Verhütung	to report sth to sb [rɪˈpɔːt tə]	jdm etw melden
favoured [ˈfeɪvəd]	bevorzugt	authorities [ɔːˈθɒrətiz]	Behörden
energy recovery [ˌenədʒi rɪˈkʌvəri]	Energierückgewinnung	listening comprehension [ˈlɪsnɪŋ ˌkɒmprɪˈhenʃn]	Hörverstehen, Hörverständnis
disposal [dɪˈspəʊzl]	Beseitigung, Entsorgung	transparency [trænsˈpærənsi]	(OHP-)Folie
96 to service the demand [ˌsɜːvɪs ðə dɪˈmɑːnd]	die Nachfrage decken	oral [ˈɔːrəl]	mündlich
		involved [ɪnˈvɒlvd]	beteiligt
sandwiched [ˈsænwɪdʒd]	eingeklemmt	fire drill [ˈfaɪə drɪl]	Probealarm
roaring [ˈrɔːrɪŋ]	dröhnend, donnernd	cure [kjʊə]	Heilen
giant [ˈdʒaɪənt]	riesig	alarm plan [əˈlɑːm plæn]	Alarmplan

Chronological word list

	smoke detector [ˌsməʊk dɪˈtektə]	Rauchmelder
	sprinkler [ˈsprɪŋklə]	Sprinker(anlage)
	escape route [ɪˈskeɪp ruːt]	Fluchtweg
	assembly point [əˈsembli pɔɪnt]	Sammelpunkt
	to simulate [ˈsɪmjuleɪt]	simulieren
98	to unpack [ˌʌnˈpæk]	auspacken
	one by one [ˌwʌn baɪ ˈwʌn]	nacheinander
	demonstration [ˌdemənˈstreɪʃn]	Demonstration, Vorführung
	to rethink [ˌriːˈθɪŋk]	überdenken
	aware [əˈweə]	bewusst, aufmerksam
	to preserve [prɪˈzɜːv]	bewahren, erhalten
	resources [rɪˈsɔːsɪz]	Ressourcen
	eco-friendliness [ˌiːkəʊ ˈfrendlinəs]	Umweltfreundlichkeit
	to recharge [ˌriːˈtʃɑːdʒ]	wieder aufladen
	printer cartridge [ˌprɪntə ˈkɑːtrɪdʒ]	Druckerpatrone

UNIT 9

99	after-sales [ˌɑːftə ˈseɪlz]	nach Verkauf
	interval [ˈɪntəvl]	(Zeit-)Abstand
	approved agent [əˌpruːvd ˈeɪdʒənt]	zugelassene/r Händler/in
	working order [ˌwɜːkɪŋ ˈɔːdə]	Betriebsfähigkeit
	commissioning [kəˈmɪʃnɪŋ]	Inbetriebnahme
	to assemble [əˈsembl]	zusammensetzen, -bauen
	to connect to power [kəˌnekt tə ˈpaʊə]	an die Stromversorgung anschließen
	servicing [ˈsɜːvɪsɪŋ]	Wartung
	handover [ˈhændəʊvə]	Übergabe
	reliable [rɪˈlaɪəbl]	zuverlässig
	procedure [prəˈsiːdʒə]	Verfahren, Vorgehensweise
	to mend [mend]	reparieren
	light goods vehicle [ˌlaɪt ɡʊdz ˈviːəkl]	leichter Lieferwagen
	conveyor belt [kənˈveɪə belt]	Fließ-, Förderband
	solar panel [ˌsəʊlə ˈpænl]	Sonnenkollektor
	CNC (Computerized Numerical Control) [ˌsiː en ˈsiː, kəmˌpjuːtəraɪzd ˌnjuːmerɪkl kənˈtrəʊl]	computerisierte numerische Steuerung
	milling machine [ˈmɪlɪŋ məʃiːn]	Fräsautomat
	HVAC (heating, ventilation and air conditioning) [ˌeɪtʃ viː eɪ ˈsiː]	Klimaanlage
	economical [ˌiːkəˈnɒmɪkl]	wirtschaftlich
100	to absorb [əbˈsɔːb]	absorbieren
	congratulations [kənˌɡrætʃʊˈleɪʃnz]	Glückwunsch
	water heater [ˈwɔːtə hiːtə]	Warmwasserbereiter
	trouble-free [ˈtrʌbl friː]	störungsfrei
	in addition to [ɪn əˈdɪʃn tə]	zusätzlich
	precious [ˈpreʃəs]	wertvoll, kostbar
	roof-mounted [ˈruːf maʊntɪd]	auf dem Dach installiert
	to transfer [trænsˈfɜː]	umwandeln
	naturally occurring [ˌnætʃrəli əˈkɜːrɪŋ]	in der Natur vorkommend
	phenomenon [fəˈnɒmɪnən]	Phänomen
	dark-coloured [ˌdɑːk ˈkʌləd]	dunkel gefärbt
	light-coloured [ˌlaɪt ˈkʌləd]	hell gefärbt
	to rise [raɪz]	(an)steigen
	to coat [kəʊt]	beschichten
	heat-absorbent [ˌhiːt əbˈsɔːbənt]	Wärme absorbierend
	to displace [dɪsˈpleɪs]	verdrängen
	to flow [fləʊ]	fließen
	closed circuit [ˌkləʊzd ˈsɜːkɪt]	geschlossener Kreislauf
	heat-transfer fluid [ˌhiːt ˌtrænsfə ˈfluːɪd]	Wärmeträgerflüssigkeit
	non-toxic [ˌnɒn ˈtɒksɪk]	ungiftig, nicht toxisch
	heat exchanger jacket [ˌhiːt ɪksˌtʃeɪndʒə ˈdʒækɪt]	Wärmetauscherummantelung
	to surround [səˈraʊnd]	umgeben
	potable [ˈpəʊtəbl]	trinkbar
	storage tank [ˈstɔːrɪdʒ tæŋk]	Wasserspeicher
	to force back [ˌfɔːs ˈbæk]	zurückdrängen
	circulation [ˌsɜːkjəˈleɪʃn]	Kreislauf
	to fit [fɪt]	ausstatten
	booster system [ˌbuːstə ˈsɪstəm]	Ersatzanlage, Notaggregat
102	to build up [ˌbɪld ˈʌp]	(sich) auftürmen
	ridge [rɪdʒ]	Rand, Kante
	valve [vælv]	Ventil
	insulation [ˌɪnsjuˈleɪʃn]	Isolierung, Dämmung

Chronological word list

	electric heater tape [ɪˌlektrɪk 'hi:tə]	Elektroerhitzerband
	heat output [ˌhi:t 'aʊtpʊt]	Heizleistung
	thermostat ['θɜ:məstæt]	Thermostat
	set at ['set ət]	eingestellt auf
	sealed [si:ld]	versiegelt
	storage cylinder [ˌstɔ:rɪdʒ 'sɪlɪndə]	Speichertank
	circumstance ['sɜ:kəmstəns]	Umstand
	other than ['ʌðə ðən]	außer
	in conjunction with [ɪn kən'dʒʌŋkʃn wɪð]	zusammen mit
	air bursts ['eə bɜ:sts]	Lufteinschlüsse
	to pressurize ['preʃəraɪz]	unter Druck setzen
	watertight ['wɔ:tətaɪt]	wasserdicht
	pressure relief valve [ˌpreʃə rɪ'li:f vælv]	Druckentlastungsventil
	to be functional [bi 'fʌŋkʃənl]	funktionieren
	to commission [kə'mɪʃn]	in Betrieb nehmen
	authorised technician [ˌɔ:θəraɪzd tek'nɪʃn]	autorisierte/r Techniker/in
104	installer [ɪn'stɔ:lə]	Installateur/in
	step-by-step instructions [ˌstep baɪ ˌstep ɪn'strʌkʃnz]	schrittweise Anweisungen
	to talk sb through sth [ˌtɔ:k 'θru:]	jdm etw erklären/erläutern
	removal [rɪ'mu:vl]	Entfernen
	front cover ['frʌnt kʌvə]	Vorderseite
	to expose [ɪk'spəʊz]	freigeben
105	basin ['beɪsn]	Becken, Schüssel
	unused [ˌʌn'ju:zd]	unbenutzt
	hydrogen gas ['haɪdrədʒən]	Wasserstoff
	to accumulate [ə'kju:mjəleɪt]	(sich) ansammeln
	to escape [ɪ'skeɪp]	entweichen
T	vent pipe ['vent paɪp]	Lüftungsrohr
	over-pressurization [ˌəʊvə ˌpreʃəraɪ'zeɪʃn]	Drucküberschreitung
	incorrect [ˌɪnkə'rekt]	falsch, unrichtig
	abnormal [æb'nɔ:ml]	ungewöhnlich, unnormal
	to discharge [dɪs'tʃa:dʒ]	austreten
	to attempt [ə'tempt]	versuchen
107	binding commitment [ˌbaɪndɪŋ kə'mɪtmənt]	bindende Verpflichtung, Vereinbarung
	nuclear plant [ˌnju:klɪə 'paʊə pla:nt]	Kernkraftwerk
	turning point ['tɜ:nɪŋ pɔɪnt]	Wendepunkt
	coal-fired power plant [ˌkəʊl faɪəd 'paʊə pla:nt]	Kohlekraftwerk
T	energy policy [ˌenədʒi 'pɒləsi]	Energiepolitik
	agenda [ə'dʒendə]	Tagesordnung
	fossil fuel ['fɒsl fju:əl]	fossiler Brennstoff
	toward [tə'wɔ:d]	auf ... zu, in Richtung (auf)
	exploitation [ˌeksplɔɪ'teɪʃn]	Ausbeutung, Nutzung
	bio mass ['baɪəʊ mæs]	Biomasse
	hydro power ['haɪdrəʊ paʊə]	Wasserkraft
	geothermal energy [ˌdʒi:əʊˌθɜ:ml 'enədʒi]	Erdwärmeenergie
	to commit oneself [kə'mɪt wʌnself]	sich verpflichten
	ambitious [æm'bɪʃəs]	ehrgeizig
	courageous [kə'reɪdʒəs]	mutig
	utility company [ju:ˌtɪləti 'kʌmpəni]	Versorgungsbetrieb, Stromkonzern
	in the long run [ɪn ðə ˌlɒŋ 'rʌn]	auf die Dauer
	reduction [rɪ'dʌkʃn]	Reduzierung, Senkung
	obliged [ə'blaɪdʒd]	verpflichtet
	profitability [ˌprɒfɪtə'bɪləti]	Rentabilität
	moreover [mɔ:r'əʊvə]	außerdem, zudem
	to phase out [ˌfeɪz 'aʊt]	aussteigen, auslaufen lassen
	unbelieving [ˌʌnbɪ'li:vɪŋ]	ungläubig
	stunning ['stʌnɪŋ]	umwerfend
	to bring about [ˌbrɪŋ ə'baʊt]	herbeiführen
	radical ['rædɪkl]	radikal
	catastrophe [kə'tæstrəfi]	Katastrophe
	to back [bæk]	unterstützen
	energy turnaround [ˌenədʒi 'tɜ:nəraʊnd]	Energiewende
	compromise ['kɒmprəmaɪz]	Kompromiss
	parliamentary opposition [ˌpɑ:ləˌmentri ˌɒpə'zɪʃn]	parlamentarische Opposition
	insight ['ɪnsaɪt]	Einblick
108	air source ['eə sɔ:s]	Luftquelle
	ground source ['graʊnd sɔ:s]	Erdquelle

171

Chronological word list

integration [ˌɪntɪˈɡreɪʃn]	Eingliederung, Einsatz	Class 1 and 2 HGVs [klɑːs wʌn ən ˈtuː ˌeɪtʃ dʒiː ˈviːz]	Führerschein-)Klasse 1 und 2 Lkw
versatility [ˌvɜːsəˈtɪləti]	Vielseitigkeit	day-to-day duties [ˌdeɪ tə ˌdeɪ ˈdjuːtiz]	tagtägliche Pflichten
respectively [rɪˈspektɪvli]	beziehungsweise	permanent position [ˌpɜːmənənt pəˈzɪʃn]	unbefristete (Arbeits-)Stelle
to evaporate [ɪˈvæpəreɪt]	verdampfen, verdunsten	extensive [ɪkˈstensɪv]	umfangreich
to condense [kənˈdens]	kondensieren	tool allowance [tuːl əˈlaʊəns]	Werkzeugzulage
compressor [kəmˈpresə]	Kompressor	career progression [kəˌrɪə prəˈɡreʃn]	beruflicher Aufstieg
to reverse [rɪˈvɜːs]	umkehren	sickness pay [ˈsɪknəs peɪ]	Krankengeld
ambient air [ˈæmbiənt eə]	Umgebungsluft	company pension [ˈkʌmpəni penʃn]	Betriebsrente
soil [sɔɪl]	(Erd-)Boden	private medical insurance [ˌpraɪvət ˌmedɪkl ɪnˈʃʊərəns]	private Krankenversicherung
bedrock [ˈbedrɒk]	Grundgestein		
collection loop [kəˈlekʃn luːp]	Sammelkreislauf	employment [ɪmˈplɔɪmənt]	Beschäftigung, Anstellung
to incorporate [ɪnˈkɔːpəreɪt]	einbauen, einsetzen	covering letter [ˌkʌvərɪŋ ˈletə]	Begleitschreiben
suited [ˈsuːtɪd]	geeignet	accredited [əˈkredɪtɪd]	zugelassen, anerkannt
comprehensive [ˌkɒmprɪˈhensɪv]	umfassend	heavy vehicles mechanic [ˌhevi ˌviːəklz mɪˈkænɪk]	Lkw-Mechaniker/in
horizontally [ˌhɒrɪˈzɒntəli]	horizontal, waagerecht	to prioritize [praɪˈɒrətaɪz]	Prioritäten setzen
vertically [ˈvɜːtɪkli]	senkrecht, vertikal	workload [ˈwɜːkləʊd]	Arbeitsbelastung, -pensum
life expectancy [ˈlaɪf ɪkspektənsi]	Lebenserwartung, -dauer	communication skills [kəˌmjuːnɪˈkeɪʃn skɪlz]	Kommunikationsfähigkeiten
reliability [rɪˌlaɪəˈbɪləti]	Zuverlässigkeit	GCE O level (General Certificate of Education Ordinary Level) [ˌdʒenrəl səˌtɪfɪkət əv ˌedʒuˈkeɪʃn ˈɔːdnri levl]	(etwa) Realschulabschluss
renovated [ˈrenəveɪtɪd]	renoviert		

UNIT 10

109	pension [ˈpenʃn]	Rente, Pension	
	to retire [rɪˈtaɪə]	in Rente/Pension gehen	
	ought to be [ˈɔːt tə]	sollte/n sein	
	opportunity [ˌɒpəˈtjuːnəti]	Chance, Möglichkeit	
	flexi-time [ˈfleksi taɪm]	Gleitzeit	
	MOT (test) (= Ministry of Transport) [ˌmɪnɪstri əv ˈtrænspɔːt]	TÜV-Untersuchung	
	self-employed [ˌself ɪmˈplɔɪd]	selbständig	
	freelance [ˈfriːlɑːns]	freiberuflich, freischaffend	
	perks [pɜːks]	freiwillige Sozialleistungen, Zusatzvergünstigungen	
	work-life balance [ˌwɜːk ˈlaɪf bæləns]	Gleichgewicht zwischen Arbeit und Freizeit	
110	motivated [ˈməʊtɪveɪtɪd]	motiviert	
	fleet (of vehicles) [fliːt]	(Fahrzeug-)Flotte, Fuhrpark	

GCSE (General Certificate of Secondary Education) [ˌdʒenrəl səˌtɪfɪkət əv ˌsekəndri edʒuˈkeɪʃn]	Sekundarabschluss	
numeracy skills [ˈnjuːmərəsi skɪlz]	rechnerische Fähigkeiten	
literacy skills [ˈlɪtərəsi skɪlz]	Lese- und Schreibfähigkeit	
equal opportunities employer [ˌiːkwəl ˌɒpəˈtjuːnətiz ɪmˈplɔɪə]	Unternehmen mit Gleichberechtigung	
to select [sɪˈlekt]	auswählen	
regardless of [rɪˈɡɑːdləs əv]	unabhängig von	
gender [ˈdʒendə]	Geschlecht	
ethnicity [eθˈnɪsəti]	ethnische Zugehörigkeit	
sexual orientation [ˌsekʃuəl ˌɔːriənˈteɪʃn]	sexuelle Orientierung	
recruitment policy [rɪˈkruːtmənt pɒləsi]	Personalpolitik	

Chronological word list

111	rapid ['ræpɪd]	schnell
	overview ['əʊvəvjuː]	Überblick, -sicht
	chronological [ˌkrɒnə'lɒdʒɪkl]	in zeitlicher Reihenfolge, chronologisch
	mandatory ['mændətəri]	vorgeschrieben, obligatorisch
	concise [kən'saɪs]	präzise, knapp
112	certificate [sə'tɪfɪkət]	Zeugnis, Urkunde
	exemplary [ɪg'zempləri]	vorbildlich, beispielhaft
	time keeping record [ˌtaɪm kiːpɪŋ 'rekɔːd]	Zeiteinhaltungsstatistik
	attendance record [ə,tendəns 'rekɔːd]	Anwesenheitsstatistik
	all-round [ˌɔːl 'raʊnd]	umfassend
	expertise [ˌekspɜː'tiːz]	Fachkenntnis(se)
	dependable [dɪ'pendəbl]	zuverlässig
	adaptable [ə'dæptəbl]	anpassungsfähig
	franchise ['fræntʃaɪz]	Franchise-Unternehmen
	warranty repair [ˌwɒrənti rɪ'peə]	Garantie reparatur
	guidelines ['gaɪdlaɪnz]	Richtlinien
	suspension [sə'spenʃn]	Federung, (Rad-)Aufhängung
	CEFR (= Common European Framework of Reference for Languages) [ˌkɒmən jʊərə,piːən ˌfreɪmwɜːk fə 'læŋgwɪdʒɪz]	Gemeinsamer Europäischer Referenzrahmen für Sprachen
	kit car ['kɪt kaː]	Bausatzauto
	gaming ['geɪmɪŋ]	Computerspiele
113	letter of application [ˌletər əv æplɪ'keɪʃn]	Bewerbungsschreiben
	vacancy ['veɪkənsi]	freie/ offene Stelle
	enclosed [ɪn'kləʊzd]	beigefügt
	haulage company [ˌhɔːlɪdʒ 'kʌmpəni]	Transportfirma, Fuhrunternehmen
	running ['rʌnɪŋ]	in Folge, hintereinander
	to catch sb's eye [ˌkætʃ 'aɪ]	jdm ins Auge fallen
	learner ['lɜːnə]	Lerner/in
	to adapt [ə'dæpt]	(sich) anpassen
	to be delighted [bi dɪ'laɪtɪd]	sich (sehr) freuen
	notice ['nəʊtɪs]	Kündigung
114	post [pəʊst]	(Arbeits-)Stelle
	at present [ət 'preznt]	im Moment
	to seek [siːk]	suchen
	enthusiasm [ɪn'θjuːziæzəm]	Begeisterung(sfähigkeit)
	adaptability [əˌdæptə'bɪləti]	Anpassungsfähigkeit
	at any time [ət ˌeni 'taɪm]	jederzeit
	Yours faithfully [jɔːz 'feɪθfʊli]	Mit freundlichen Grüßen
	in charge of [ɪn 'tʃɑːdʒ əv]	verantwortlich für
115 T	to take sb through sth [ˌteɪk 'θruː]	mit jdm etw durchgehen
	vocational training [vəʊˌkeɪʃnl 'treɪnɪŋ]	Berufsausbildung
	to settle down [ˌsetl 'daʊn]	sesshaft werden, eine Familie gründen
	varied ['veərid]	abwechslungsreich
	to pick up [ˌpɪk 'ʌp]	lernen, erwerben
	experienced worker [ɪkˌspɪəriənst 'wɜːkə]	erfahren e/r Mitarbeiter/in
	weakness ['wiːknəs]	Schwäche
	punctual ['pʌŋktʃʊəl]	pünktlich
	hardly ever [ˌhɑːdli 'evə]	fast nie, kaum jemals
	foundation [faʊn'deɪʃn]	Grundlage
	airplane ['eəpleɪn]	Flugzeug
	shift work ['ʃɪft wɜːk]	Schichtarbeit
	skilled [skɪld]	ausgebildet, geschickt
118	to fall into the trap [ˌfɔːl ɪntə ðə 'træp]	den Fehler begehen
	self-orientated [ˌself 'ɔːriənteɪtɪd]	selbstbezogen
	consequently ['kɒnsɪkwəntli]	infolgedessen
	to gain [geɪn]	sammeln
	suitability [ˌsuːtə'bɪləti]	Eignung
	in-between [ɪn bɪ'twiːn]	(da)zwischen
	marketplace ['mɑːkɪtpleɪs]	Markt(platz)
	to graduate from ['grædʒueɪt frəm]	absolvieren
	to obtain [əb'teɪn]	erhalten, erzielen
	to relate to [rɪ'leɪt tə]	sich auswirken auf
	unique selling point [juˌniːk 'selɪŋ pɔɪntʃ]	Alleinstellungsmerkmal
	prospective [prə'spektɪv]	(zu)künftig, potentiell
	to spot [spɒt]	herausfinden, bemerken
	achievement [ə'tʃiːvmənt]	Leistung, Errungenschaft
	addition [ə'dɪʃn]	Ergänzung
	tailored to ['teɪləd tə]	zugeschnitten auf
	targeted ['tɑːgɪtɪd]	zielgerichtet
	overlong [ˌəʊvə'lɒŋ]	überlang, zu lang

Chronological word list

119 **tablet computer** [ˌtæblɪt kəmˈpjuːtə] — Tablet-Computer

surfstick [ˈsɜːfstɪk] — USB-Datenstick (zum Surfen im Internet)

dongle [ˈdɒŋl] — Kopierschutzstecker

USB port [ˌjuː es ˈbiː pɔːt] — USB-Anschluss

provider [prəˈvaɪdə] — Anbieter

sim card [ˈsɪm kɑːd] — SIM-Karte

120 **personal details** [ˌpɜːsənl ˈdiːteɪlz] — persönliche Angaben

print job [ˈprɪnt dʒɒb] — Druckauftrag

flyer design [ˌflaɪə dɪˈzaɪn] — Entwerfen von Flugblättern

diploma [dɪˈpləʊmə] — Abschlusszeugnis, Diplom

distinction [dɪˈstɪŋkʃn] — Auszeichnung

referee [ˌrefəˈriː] — Referenz(geber)

Alphabetical word list

Diese Liste enthält alle Wörter in alphabetischer Reihenfolge. Nicht aufgeführt sind die Wörter aus der Liste des Grundwortschatzes (Basic word list). Die Zahl nach dem Stichwort bezieht sich auf die Seite, auf der das Wort zum ersten Mal erscheint.
P = das Wort befindet sich in den *Partner files*.
T = das Wort befindet sich in den *Transcripts* (Hörverständnistexte in der HRU).

A

a.s.a.p. so bald/schnell wie möglich *19*
abbreviation Abkürzung *40*
ability Fähigkeit *91P*
abnormal ungewöhnlich, unnormal *105T*
aboard an Bord *15*
to absorb absorbieren *100*
to accelerate beschleunigen, Gas geben *71*
to access besichtigen *89*
accident report Unfallbericht *81T*
accidental zufällig, unbeabsichtigt *59*
accidentally aus Versehen *15*
accidently versehentlich *90*
to account for ausmachen *86*
accounts department Buchhaltung *19*
accredited zugelassen, anerkannt *110*
to accumulate (sich) ansammeln *105*
accurate genau *54*
to achieve erreichen, erzielen *34*
achievement Leistung, Errungenschaft *118*
to adapt (sich) anpassen *113*
adaptability Anpassungsfähigkeit *114*
adaptable anpassungsfähig *112*
addition Ergänzung *118*; **in ~ to** zusätzlich *100*
additional zusätzlich *38*
to adjust anpassen, einstellen *34*
adjusting nut Einstellschraube *59*
adjustment dial Einstellknopf *57*
administration Verwaltung *18T*
administrative Verwaltungs- *12*
admittance Zutritt, Durchgang *77*
to advance aufstellen, vorbringen *15*; **~d facilities** moderne Einrichtungen *25*; **~d plastics** fortgeschrittene Kunststoffe *8*; **~d users** fortgeschrittene Nutzer *74*
aerodynamic aerodynamisch *16*
aerosol Sprühdose *77*
aerospace Raumfahrt- *7*; **~ engineer** Raumfahrtingenieur/in *9*
affordable erschwinglich *16*
after-sales nach Verkauf *99*
agency Agentur, Büro *84*
agenda Tagesordnung *107T*
aggregate Zuschlag(stoff) *41*
agricultural landwirtschaftlich *30*
ahead of schedule vor dem Zeitplan *18T*
to aim beabsichtigen *96*
airbag Airbag *39*
air blast (Luft-)Gebläse *91P*
air bursts Lufteinschlüsse *102*
aircraft Flugzeug *11T*
air filter Luftfilter *87*
airliner Verkehrsflugzeug *11T*
airplane Flugzeug *115T*
air source Luftquelle *108*
alarm plan Alarmplan *97*
to align ausrichten *67P*
alignment Ausrichtung *74*
alkaline Alkali, alkalischer Stoff *91*
alloy Legierung *10*
all-round umfassend *112*
alright in Ordnung *81T*
alteration Änderung *86*
alternative Alternative *36*; **~ energy** alternative Energie *93*
alternator Lichtmaschine *71*
ambient Umgebungs-, Raum- *34*; **~ air** Umgebungsluft *108*
ambitious ehrgeizig *107T*
ammonia vapour Ammoniakdampf *15*
amplifier Verstärker *65*
analogue analog *70*
angle Winkel *22*
antenna cable Antennenkabel *76*
antenna connector Antennenanschluss *76*
anti-freeze Gefrier(mittel), Frostschutz(mittel) *87*
anti-lock braking system (ABS) Antiblockiersystem *39*
anti-theft protection Diebstahlsicherung *39*
anti-virus Antiviren- *66T*
to apologize for sich entschuldigen für *28*
appliance Gerät *10*
applicant Bewerber/in *51*
to apply the brakes die Bremsen betätigen *71*
apprentice Auszubildende/r *12*
appropriate entsprechend *78*
approved agent zugelassene/r Händler/in *99*
architectural Architektur- *26*
arena Arena, Stadion *40*
argument Streit *84*
armature Armatur *90*
arrangement Vereinbarung, Termin *49T*
asphalt Asphalt *41*
to assemble zusammensetzen, -bauen *99*
assembly Montage(halle) *19*; **~ line** Montage-, Fließband; *17*; **~ point** Sammelpunkt *97*
to assist assistieren, unterstützen *26*
to assume annehmen *36*
to attempt versuchen *105T*
to attend teilnehmen (an) *15*
attendance record Anwesenheitsstatistik *112*
audio-visual audiovisuell *31*
authentic authentisch, echt *97*
authorised technician autorisierte/r Techniker/in *102*
authorities Behörden *97*
to authorize autorisieren, bevollmächtigen *73*
autoclave Autoklav, Druckbehälter, -kammer *19*
automatically automatisch *39*
automotive Auto(mobil)- *7*; **~ material** Autozubehör *88*; **~ technician** Kfz-Techniker/in *9*
availability Verfügbarkeit *51*
to avoid (ver)meiden, verhüten *24*
aware bewusst, aufmerksam *98*

B

to back unterstützen *107T*; **~ into sth** rückwärts in etw hineinfahren *82*
backing Rückseite *58T*
backlight Rücklicht *39*
backup Sicherungskopie *68*
badge Namensschild *8*
ballast power Ballastleistung *36*
balloon Ballon *14*
ball-peen hammer Tischlerhammer (mit Kuhfuß) *54*
to ban verbieten *93*
band saw Bandsäge *59*
bar chart Säulen-, Balkendiagramm *46*
barrier Absperrung, Barriere *44*
to based, be ~ in seinen Hauptsitz haben in *11*
basecourse Tragschicht *50*
basically im Grunde, eigentlich *65*
basin Becken, Schüssel *105*
battery charge level Batterieladezustand *39*

Alphabetical word list

battery-powered batteriebetrieben *57*
Bavarian bayerisch *15*
to be out of fehlen *71*
bearing Lager *71*
bedding Einbettung *44*
bedrock Grundgestein *108*
belongings Sachen, Habseligkeiten *15*
bench grinder Schleifbock *59*
to bend (sich) (ver)biegen; Kurve *50*
beneath unter(halb) *39*
benefit Vorteil, Vorzug *86*; **~s package** Zusatzleistungen *26*
Best regards Freundliche Grüße *72*
beverage Getränk *7*
biker Radfahrer/in *84*
billboard Werbeplakat *40*
billion Milliarde *13*
bin bag Müll(eimer)beutel *93*
to bind binden *29*
binder Bindemittel, Bindeschicht *42*
binding commitment bindende Verpflichtung, Vereinbarung *107*
bio-degradable biologisch abbaubar *95*
biogas Biogas *10*
bio mass Biomasse *107T*
bit Bit, Aufsatz *57*; **~ driver** Ratsche *62*
bituminous bituminös *43*
blacktop Asphalt *50*
blade Blatt, Klinge *57*; **~ knife** Messerklinge *62*
blank leer *66T*
blast furnace Hochofen *41*
to bleed bluten *81T*
blind spot toter Winkel *39*
to block verstopfen *75*
blockage Verstopfung *67P*
blocked drain verstopfter/s Abfluss(rohr) *64*
body panel Karosserieteil *91P*
bodywork Karosserie *64*
bold stark, kräftig *16*
bolt Schraube *55*
bonnet Motorhaube *16*
bookkeeper Buchhalter/in *23*
booster system Ersatzanlage, Notaggregat *100*
to bore langweilen *12T*; bohren *57*
to boss sb around jdn herumkommandieren *23*
bottle opener Flaschenöffner *62*
bracket (runde) Klammer *14*
brake Bremse *39*; **~ disc** Bremsscheibe *71*; **~ fluid** Bremsflüssigkeit *71*; **~ light** Bremslicht *39*; **~ line** Bremsleitung, -schlauch *71*; **~**

pad Bremsbelag *71*; **~ pedal** Bremspedal *73*
branch Zweig, Branche, Bereich *10*
brand Marke, Typ *40*
to break down sich zersetzen, zersetzt werden *93*
breakdown Panne *85*; **~ lorry** Pannenwagen *72*
to breathe in einatmen *24*
brick Ziegel(stein) *24*
brickie Maurer/in *82*
bricklayer Maurer/in *17*
brightness Helligkeit *40*
to bring about herbeiführen *107T*
brittle brüchig, spröde *91*
brochure Prospekt *9*
bronze (aus) Bronze *59*
bruise Bluterguss, blauer Fleck *81T*
brush Pinsel *67P*
bucket Eimer *76*
budget Etat, Budget *18*
to build up (sich) auftürmen *102*
builder Bauarbeiter/in *17*
building site Baustelle *17*
built-in eingebaut *65*
bulb Glühbirne, -lampe *33*
bulk order Großauftrag, -bestellung *22*
bulldozer Planierraupe *43*
bump Erhöhung *63*
bumper Stoßstange *10*
burnout Ausbrennen, Brennschluss *74*
burr Grat, Naht, raue Kante *59*
burst pipe (Wasser-)Rohrbruch *64*
business convention Firmenkonferenz *51*
butane Butan *57*
buzzing Summ(ton) *65*
by mal *34*

C

cabinet (Werkzeug-)Schrank *58*
cabling Verkabelung *22*
to calculate kalkulieren *29*
calculation Rechenoperation *66T*
calculator (Taschen-)Rechner *23*
can opener Büchsen-, Dosenöffner *62*
to cancel stornieren, streichen *46T*
canteen Kantine, Cafeteria *18T*
canvas bag Stofftasche *94*
capable, to be ~ of in der Lage sein *28*; fähig sein zu, imstande sein zu *58*
capacity Kapazität, Leistung *39*
carmaker Autohersteller *16*
car manufacturing plant Automobilwerk *25*
carbon footprint ökologischer Fußabdruck, CO_2-Bilanz *94*

carbon-fibre-reinforced plastic kohlefaserverstärkter Kunststoff *16*
career progression beruflicher Aufstieg *110*
car-maker Autohersteller *16*
carpentry Tischlerei *58*
carpet Teppich(boden) *91P*
to carry out durchführen *44*
casing Gehäuse *66T*
catalytic converter Katalysator *87*
catastrophe Katastrophe *107T*
to catch sb's eye jdm ins Auge fallen *113*
caustic soda Ätznatron *96*
caution Vorsicht *77*
CEFR (= Common European Framework of Reference for Languages) Gemeinsamer Europäischer Referenzrahmen für Sprachen *112*
ceiling (Zimmer-)Decke *18*
cement Zement *22*; **~ mixer** Betonmischmaschine *19*
centre head Zentrierkopf *63*
centred in der Mitte *59*
CEO (Chief Executive Officer) Vorstandsvorsitzende/r, Generaldirektor/in *16*
ceramic Keramik *41*
certain sicher *73*
certificate Zeugnis, Urkunde *112*; **~ of destruction** Abwrackbescheinigung *89*
certification Zertifikat, Anerkennung *22*
challenge Herausforderung *27*
to change gears (in einen anderen Gang) schalten *71*
characteristics Eigenschaften *41*
charge, in ~ of verantwortlich für *114*
charges (Un-)Kosten *75*
chassis Fahrgestell *16*
to chatter klappern *74*
checker Überprüfer/in *96*
check-up (Nach-)Untersuchung *83*
cheerful fröhlich, vergnügt *76*
chemical engineering Verfahrenstechnik *7*
chisel Meißel, Stemmeisen *54*
to choke the drains die Abwasserrohre verstopfen *95*
chronological in zeitlicher Reihenfolge, chronologisch *111*
chunk Klumpen, Brocken *90*
circuit (Strom-)Kreis *70*
circular saw Kreissäge *57*
circulation Kreislauf *100*
circumstance Umstand *102*
civil engineering Tiefbau, Bauingenieurwesen *10*

Alphabetical word list

to claim behaupten, erklären *16*; beanspruchen *96*
to clamp einspannen, festschrauben *60T*
to clarify erläutern *66T*
Class *1* **and** *2* **HGVs** (Führerschein-)Klasse *1* und *2* Lkw *110*
claw hammer Kugelhammer *54*
clay Ton, Lehm *41*
clean room Waschraum *19*
cleaning agent Reinigungsmittel *77*
cleaning fluid Reinigungsmittel *77*
to clear up aufräumen *46T*
client Kunde/Kundin *25*
clip point knife Klipppunktmesser *62*
to clog verstopfen *66T*
closed circuit geschlossener Kreislauf *100*
cloth Tuch, Lappen *67P*
clutch Kupplung *71*
CNC (Computerized Numerical Control) computerisierte numerische Steuerung *99*
coal-fired power plant Kohlekraftwerk *107*
coarse grinding wheel grobe Schleifscheibe *59*
to coat beschichten *100*; ~ **hanger** Kleiderbügel *71*
coated beschichtet *91P*
coating Beschichtung *91P*
cold chisel Flachmeißel *54*
colleague Kollege/Kollegin *8*
collection loop Sammelkreislauf *108*
column drill Ständerbohrmaschine *59*
combination Verbindung *10*; ~ **square** Universalwinkelmesser *63*
commercial gewerblich *10*; ~ **building** Geschäftsgebäude *11T*; ~ **traffic** gewerblicher Verkehr *50*
to commission in Betrieb nehmen *102*
commissioning Inbetriebnahme *99*
to commit oneself sich verpflichten *107T*
to commit suicide Selbstmord begehen *15*
common sense gesunder Menschenverstand *56T*
communication skills Kommunikationsfähigkeiten *110*
commutator Kollektor, Stromwender *74*
to commute pendeln, zum Arbeitsplatz fahren *26*
to compact verdichten *44*

company pension Betriebsrente *110*
comparable vergleichbar *89*
to compete with konkurrieren mit *27*
competitive konkurrenzfähig *26*
complaint Beanstandung, Reklamation *29*
complex of offices Bürokomplex *27*
complicated kompliziert *16*
component (Bau-)Teil *8*
composite Bauteile *18T*
composition Aufbau, Zusammensetzung *88*
comprehensive umfassend *108*
compressed komprimiert *15*; ~ **air** Druckluft *57*
compression Kompression, Druck *15*
compressor Kompressor *108*
to comprise umfassen *10*
compromise Kompromiss *107T*; **to ~ on** Kompromisse eingehen bei *27*
concept Konzept *10*
concerned besorgt *36*
concise präzise, knapp *111*
concrete Beton *21*
to condense kondensieren *108*
condenser coil Kondensatorspule *67P*
condition Zustand *51*
conductor Leiter *90*
conduit Kabelrohr *10*
cone Kegel *44*
conference Konferenz, Tagung *23*
confetti Konfetti *90*
configuration Konfiguration *65*
confined space geschlossener Raum *78*
to confirm bestätigen *73*
confusion Verwirrung *40*
congratulations Glückwunsch *100*
conjunction, in ~ with zusammen mit *102*
to connect to power an die Stromversorgung anschließen *99*
connection Anschluss *65*
connector Verbindungsstecker *67*
consequently infolgedessen *118*
to consider berücksichtigen *26*; erwägen *40*
considerable beträchtlich *72*
considerably beträchtlich *89*
to consist of bestehen aus *19*
construction Konstruktion *10*; ~ **company** Bauunternehmen, -firma *11T*; ~ **industry** Bauindustrie *7*
to consume verbrauchen *15*
consumer Verbraucher/in *94*; ~ **electronics**

Unterhaltungselektronik *7*
~ **vehicle** Fahrzeug für den Normalverbraucher *16*
consumption Verbrauch *91P*
contest Wettbewerb *52*
continuous ununterbrochen, durchgehend *50*; ~ **cycle** ununterbrochener Kreislauf *96*
to contract schrumpfen *25*
contract Vertrag *23*; ~**s manager** Projektleiter/in *23*
contraction Zusammenziehung *50*
contractor Bauunternehmer/in *32*
contrasting gegensätzlich *89*
to contribute beitragen *95*
control panel Kontrollpult, Bedienungsfeld *65*
convenient bequem, praktisch *58*
conventional herkömmlich, konventionell *16*
conversion Umwandlung, -stellung *14*
to convert umbauen *8*
convertible Kabrio *90*
conveyor belt Fließ-, Förderband *99*
to convince überzeugen *36*
to cool down (sich) abkühlen *65*
co-ordinator Koordinator/in *8*
to cope (damit) zurechtkommen *66T*
coping saw Handstichsäge *54*
copper Kupfer *41*
cordless schnur-, kabellos *57*
corkscrew Korkenzieher *62*
corporate client Firmenkunde, -kundin *25*
corrosion resistant korrosionsbeständig, rostfrei *91P*
corrupt beschädigt *66T*
cost effective kostengünstig *16*
counter Schalter, Tresen *21*
courageous mutig *107T*
to cover (be-, zu-, ab)decken *58T*; (ab)decken *86*; (be)decken *96*
covering letter Begleitschreiben *110*
to crack brechen, reißen *50*
craft knife Tapezier-, Schneidemesser *63*
craftsperson Handwerker/in *57*
crane Kran *19*; ~ **driver** Kranfahrer/in *68*
crash helmet Sturzhelm *85*
crèche Kindertagesstätte *18T*
crimper Quetschzange *62*
crimping pliers Kombizange *70*
critical kritisch *52*
crosscut saw Fuchsschwanz(säge) *54*
cross-head screwdriver Kreuzschlitz-Schraubendreher *62*
crushed stone Schotter *50*

177

Alphabetical word list

crusher Presse, Brechwerk(anlage) *91P*
to crystallise kristallisieren *96*
culprit Schuldige/r, Übeltäter/in *66T*
cup mask Atem(schutz)maske, Mundschutz *24*
cure Heilen *97*
current Strom *70*
custom-made maßgeschneidert *21*
to cut to size zurechtschneiden *58T*
cutter Schneider *43*
cutting angle Span-, Schnittwinkel *55*
cutting edge Schnittkante *59*; Speerspitze *96*
cylindrical zylindrisch *63*

D

to damage beschädigen *56T*; Schaden, Schäden *72*; **~d** beschädigt *44*
damn verdammt, verflucht *82*
dark-coloured dunkel gefärbt *100*
darkness Dunkelheit *40*
dashboard Armaturenbrett *71*
data Daten *10*; **~ bank** Datenbank *29*; **~base** Datenbank *89*
day-glo jacket reflektierende Warn(schutz)weste *21T*
day-to-day duties tagtägliche Pflichten *110*
day nursery (AE) Kindertagesstätte *20*
to deactivate deaktivieren *39*
deadline Liefertermin, Frist *27*
to deal with bearbeiten, erledigen *29*
dealer Händler/in *73*; **~ship** Vertretung(en) *73*
Dear Sir or Madam Sehr geehrte Damen und Herren, *73*
to de-bale entpaketieren *96*
decontaminated dekontaminiert, entgiftet *96*
decontamination Dekontamination, Entgiftung *96*
decorator Maler/in, Tapezierer/in *22*
to decrease abnehmen, (sich) verringern *88*
deep tief, stark *40*
deer Reh, Hirsch *72*
defect Schaden, Defekt *44*
defective fehlerhaft *55*
to defragment (in einzelne Teile) zerlegen *66T*
delighted, to be ~ sich (sehr) freuen *113*
delivery bay Lieferzone *19*

demand Nachfrage, Bedarf *25*; **~ for** Nachfrage nach *91P*
demonstration Demonstration, Vorführung *98*
dense dicht *50*
department Ressort, Abteilung *13*
dependable zuverlässig *112*
to depollute entsorgen, reinigen *89*
de-pollution Säuberung, Schadstoffbeseitigung *89*
to depress (nieder)drücken *65*
depth Tiefe *44*; **~ gauge** Tiefenmesser *63*
to de-register abmelden *89*
derelict verfallen, baufällig *91*
desktop (computer) Bürocomputer *65*
despite trotz *25*
destruction Zerstörung, Vernichtung *89*
deterioration Verschleiß *74*
to determine bestimmen. feststellen *96*; **~d by** bestimmt durch *50*
to develop entwickeln *10*
development Entwicklung *10*
to diagnose diagnostizieren *53*
diagnostic Diagnose- *67*
diameter Durchmesser *59*
diamond-coated file diamantbeschichtete Feile *62*
to die ausgehen *67*; **~ for** sterben für *77T*
difficulty Schwierigkeit *15*
to dig graben, ausheben *18*
digital imaging technology digitale bildgebende Technologie *28*
dimension Abmessung, Maß *55*
dimmer switch Dimmerschalter *34*
diploma Abschlusszeugnis, Diplom *120*
directional lighting bewegliche Leuchten *34*
to discharge austreten *105T*
to disconnect abklemmen, entfernen *36*
to discuss besprechen *34*
to disinfect desinfizieren *81T*
to disintegrate zerfallen, sich auflösen *95*
to dismantle zerlegen, auseinander nehmen *91P*
dismantler Abwrackbetrieb *88*
dispenser Verteiler *67*
to displace verdrängen *100*
to display zeigen, ausstellen *31*
disposable Einweg-, Wegwerf- *88*
disposal Beseitigung, Entsorgung *95*
to dissolve auflösen *43*
distance Entfernung, Abstand *22*

distinction Auszeichnung *120*
to distract ablenken *79*
to distribute verteilen *85*
distribution Vertrieb, (Aus-)Lieferung *12*
diverse unterschiedlich *10*
diversion Umleitung *44*
division (Betriebs-)Sparte, Abteilung *13*
DIY Heimwerker-, Do it yourself- *57*
domestic häuslich, privat *31*; **~ building** Wohngebäude *27*; **~ contract** Wohnungsbauauftrag *45*; **~ job** Wohnungsbau *46T*
dongle Kopierschutzstecker *119*
downlight Deckenstrahler *34*
draftsman, pl draftsmen Zeichner/in *26*
drain Abfluss(rohr) *75*; **~ cycle** Abpumpen *65* **~ off** ablassen *89*; **~ pan** Abflussbehälter *67P*
drainage Entwässerung, Drainage *41*
dramatically dramatisch, drastisch *91P*
to draw up etw ausfertigen *22*; **~ a plan** einen Plan aufstellen *34*
drawer Schub(lade) *58*
drill Bohrer, Bohrmaschine *57*
to drive (nails into) (Nägel ein)schlagen *57*
to drop abfallen, sinken *71*
drum Trommel *65*
dryer (Wäsche-)Trockner *10*
duckstone großer Kieselstein *43*
ductile (ver)formbar *91*
due to aufgrund von *88*; **to be ~** etw tun sollen *49T*
durability (Lebens-)Dauer, Haltbarkeit *16*
duration Dauer *42*
dust Staub *21*; **~proof** staubdicht *86*

E

ear protectors Ohrenschützer *24*
eco-friendliness Umweltfreundlichkeit *98*
economical wirtschaftlich *99*
eddy current Wirbelstrom *90*; **~ separator** Wirbelstromabscheider *90*
edge Rand, Kante *40*
edged tool Schneidwerkzeug *55*
edging Einfassung *42*
educational building Schulgebäude *25*
effectiveness Effektivität *25*
efficient effizient, leistungsfähig *15*
effort Bemühung *10*
electric heater tape Elektroerhitzerband *102*

Alphabetical word list

electrical circuit Stromkreis 55
electrician Elektriker/in, Elektrotechniker/in 17
electricity supply Netz-, Stromanschluss 21
to electrocute durch Stromschlag verletzen/töten 21T
electronics Elektronik 91P
to eliminate eliminieren, beseitigen 68
ELV (= end-of-life vehicle) Schrottwagen 88
emergency Notfall 79
emission Emission, Abgase 93; ~ **regulation** Abgasregelung 91P
emphasis Betonung 56T
employee Mitarbeiter/in 12
employment Beschäftigung, Anstellung 110
to enable ermöglichen 96
enclosed beigefügt 113
to endure aushalten 50
energy efficient energiesparend 34
energy policy Energiepolitik 107T
energy recovery Energierückgewinnung 95
energy turnaround Energiewende 107T
engine coolant Motorkühlmittel 89
engine oil Motoröl 89
engineering characteristics technische Eigenschaften 91P
to enquire about sich erkundigen nach, fragen nach 75
to ensure sicherstellen, gewährleisten 74
enthusiasm Begeisterung(sfähigkeit) 114
enthusiast Begeisterte/r 57
entire ganz, vollständig 40
entrance, (car park) ~ (Parkplatz-) Einfahrt 85
environment Umwelt 92
environmentally friendly umweltfreundlich 34
equal entsprechen 88; ~ **opportunities employer** Unternehmen mit Gleichberechtigung 110
to equip ausrüsten, ausstatten 39
equipment cage Maschinenschutzkäfig 79
equivalent Entsprechung, Übersetzung 54
to erect errichten, (auf)bauen 18
ergonomic ergonomisch 16
erratically ungleichmäßig 65
error Fehler 65
to escape entweichen 105; ~ **route** Fluchtweg 97
to establish errichten, aufbauen 44

establishment Einrichtung 13P
estimate (Kosten-)Voranschlag 36; schätzen 46 **~d** geschätzt 73
ethnicity ethnische Zugehörigkeit 110
to evaluate bewerten 22
to evaporate verdampfen, verdunsten 108
evenly gleichmäßig 67P
eventually schließlich, zum Schluss 71
excavation Graben, Ausschachtung 80; **~ work** Erdarbeiten 78
excerpt Auszug 85
excessive überflüssig 74
executive office Managerbüro 19
exemplary vorbildlich, beispielhaft 112
exhaust Auspuff(rohr) 71; **~ gas** Abgas(e), Auspuffgas(e) 15
exhibition Ausstellung 34
exit, (car park) ~ (Parkplatz-) Ausfahrt 85
to expand wachsen 25
expansion Ausdehnung 50
experienced worker erfahrene/r Mitarbeiter/in 115T
expertise Fachkenntnis(se) 112
to explode explodieren 15
exploitation Ausbeutung, Nutzung 107T
explosive charge Sprengladung 57
to export ausführen, exportieren 90
to expose freigeben 104
to extend vergrößern, erweitern 21; sich erstrecken 73
extensive umfangreich 110; **~ly** umfassend, vielfach 91P
exterior Außen- 10
external äußer(lich) 27
to extract extrahieren, gewinnen 41
extractor fan Entlüfter, Abzugshaube 21

F
fabric Stoff 57
face shield Gesichtsschutz 79
faceplate Front-, Schutz-, Richtplatte 59
facility Einrichtung 18T
failure Fehler, Versagen 66T
to fall into the trap den Fehler begehen 118
family-owned business Familienunternehmen 11T
fan belt Keilriemen 71
fan motorcircuit Stromkreis des Ventilatormotors 67
fan Lüfter, Ventilator 66T

fancy furniture schicke Möbel 19
fatal tödlich, fatal 95
faulty fehlerhaft, defekt 37
favoured bevorzugt 95
to fear (be)fürchten 15
feature Eigenschaft 16
ferrous Eisen- 90; **~ metal** Eisenmetall 88
to fetch holen 81T
field engineer Ingenieur/in im Außendienst 8
file Feile 55
to fill in ausfüllen 48
final exam Abschlussprüfung 84
finance Finanzabteilung 19
fine grinding wheel feine Schleifscheibe 59
finish Finish, letzter Schliff 58
to fire verbrennen 41; **~ drill** Probealarm 97
firm fest 50
first floor (AE) Erdgeschoss 20
first-aid kit Verbandskasten 79
fisherman, pl fishermen Fischer 15
fish scaler Fischentschupper 62
to fit ausstatten 100
fitter Monteur/in, Installateur/in 17
fitting Teil 74
to fix a date einen Termin ausmachen 49T
fixture (Elektro-)Installation 35
flag Steinplatte 43; **~stone** Steinplatte 42
flake Flocke 96
flammable (leicht) brennbar, feuergefährlich 77; **~ gas** (leicht) brennbares Gas 57
to flash blinken 39
flat platter Reifen 71; **~ bedding** Verfüllung, Lager 42; **~ panel television** Flachbildfernseher 40
to flatten einebnen, platt machen 50
fleet (of vehicles) (Fahrzeug-) Flotte, Fuhrpark 110
flex Netzkabel 57
flexible flexibel, biegbar 10; **~ auger** Rohrreinigungsspirale 76
flexi-time Gleitzeit 109
to float (im Wasser) treiben 15
flood Überschwemmung, -flutung 95
flooded überschwemmt 75
to flow fließen 100; **~ chart** Flussdiagramm 46
fluency fließende Sprachkenntnisse 26
fluid Flüssigkeit 71
fluorescent tube lighting Neonlicht 31
to flush the toilet die Toilettenspülung betätigen 27

Alphabetical word list

flyer design Entwerfen von Flugblättern *120*
foam Schaum(stoff) *22*
to fold out ausklappen *39*
food and catering Versorgung mit Speisen und Getränken *86*
food chain Nahrungskette *93*
food-grade lebensmitteltauglich *96*
foolproof idiotensicher *49T*
footbridge Fußgängerbrücke *42*
footpath Fußweg *42*
footrest Fußstütze *39*
footwear Schuhwerk *77*
to force back zurückdrängen *100*
force sb to do sth jdn zwingen, etw zu tun *15*
forecourt Vorplatz, Vorhof *43*
foreman Vorarbeiter *44*
forklift Gabelstapler *17*; ~ **operator** Gabelstaplerfahrer/in *17*
forwards vorwärts *39*
fossil fuel fossiler Brennstoff *107T*
to found gründen *14*
foundation Fundament *18*; Grundlage *115T*
foundry Gießerei *17*
fragmented zerstört *66T*
frame Rahmen *18*
franchise Franchise-Unternehmen *112*
freelance freiberuflich, freischaffend *109*
freezer Gefrierschrank, -truhe *10*
friction Reibung *15*
front cover Vorderseite *104*
frozen eingefroren *74*
to fuel antreiben *15*; ~ **efficiency** Kraftstoffwirkungsgrad *16*; ~**-efficient** Treibstoff sparend, mit geringem Treibstoffverbrauch *16*
fully-equipped vollständig eingerichtet *18T*
fully-qualified vollständig ausgebildet *22*
to function funktionieren *57*
functional, be ~ funktionieren *102*

G

to gain sammeln *118*
gaming Computerspiele *112*
Gantt chart Gantt-Diagramm *46*
gas-filled mit Gas gefüllt *33*
gauze pad Mullverband *81T*
GCE O level (General Certificate of Education Ordinary Level) (etwa) Realschulabschluss *110*
GCSE (General Certificate of Secondary Education) Sekundarabschluss *110*
gear box oil Getriebeöl *89*
gender Geschlecht *110*
to generate herstellen *26*
generator Generator *39*
generous großzügig *26*
geographical geographisch *12T*
geothermal energy Erdwärmeenergie *107T*
to get off sb's back jdn in Ruhe lassen *27*
giant riesig *96*
gizmo (elektronisches) Kleingerät *70*
glad, (I'm) ~ ich freue mich *8*
global global, weltweit *8*
gloves Handschuhe *24*
to go ahead anfangen *24*
goggles Schutzbrille *78*
gradient Steigung *50*
to graduate from absolvieren *118*
gravel Kies, Kieselsteine *41*
grease Schmiere, Fett *67P*
greenhouse gas Treibhausgas *92*
to grind, ground, ground schleifen *59*
grinder Schleifmaschine *77*
grinding schleifend *71*
to grip festhalten *55*
groove Rille, Profil *57*
ground geschliffen *55*; ~ **floor (BE)** Erdgeschoss *20*; ~ **source** Erdquelle *108*
guarantee garantieren *27*
guided tour Führung, Besichtigung *18*
guideline Richtlini *91P*; ~**s** Richtlinien *112*

H

hacksaw Handbügelsäge, Metallsäge *54*
hammer Hammer *54*
hand tool Handwerkzeug *54*
handbook Bedienungsanleitung, Handbuch *58*
handle (Hand-)Griff *55*
handlebars (Fahrrad-)Lenker *39*
handout Merkblatt *8*
handover Übergabe *99*
handsaw Handsäge *54*
handy praktisch *63*
handyman Handwerker *75*
hard hat (AE) Schutzhelm *24*
hard reset komplette Neuinstallation *65*
to harden härten, hart werden *44*
hardly ever fast nie, kaum jemals *115T*
hard-wire cutter Drahtschneider *62*
harmful schädlich *24*
harsh hart, (Licht) grell *34*
haulage company Transportfirma, Fuhrunternehmen *113*
hazard Risiko, Gefahr *77*
hazardous gefährlich, schädlich *22*
HDPE (high-density polyethylene) hochverdichtetes Polyäthylen *96*
head-height Kopfhöhe *89*
headlamp Scheinwerfer *39*
headlight Scheinwerfer *10*
head office Zentrale *12T*
headquarters Zentrale, Firmensitz *12*
health and safety executive Arbeitsschutzbeauftragt/r *86*
health and safety manager Arbeitsschutzbeauftragte/r *21*
healthcare Gesundheitsfürsorge, medizinische Versorgung *25*
health risk Gesundheitsrisiko *22*
heaps of Unmengen von *92*
heat-absorbent Wärme absorbierend *100*
heat exchanger jacket Wärmetauscherummantelung *100*
heating system Heizungsanlage *9*
heat output Heizleistung *102*
heat pump Wärmepumpe *10*
heat radiation Wärme(ab)strahlung *15*
heat sink Wärmeableiter, Kühlkörper *65*
heat-transfer fluid Wärmeträgerflüssigkeit *100*
heavy stark, dicht (Verkehr) *9*; ~**-duty** Hochleistungs- *10*; ~ **industrial** Schwerindustrie- *30*; ~ **vehicles mechanic** Lkw-Mechaniker/in *110*
to help yourself to sich bedienen mit *8*
hemp Hanf *10*
herringbone pattern Fischgrätmuster *44*
to hesitate zögern *37*
HGV (Heavy Goods Vehicles) LKW *50*
hierarchy Rangfolge *86*
high-density Dichte *96*
high-end im gehobenen Marktsegment *16*
to highlight hervorheben, auswählen *74*
high-pressure Hochdruck- *21T*
high priority hohe Priorität *44*
high-resolution mit hoher Auflösung *40*
high-speed Hochgeschwindigkeits- *57*
high-strength extrem stabil *16*
high-visibility jacket reflektierende Warn(schutz)weste *77*
high-voltage Hochspannungs- *77*

Alphabetical word list

high volume umfangreich 28
to hire (an)heuern 15
to hiss zischen, fauchen 71
to hit the brakes auf die Bremsen treten 72
holder Halterung 74
hollow Senke, Mulde 50
hook disgorger (Angel-) Hakenentferner 62
horizontally horizontal, waagerecht 108
horse Pferd 82
hose Schlauch 10
hourly rate Stundenlohn, -satz 22
to house unterbringen, enthalten 19
HR (human resources) Personalwesen, -abteilung 19
hub (Rad-)Nabe 39
HVAC (heating, ventilation and air conditioning) Klimaanlage 99
hydraulic hydraulisch 78
hydro power Wasserkraft 107T
hydrogen gas Wasserstoff 105

I

icy vereist 85
to identify identifizieren 15
to ignite (sich) entzünden 15
ignition Zündung 5; **~ box** Zündung, Anlasser 71; **~ switch** Zündschalter 71
to ignore ignorieren, nicht beachten 71
to illustrate illustrieren, veranschaulichen 13
illustration Abbildung 29
image content Bildinhalt 40
imbalance Unausgeglichenheit 74
immobilizer Wegfahrsperre 39
impact resistant stoßfest 91P
impact (Aus-)Wirkung, Effekt 88
impermeable undurchlässig 89
to implement einführen, einsetzen 91P
impressive beeindruckend, eindrucksvoll 16
inaccurate ungenau, falsch 63
inappropriate falsch, unangemessen 66T
inauguration Eröffnung 28
in-between (da)zwischen 118
inception Beginn 25
inclined geneigt, mit Gefälle 50
income Einkommen, Einnahmen 52
incompatible nicht (zueinander) passend 66T
inconvenience Unbequemlichkeit, Unannehmlichkeit 73
to incorporate einsetzen, verwenden 88; einbauen, einsetzen 108

incorrect falsch, unrichtig 105T; **~ly** falsch, unrichtig 56T
increase Steigerung, Erhöhung 28; (an)steigen, (sich) erhöhen 71
to indicate (an)zeigen 65
indication Anzeichen 68
indicator Anzeige 67
to induce auslösen 90
induction Arbeitseinführung 80
industrial tools Industriemaschinen 9
inefficient unwirtschaftlich 33
inexpensive preiswert 16
to inform informieren, unterrichten 51
infrastructure Infrastruktur 25
inhabitant Einwohner/in 51
initial anfänglich 49T
to inject (ein)spritzen 15
to injure verletzen 21T; **to get ~d** verletzt werden 21T
injury Verletzung 24
innovative innovativ, aufgeschlossen 25
to insert einsetzen 60T
insight Einblick 107T
insoluble unlöslich 91
to inspect untersuchen 37
inspection Untersuchung 37; **~ shaft** Inspektionsschacht 77
installer Installateur/in 104
institutional client institutionelle/r Kunde/Kundin 25
instruction manual Bedienungsanleitung, Benutzerhandbuch 58
instructor Dozent/in, Ausbilder/in 8
insulated isoliert 10
insulation Isolierung, Dämmung 102
insulator Isolator, Nichtleiter 91
insurance Versicherung 86; **~ company** Versicherungsgesellschaft 72; **~ cover** Versicherungsschutz 85
to integrate einbauen 39
integration Eingliederung, Einsatz 108
to intend to do sth beabsichtigen etw zu tun 31
interior Innen- 67
internal Innen- 10
intersection Kreuzung 85
interval (Zeit-)Abstand 99
to introduce einbringen 74; **~ sb to sb** jdn jdm vorstellen, jdn mit jdm bekannt machen 8
to invent erfinden 14
inventor Erfinder/in 15
to invest investieren 93
investment Investition 52
investor Investor/in, Anleger/in 51

involved beteiligt 97; damit verbunden 75
iron Eisen 41
irrelevant unwesentlich 89
to irrigate bewässern 27
to issue ausstellen, erteilen 89
IT (Information Technology) Informationstechnologie 17
item Gegenstand, Ding 55

J

jaw Backe 63
jib Kranbalken, Ausleger 43
jigsaw Laub-, Stichsäge 57
job title Berufsbezeichnung 21
joiner Tischler/in, Schreiner/in 17
joint Naht(stelle), Stoßfuge 50
junction (Straßen-)Kreuzung 72
jute Jute 10

K

kettle (Wasser-)Kessel 72
key to symbols Zeichenerklärung 35
keyhole saw Stichsäge 54
killer Killer/in, Mörder/in 15
kiln Brennofen 41
kingdom Königreich 71
kit car Bausatzauto 112
knot Knoten 63

L

to label bezeichnen, nennen 40
laboratory Labor(atorium) 17
lad Bursche 82
ladder Leiter 79
landfill Mülldeponie 88
to last ausreichen 27; (durch)halten 61
laundry Wäsche; Wäscherei 72
to lay (the foundations) (die Fundamente) legen 19
to lay down anlegen, aufstellen 42
lead Blei 91P
to leak tropfen 64; undichte Stelle, Leck 71
leakage Leck(stelle) 22
learner Lerner/in 113
to lease leasen, mieten 31; Mietvertrag 51
letter of application Bewerbungsschreiben 113
levelling instrument Vermessungsgerät, Theodolit 19
lever Hebel 23
licence Lizenz, Führerschein 82
to lie down sich hinlegen 81T
life expectancy Lebenserwartung, -dauer 108
lifespan Lebenszeit, -dauer 88
lifetime Lebenszeit 16
lifting Kranarbeiten 78
light-coloured hell gefärbt 100

Alphabetical word list

light-duty (Werkzeug) Leicht-arbeiten, nur leicht belastbar *57*
lighted eye shield erleuchteter Sichtschutz *59*
light goods vehicle leichter Lieferwagen *99*
light industrial Leichtindustrie- *30*
lighting level Helligkeitsstufe *34*
lighting plan Beleuchtungsplan *34*
lightly leicht *44*
lightweight Leicht- *8*
like hell höllisch, teuflisch *81T*
limestone Kalkstein *41*
line graph (Kurven-, Linien-) Diagramm *46*
liquid Flüssigkeit *91*
listening comprehension Hörverstehen, Hörverständnis *97*
literacy skills Lese- und Schreibfähigkeit *110*
lithium-ion battery Lithium-Ionen-Batterie *39*
load Ladung, Last *18*; Ladung, (Strom-)Spannung *74*; **to ~ up** beladen *90*
loads Lasten *85*; **~ of** jede Menge an *92*
loan Kredit, Darlehen *52*
local council Stadtverwaltung *44*
to locate liegen, platzieren *63*
lock bolt Feststellschraube *63*
to lock oneself out sich aussperren *75*
logistical support officer Angestellter in der Auslieferung *22*
logistics Auslieferung *12*; **~ clerk** Logistik-Mitarbeiter/in *22*
long-handled mit langem Handgriff *86*
long-term langfristig, Langzeit- *27*
loose lose, locker *67P*
to loosen lockern, lösen *55*
lorry (AE: truck) Lastwagen, Lkw *19*
low-heat mit geringer Erwärmung *40*
low-power mit niedrigem Stromverbrauch *40*
low priority geringe Priorität *44*
lubricant Gleit-, Schmiermittel *60T*
to lubricate schmieren *74*
luggage carrier Gepäckträger *85*
luxurious luxuriös *9*
luxury Luxus *10*

M
macadam Makadam, Straßenbelag mit Teer oder Bitumen *43*
machine guard Maschinenschutz, -verkleidung *79*

machine tool Werkzeugmaschine *7*
machinery Maschinen(park), Geräte *18*
machinist Maschinist/in, Maschinenschlosser/in *18*
magnet separator Magnetabscheider *90*
magnetic field Magnetfeld *90*
magnifying lens Lupe *62*
mainly hauptsächlich, vor allem *88*
mains (Wasser-)Leitung *27*; **~ voltage** Stromnetz *57*
to maintain warten *24*
maintenance Wartung *11*
major bedeutend, größer *25*
to make it es schaffen *8*
to make up your mind sich entscheiden *84*
to make yourself familiar with sich vertraut machen mit *85*
malfunction nicht funktionieren *67*
to man besetzen *51*
management Geschäftsführung, Verwaltung *25*
managing director Geschäftsführer/in *28*
mandatory vorgeschrieben, obligatorisch *111*
manual manuell, von Hand *96*
manually manuell, von Hand *66T*
to manufacture herstellen, produzieren *12T*
manufacturer Hersteller/in *11T*
manufacturing process Herstellung, Produktionsprozess *18*
manufacturing sector produzierender Bereich *11*
marine animal Meerestier *93*
to mark out abgrenzen *44*
marketing Werbung, Vertrieb *19*
marketplace Markt(platz) *118*
masonry Mauerwerk *57*
material properties Materialeigenschaften *91*
materials section Materialabteilung *22*
to maximise maximieren *88*
to measure (ver)messen *22*; Maßnahme *73*
mechanic Mechaniker/in *17*
mechanical mechanisch *50*; **~ engineer** Maschinen(bau)ingenieur/in *15*
mechanism Mechanismus *91P*
mechatronic technician Mechatroniker/in *53*
mechatronics Mechatronik *55*
medium-sized mittelgroß *11*
meet standards Ansprüche erfüllen *10*
to melt down einschmelzen *44*

memory-hungry viel Speicher benötigend *66T*
to mend reparieren *99*
metal file Metallfeile *62*
metal shears Blechschere *55*
metalworker Metallarbeiter/in *79*
method Methode, Verfahren *40*
midprice im mittleren Preissegment *43*
midweek in der Wochenmitte *47*
migrant Gastarbeiter/in *21T*
miles per gallon Meilen pro Gallone *71*
milling machine Fräsautomat *99*
minor klein, geringfügig *46T*
misaligned verstellt, falsch ausgerichtet *74*
to mislay verlegen *84*
to mistreat misshandeln *54*
mitre face Gehrungswinkel *63*
mobile elevating work platform fahrbare Hebebühne *86*
moderate mäßig *72*
moisture Feuchtigkeit *67P*
molten flüssig, geschmolzen *18*
moped Moped *68*
moreover außerdem, zudem *107T*
mortar Mörtel *44*
MOT (test) (= Ministry of Transport) TÜV-Untersuchung *109*
motion Bewegung *57*
motivated motiviert *110*
motorcycle Motorrad *39*
to mould formen *16*; Schimmel *64*
mound Hügel, Haufen *44*
mount Halterung *39*
to move back (nach hinten) verschieben *46T*
mph m/h (Meilen pro Stunde) *72*
multimeter Vielfachmessinstrument *55*

N
to nail nageln *58T*; **~ file** Nagelfeile *62*; **~ gun** Nagler, Nagelpistole *57*
narrow eng, schmal *42*
nasty schlimm *21T*
naturally occurring in der Natur vorkommend *100*
navigation Navigation *39*
nearby in der Nähe *78*
needlenose pliers Spitzzange *62*
no offence intended nimm's mir nicht übel *82*
no-interest loan zinsfreies Darlehen *52*
none keine/r/s *71*
non-fatal nicht lebensgefährlich *86*
non-ferrous metal Nichteisenmetall *90*
non-flammable nicht brennbar *91*
non-metal Nichtmetall *90*

Alphabetical word list

non-metallic nichtmetallisch *90*
non-toxic ungiftig, nicht toxisch *100*
nor und auch nicht, noch *73*
normally normalerweise *39*
notice Kündigung *113*
nought Null *60*
nuclear plant Kernkraftwerk *107*
nuisance Ärgernis *54*
numeracy skills rechnerische Fähigkeiten *110*
nut (Schrauben-)Mutter *55*

O

to obey beachten *78*
obliged verpflichtet *107T*
to observe beobachten *74*
to obtain erhalten, erzielen *118*
obvious erkennbar, sichtbar *65*; **for ~ reasons** aus naheliegenden Gründen *19*
to occur geschehen, stattfinden *72*
off we go los geht's *39*
off-balance, to be ~ nicht waagerecht stehen *65*
off-site außerhalb der Baustelle *78*
oil filter Ölfilter *88*
oil spill Öllache *81T*
one by one nacheinander *98*
one point four (1.4) eins Komma vier *13*
ongoing (fort)laufend, andauernd *36*
on-site vor Ort, auf der Baustelle *78*
opaque undurchsichtig, nicht durchscheinend *91*
open day Tag der offenen Tür *97*
open spanner Maul-, Gabelschlüssel *54*
opening Öffnung *67P*
to operate betreiben *12*
operating director Bauleiter/in *23*
operating procedure Bedienungsanleitung *78*
operational laufend, in Betrieb *74*; **~ facility** funktionsfähige Einrichtung
operations boss Bauleiter/in *23*
operator Telefonist/in *49*
opportunity Chance, Möglichkeit *109*
optical optisch *91P*
to optimise optimieren *10*
optional wahlweise *85*
oral mündlich *97*
ore Erz *41*
organic matter organische(r) Stoff(e) *44*
oscilloscope Oszilloskop *70*
other than außer *102*
ought to be sollte/n sein *109*

outbreak Ausbruch *15*
out-of-date abgelaufen, überholt *89*
output Ausstoß *91P*
outskirts Außengebiete, Stadtrand *51*
oven Ofen, Herd *67P*
overall Overall, Arbeitsanzug *79*
overband magnet Überbandmagnet *90*
overboard über Bord *15*
overhead power cable Ober-, Freileitung *86*
overheating Überhitzung *65*
overlong überlang, zu lang *118*
over-pressurization Drucküberschreitung *105T*
overtightening Überdrehen *58*
overtime Überstunden *22*
overview Überblick, -sicht *111*
ownership Besitz, Eigentum *88*
oxidation Oxidation, Oxidierung *91P*
oxidization Oxidierung, Oxidation *91P*

P

PA (= personal assistant) persönliche/r Assistent/in *75*
padlock Vorhängeschloss *79*
painful schmerzhaft *81T*
paint removal Farblösung *91P*
paint shop Lackiererei *19*
panelling Anzeigetafel *39*
paperwork Papierkram *21T*
parabolic dish Parabolschüssel *75*
parallel parallel *34*
park parken *39*
parking bay Parkbucht *21*
parliamentary opposition parlamentarische Opposition *107T*
partial teilweise *85*
participant Teilnehmer/in *9*
to participate in teilnehmen an, sich beteiligen an *92*
particle Teil(chen) *41*
to patch up notdürftig reparieren, zusammenflicken *71*
patio Terrasse *43*
pattern Muster *70*
paver Fertiger *50*
paving block Bodenplatte *42*
paving material Pflastermaterial *43*
pebble Kieselstein *43*
to peel away abschmelzen, abtragen *96*
pellet Kügelchen, Pellet *91P*
pension Rente, Pension *109*
per annum jährlich, pro Jahr *91P*
to perform aus-, durchführen *18*
performance Leistung *16*

peripheral Peripherie(gerät) *65*
perks freiwillige Sozialleistungen, Zusatzvergünstigungen *109*
permanent dauerhaft *86*; **~ position** unbefristete (Arbeits-)Stelle *110*
permission Erlaubnis, Genehmigung *55*
to permit erlauben *63*
personal details persönliche Angaben *120*
personnel Personal, Mitarbeiter *25*
to persuade überreden *84*
PET (polyethylene terephthalate) PET *96*
to phase out aussteigen, auslaufen lassen *107T*
phenomenon Phänomen *100*
Phillips Kreuzschlitzschraubendreher *54*
to pick up lernen, erwerben *115T*
pie chart Torten-, Kreisdiagramm *46*
to pile aufschütten *44*
pillion seat Soziussitz *39*
pin Kontaktstift *67*
pipe wrench Rohrzange *76*
pipefitter Rohrleger/in *21*
pipework Rohrleitung(en) *53*
piston Kolben *15*
to place platzieren *40*
placement Praktikum *42*
plain einfach *43*
planer Hobelmaschine *57*
planing machine Hobelmaschine *43*
plant Werk, Betrieb *12*
plaster Gips *27*; **~board screw** Gipskartonschraube *76*
platform Rampe *82*
platinum Platin *87*
playground Spielplatz *44*
pleased zufrieden *84*; **P~ to meet you.** Es freut mich, Sie kennen zu lernen. *8*
pliers (Kombi-)Zange *55*
plumber Installateur/in, Klempner/in *21*
plumbing Rohrleitungen, Installationen *10*; **~ firm** Sanitärfirma *27*
plunger Ausgussreiniger, Stampfer *76*
plywood Sperrholz *58T*
poetic poetisch *66T*
point Spitze *60T*
polished sauber, poliert *74*
pollutant Schadstoff *89*
polymer Polymer(e) *8*; **~-based** aus Polymeren bestehend *10*
polystyrene foam Styropor *41*
polytechnic Fachhochschule *15*
portable transportabel, tragbar *57*

Alphabetical word list

portacabin (Bau-)Container 19
to position positionieren 78
to possess besitzen 50
possession Besitz 73
post Internetbeitrag 65; (Arbeits-)Stelle 114
poster Poster/in, Absender/in (eines Internetbeitrags) 65
potable trinkbar 100
potential möglich, potenziell 30
pothole Schlagloch 42
power generation Stromerzeugung 7
power steering fluid Servolenkungsflüssigkeit 87
power transmission system Antriebssystem 74
powered system Elektrogerät 78
PPE (= personal protective equipment) Schutzkleidung 78
precaution Vorsichtsmaßnahme 78
precautionary Vorsichts- 73
precious wertvoll, kostbar 100
precise genau, präzise 22; **~ly** genau, präzise 34
precision Präzision 26; **~-made** Präzisions- 57
to prefabricate vorfabrizieren 21T
premises (Betriebs-)Gelände 27
present, at ~ im Moment 114
to preserve bewahren, erhalten 98
pressure Druck 27; **~ relief valve** Druckentlastungsventil 102
to pressurize unter Druck setzen 102
prevailing vorherrschend 85
to prevent verhindern, verhüten 77
prevention Verhütung 95
principle Prinzip 34
print job Druckauftrag 120
printer cartridge Druckerpatrone 98
to prioritize Prioritäten setzen 110
priority Vorrang, Priorität 42
private medical insurance private Krankenversicherung 110
procedure Verfahren, Vorgehensweise 99
processing Verarbeitung 90
procurement Beschaffung 12T
production supervisor Produktionsleiter/in 9
professional professionell 30; Fachmann, Profi 57
proficiency Kompetenz, Leistungsfähigkeit 26
profile Profil 57
profit Profit, Gewinn 13P
profitability Rentabilität 107T
progress Fortschritt(e) 18
projected vorhergesagt, prognostiziert 50

to pronounce aussprechen 60
to propel (an)treiben 39
properly richtig, korrekt 12; **~-equipped** sachgerecht ausgestattet 78
properties Eigenschaften 41
property Eigenschaft 50; **~ developer** Bauträger/in 51
proportion Proportion, Verhältnis 46
pros and cons Für und Wider 87
prospective (zu)künftig, potentiell 118
protective Schutz- 77; **~ clothing** Schutz(be)kleidung 24
prototype Prototyp 72
protractor head Winkelmesser(kopf) 63
to prove sich herausstellen als 37
provider Anbieter 119
P-trap Siphon 27
to pull a lever einen Hebel betätigen 23
punctual pünktlich 115T
purchase (Ein-)Kauf, Anschaffung 30
purpose Zweck 55; **~-designed** Spezial- 89
to put a call through to sb einen Anruf zu jdm durchstellen 31

Q

qualified qualifiziert, ausgebildet 78
quantity surveyor Bauwirtschaftler/in 22
questionnaire Fragebogen 48
quick chuck Schnellspann-Bohrfutter 60T

R

rack Ständer, Gestell 54
radiator Kühler 72
radical radikal 107T
radioactive radioaktiv 78
rainwater Regenwasser 27
to raise (hoch)heben 89
rake Harke, Rechen 44
range Reihe, Auswahl, Palette 8
rapid schnell 111
rare selten 91; **~ly** selten 39
rat Ratte 93
rather ziemlich, recht 34; **~ than** anstelle von, anstatt 54
ratio Verhältnis 91P
to rattle klappern, rattern 67P
raw material Rohstoff(e) 10
reaction Reaktion 52
to readjust neu einstellen 67P
reamer (Reib-)Ahle 62
rear Hinter- 39; Hinter-, Rückseite 67; **~-view mirror** Rückspiegel 39

reasonable angemessen, günstig 43
to reattach wieder befestigen 71
to rebalance ausbalancieren 65
recall Rückruf 73
reception area Empfang(sbereich) 19
recessed eingelassen 34
recession Rezession, Wirtschaftsflaute 28
to recharge wieder aufladen 98
reciprocating saw Gattersäge 57
reclamation Wiedergewinnung 88
to recover bergen 15; zurück-, wiedergewinnen 95
recoverable wieder verwertbar 88
recovery Wiedergewinnung 89
recreation Erholung 18T
recruitment policy Personalpolitik 110
redecoration Renovierung 27
reduction Reduzierung, Senkung 107T
referee Referenz(geber) 120
to refill neu befüllen 71
reflective jacket reflektierende Warn(schutz)weste 79
refreshment Erfrischung 28
refrigerator Kühlschrank 10
to refund erstatten 37
to refurbish renovieren, herrichten 92
to refuse sich weigern 94
regardless of unabhängig von 110
region Gebiet, Bereich 12
to register anmelden 88
to regrind, reground, reground abschleifen 59
regulation Vorschrift, Regel 78
reinforce verstärken 50; **~d** verstärkt 16
to reinsert wieder einführen 67P
to reinstall neu installieren 65
to relate to sich auswirken auf 118
to relay neu verlegen 44
relevant wesentlich 13
reliability Zuverlässigkeit 108
reliable zuverlässig 99
relief Hilfe 81T
to rely on sich verlassen auf 85
remainder Rest 88
removal Entfernen 104
to render inoperative stilllegen, abschalten 71
renewable erneuerbar 10
renovated renoviert 108
replacement Ersatz(teil) 37
to report sth to sb jdm etw melden 97
to report to unterstehen 23
repulsion Abstoßung 90
to request bitten (um) 73
requirement Anforderung 10

Alphabetical word list

research Forschung *10*
researcher Forscher/in *18*
to resell wieder verkaufen *88*
to reserve for reservieren für *54*
reservoir Behälter *10*
to reset zurückstellen *66T*
resident An-, Einwohner/in *44*
residential Wohn- *30*; ~ **building** Wohngebäude *11T*
residual Rest-, restlich *91P*
resin (Kunst-)Harz *91P*
to resist widerstehen *50*
resistance Widerstand *39*
resistant widerstandsfähig *50*
resources Ressourcen *98*
respectively beziehungsweise *108*
respirator Atemschutzmaske *79*
to respond reagieren *65*
responsibility Verantwortung *22*
to rest aufsetzen *57*; ~ **room (AE)** Toilette *20*
to restore wiederherstellen *68*
to result in ergeben, zur Folge haben *16*
resulting daraus folgend *91P*
résumé Lebenslauf *26*
retail Einzelhandel *31*
to retard verlangsamen, verzögern *39*
to rethink überdenken *98*
to retire sich zurückziehen *15*; in Rente/Pension gehen *109*
re-usable wieder verwendbar *94*
reuse Wiederverwendung *88*
revenue Einkünfte, Einnahmen *93*
to reverse rückwärts fahren, zurücksetzen *80*; umkehren *108*; ~ **drive** Rückwärtsgang *57*
ridge Rand, Kante *102*
ridiculous lächerlich *93*
rigid starr, steif *50*
ring spanner Ringschlüssel *54*
to rise (an)steigen *100*
risk, at ~ in Gefahr *86*
roadbase Unterbau *50*
road conditions Straßenverhältnisse *85*
road marking Straßenmarkierung *44*
roadworthiness Verkehrssicherheit *85*
roaring dröhnend, donnernd *96*
to roll walzen *50*
roof Dach *58T, 78*; **~-mounted** auf dem Dach installiert *100*
to rotate drehen *63*
rough Roh(skizze) *26*
roughly ungefähr, etwa *16*
to round (ab)runden *43*; **~-the-clock** rund um die Uhr, *24* Stunden *75*
route, en ~ unterwegs, auf der Strecke *89*
router Fräsmaschine, Oberfräse *57*
row Reihe *34*
to ruin ruinieren *56T*
rumour Gerücht *73*
to run verlegen *21*; ~ **a business** ein Geschäft führen *31*; ~ **on (electricity)** durch (Strom) angetrieben werden, mit (Strom) fahren *8*; **in the long** ~ auf die Dauer *107T*
running in Folge, hintereinander *113*

S

sack Tüte *95*
safety attendant Sicherheitsbeauftragte/r *78*
safety harness Sicherheitsgurt *78*
safety helmet Schutzhelm *24*
safety inspector Sicherheitsbeauftragte/r *22*
safety seat Sicherheitssitz *92*
salary Gehalt *22*
sales office Verkaufsbüro *12*
sample Muster, (Kost-)Probe *13*
sand Sand *41*
sandwiched eingeklemmt *96*
satellite Satellit *11T*
sat-receiver Satellitenempfänger *75*
scaffolder Gerüstbauer/in *17*
scaffolding (Bau-)Gerüst *78*; ~ **rig** (Bau-)Gerüst *77*
scale Maß(stab) *26*; **to** ~ maßstabgerecht, nach Maß *26*
scavenger Aasfresser *93*
schedule, on ~ planmäßig, pünktlich *25*
scheduled planmäßig, regelmäßig *74*
scholarship Stipendium *15*
scissors Schere *55*
sconce Wandleuchte *35*
scooter (Motor-)Roller *39*
scrap Abfall *60T*; verschrotten *88*
screeching noise kreischendes Geräusch *71*
to screed glattstreichen, einebnen *42*
screw Schraube *55*
screwdriver Schraubenzieher, -dreher *54*
to scribe anreißen, vorzeichnen *63*
scriber Reißahle, -nadel *63*
seagull Möwe *93*
seal Dichtung *10*; **~ed** versiegelt *102*
search phrase Suchbegriff *35*
seat (Sitz-)Platz *18T*; **~-mounted** am Sitz montiert *72*
second to none an erster Stelle *91P*
secure sicher *78*; **~ly fixed** sicher befestigt *55*
security bars Sicherheitsgitter *21*
security measures Sicherheitsvorkehrungen *24*
seek suchen *114*; ~ **instruction** Anweisung(en) einholen *55*
to select auswählen *110*
selection Trennung *91P*
self-employed selbständig *109*
self-orientated selbstbezogen *118*
sellotape Tesafilm *70*
semiconductor Halbleiter *33*
sense Verstand *82*
to separate trennen *96*
separator Trenner *91P*
sequence Reihenfolge *50*
serrated knife Sägemesser, Messer mit Wellschliff *62*
to service eine Inspektion durchführen *85*; ~ **and maintenance plan** Inspektions- und Wartungsplan *85*; ~ **manual** Wartungshandbuch *85*; ~ **patch** Softwareaktualisierung *68*; ~ **the demand** die Nachfrage decken *96*
servicing Wartung *99*
set at eingestellt auf *102*
to set the pace wegweisend sein *26*
to set up a business ein Geschäft eröffnen *31*
setting Einstellung *66T*
to settle down sesshaft werden, eine Familie gründen *115T*
several einige, mehrere *40*
severe ernst, schwer *86*
sewing eye Nadelöhr *62*
sexual orientation sexuelle Orientierung *110*
shaft Welle *74*
shape Form *16*; formen *50*
sharp scharf, spitz *24*
to sharpen schärfen *55*
to shatter zerbrechen *58*
shift work Schichtarbeit *115T*
to shine a beam of light at einen Lichtstrahl richten auf *96*
shock absorber Stoßdämpfer *87*
shoddy schludrig, minderwertig *27*
short Kurzschluss *67*
shovel Schaufel *44*
showroom Ausstellungsraum *38*
to shred shreddern, zerkleinern *90*
shredder Shredder, Reißwolf *90*; ~ **process** Shredderprozess *89*
shrinking schrumpfend *25*
to shut down ab-, ausschalten *65*
sickness pay Krankengeld *110*
sideways seitwärts, zur Seite *72*
sieving Sieben *96*

Alphabetical word list

sightseeing Besichtigung (von Sehenswürdigkeiten) *49T*
significantly erheblich, deutlich *16*
silly sod Dummkopf *82*
silt Schlick *41*
sim card SIM-Karte *119*
similarity Ähnlichkeit *91P*
to simulate simulieren *97*
simultaneously gleichzeitig *39*
Sincerely Mit freundlichen Grüßen *73*
siren Sirene *79*
site Standort *12T*; ~ **manager** Bauleiter/in *9*
size-reduction Verkleinerung *90*
to skid schleudern *50*
skilled ausgebildet, geschickt *115T*; ~ **labourer** Facharbeiter/in *23*
slab Platte, Tafel *43*
slight gering, leicht *39*; ~**ly** leicht, geringfügig *89*
to slip (ver)rutschen *63*
slippery glatt, glitschig *72*
slippy rutschig, glatt *43*
slot Nut(e), Schlitz *57*; ~**-head screwdriver** Schlitzschraubendreher *54*
small production Kleinproduktion *8*
smart drive kit Smart-Drive-Kit *39*
to smash zerschlagen, zertrümmern *90*
smoke, a ~ eine Zigarette*;77* T; ~ **detector** Rauchmelder *97*
smooth glatt *50*; glätten *55*
to soak einweichen *67T*
socket Steckdose *39*; Stecknuss *54*; ~ **spanner** Steckschlüssel *54*
soil (Erd-)Boden *108*
solar panel Sonnenkollektor *99*
solar-powered mit Solarantrieb *15*
soldering iron Lötkolben *55*
solid fest *33*; fester Körper *91*
soluble löslich *91*
to sort (aus)sortieren *90*; Sortierung, Sortiergang *96*; ~ **out** in Ordnung bringen *64*; ~ **sth out** sich um etw kümmern *23*
sorter Sortiermaschine *90*
soundproof schalldicht *72*
spanner Schraubenschlüssel *54*
spare time Freizeit *65*
spark Funke *79*; ~ **arrestor** Funkenfänger *59*; ~ **plug** Zündkerze *15*
sparking Funken auslösen *74*
speaker Lautsprecher *65*
specialist Spezialist/in, Fachmann/frau *17*
to specialize in sich spezialisieren auf *25*
specification Angabe *10*

speed Geschwindigkeit *39*; ~ **chart** Geschwindigkeitstabelle *60T*; ~ **limit** Geschwindigkeitsbegrenzung *85*; ~ **up** beschleunigen *46*
spillage Pfütze, Lache *43*
to spin (sich) drehen *90*; ~ **cycle** Schleudern *65*
spirit level Wasserwaage *63*
splinter Splitter *24*; splittern *60T*
to spot herausfinden, bemerken *118*
spotlight Scheinwerfer *34*
to spread (sich) verbreiten, verteilen *40*
spring tension Federspannung *74*
sprinkler Sprinker(anlage) *97*
square head Vierkant(kopf) *63*
squealing Quietschen *74*
to stabilize stabilisieren *78*
stack Stapel *80*
staff Mitarbeiter(stab) *10*
stage Stadium *89*
to stall ausgehen *66T*
standby Standby, Ruhezustand *94*; ~ **worker** Ersatzarbeiter/in *78*
standpoint Standpunkt *16*
staple Heftklammer *70*
starter motor Anlasser *15*
state-of-the-art letzter Stand der Technik *18T*
statistics statistische Angaben *13*
steady stetig *28*
steam Dampf *71*; ~ **engine** Dampfmaschine *15*
steamer Dampfer *15*
steel mill Stahlwerk *90*
steel rule Stahllineal *63*
steelworker Stahlarbeiter/in *17*
steering wheel Lenkrad, Steuer *71*
step-by-step instructions schrittweise Anweisungen *104*
to stick (fest)klemmen *73*
sticky klebrig *41*; ~ **bitumen** klebriger Bitumen *58T*
stiff steif *50*
to stitch nähen; Stich *83*
stock Vorrat, Lager *28*
storage area Baumateriallager *77*
storage cylinder Speichertank *102*
storage facility Lagerhalle *19*
storage tank Wasserspeicher *100*
to store aufbewahren *89*
storeroom Lagerraum *77*
storey (AE) Stock(werk), Etage *20*
story (BE) Stock(werk), Etage *20*
straight pin Zylinderstift *62*
to straighten gerade machen, begradigen *64*
stranded-wire cutter Litzenschneider *62*
stream Strom, Anteil *90*
to strengthen verstärken *50*

stretch Ausdehnung *50*; sich ausdehnen *50*
structural baulich *31*
studio Studio, Atelier *31*
stunning umwerfend *107T*
sub-base Untergrund, Fundament *44*
subsidiary Tochter(gesellschaft) *8*
substantially wesentlich, erheblich *88*
to suck saugen *90*
to suffer leiden *94*; ~ **damage** Schaden erleiden *50*
to suffice genügen *39*
suicide Selbstmord *15*
to suit passen *32*
suite, a ~ of eine Reihe von *19*
suitability Eignung *118*
suitable geeignet, passend *43*
suited geeignet *108*
to sum up zusammenfassen *52*
to supervise beaufsichtigen *22*
supervisor Aufseher/in, Leiter/in, Ausbilder/in *17*
supplier Lieferant/in, Zulieferer *26*
to supply liefern, bereitstellen, versorgen (mit) *10*
support frame Fahrzeugrahmen *16*
surface (Ober-)Fläche, (Straßen-)Belag *19*
surfstick USB-Datenstick (zum Surfen im Internet) *119*
to surround umgeben *100*
surrounding um ... herum *40*
surveyor Landmesser/in *19*
susceptible to anfällig für *91P*
suspension Federung, (Rad-)Aufhängung *112*; ~ **bridge** Hängebrücke *91P*
sweaty verschwitzt, Schweiß- *71*
to sweep up, swept, swept zusammenfegen *27*
to swing drehen, reißen *72*
to switch off ab-, ausschalten *72*
to switch on an-, einschalten *60T*
symptom Symptom *65*

T

table saw Tischsäge *59*
tablet computer Tablet-Computer *119*
tailored to zugeschnitten auf *118*
to take a class einen Kurs mitmachen *71*
to take into account berücksichtigen *36*
to take sb through sth mit jdm etw durchgehen *115T*
to talk sb through sth jdm etw erklären/erläutern *104*
tangled up verstrickt in *95*
tap (Wasser-)Hahn *64*

Alphabetical word list

targeted zielgerichtet *118*
tariff Tarif, Gebühr *36*
tarmac Asphalt *42*
task-specific arbeitsgerecht, der Aufgabe entsprechend *78*
to tax besteuern *93*
technical development technische Entwicklung *12*
technique Methode *12*; ~s Methoden, (Arbeits-)Technik *25*
technological technologisch *16*
teflon packing tape Teflonklebeband *76*
telecommunications Fernmeldewesen *25*
temporary vorübergehend *86*
tenant Mieter/in *51*
tender Angebot *25*
ten-stage zehnstufig *50*
terminal Anschluss *70*
textile Textilie, Gewebe *7*
Thank goodness! Gott sei Dank! *72*
theodolite Theodolit, Winkelmessgerät *43*
theory Theorie *15*
therefore deshalb *91P*
thermal thermisch *78*
thermostat Thermostat *102*
thick dick, stark *40*
thickness Dicke, Stärke *50*
throughout die ganze Zeit hindurch, während *46*
thumb Daumen *84*
thunderstorm Gewitter *38*
tight fest(sitzend) *74*
to tighten anziehen, festschrauben *55*
to tile kacheln, fliesen *21*
tiler Fliesenleger/in *24*
timber Holz(balken) *18*
time, at any ~ jederzeit *114*; on ~ pünktlich, rechtzeitig *27*; ~-consuming zeitaufwendig *43*; ~ frame Zeitrahmen *42* ~ keeping record Zeiteinhaltungsstatistik *112*
tin Zinn *91P*; ~ opener Dosenöffner *62*
to tolerate tolerieren *84*
tool allowance Werkzeugzulage *110*
tool rest Werkstückauflage *59*
toolbox Werkzeugkasten *81T*
toolkit Werkzeugkasten *57*
toolstore Werkzeugkasten *58*
torch Taschenlampe *76*
torque Drehmoment, -kraft *57*; ~ wrench Drehmomentschlüssel *54*
total (ins)gesamt *12*
tough robust, hart *58*
to tow (ab)schleppen *72*

toward auf ... zu, in Richtung (auf) *107T*
toxic giftig, toxisch *93*
track light Systemleuchte *35*
tracking app Suchfunktion *39*
traction Zugkraft *41*
trade fair Handelsmesse *51*
traffic flow Verkehrsfluss *47*
trailing herabhängend *86*
to train ausbilden, schulen *8*
trainee Auszubildende/r, Praktikant/in *14*
training course Lehrgang, Schulung *8*
to transfer umwandeln *100*
transmission Getriebe, Gangschaltung *16*; ~ fluid Getriebeöl *87*
to transmit übertragen *74*
transparency (OHP-)Folie *97*
transparent durchsichtig, transparent *91*
transportation Transport *91P*
to treat behandeln *57*; ~ sb to sth jdm etw anbieten *18T*
trench wall Grabenwand *78*
trial period Probezeit *22*
triangle Dreieck *39*
trigger Auslöser *65*
trillion Trillion *93*
trim shop Werkstatt für die Innenausstattung *19*
trip Stolpern *86*; ~ hazard Stolperrisiko *57*
trommel Trommel *96*
trouble-free störungsfrei *100*
to troubleshoot Störungen beseitigen *18*; ~ing Fehlersuche *64*
tube Röhre, Rohr *33*
tubing Röhren *91P*
tumble dryer Trommeltrockner *65*
tungsten wire Wolframdraht *33*
turn around copy doppelseitige Kopie *28*
turning point Wendepunkt *107*
turnover Umsatz *28*
tweezers Pinzette *62*
two-wheeler Zweirad *39*
tyre pressure Reifendruck *87*

U

ugly hässlich *31*
ultra-modern ultramodern *39*
unable unfähig, nicht in der Lage *50*
unauthorised unbefugt *77*
unauthorized unbefugt *23*
unbelievable unglaublich *39*
unbelieving ungläubig *107T*
to unblock Verstopfung beseitigen *76*
undercover Bodenverkleidung *91P*

underneath (dar)unter *42*
underside Unterseite *89*
to undo rückgängig machen, annullieren *66T*
uneven uneben *42*
unexpected unerwartet *70*
unfamiliar unbekannt, ungewohnt *55*
to uninstall deinstallieren *65*
unique selling point Alleinstellungsmerkmal *118*
unlit unbeleuchtet *86*
to unload abladen *77T*
to unpack auspacken *98*
to unplug den Stecker herausziehen *65*
unrealistic unrealistisch *93*
to unscrew abschrauben *27*
unsecured ungesichert *80*
unstable instabil *67P*
unsuitable ungeeignet, unpassend *43*
unused unbenutzt *105*
unusual ungewöhnlich *92*; ~-looking ungewöhnlich aussehend *16*
to update aktualisieren *66T*
upfront cost Vorauskosten *36*
urgent dringend, eilig *44*
usage Verbrauch *36*
USB port USB-Anschluss *119*
utility company Versorgungsbetrieb, Stromkonzern *107T*

V

vacancy freie/ offene Stelle *113*
value Wert, Nutzen *10*
valve Ventil *102*; ~ seal Ventildichtung *71*
van (Werkzeug-)Wagen *76*
vapour Dampf, Dunst *21*
varied abwechslungsreich *115T*
variety Auswahl *40*
various verschiedene *15*
varying unterschiedlich *57*
vehicle Fahrzeug *8*; ~ identification number (VIN) Kfz-Kennzeichen *73*
vent Lüftungsschlitz *65*; ~ pipe Lüftungsrohr *105T*
to verify nachprüfen *78*
vernier calliper Messschieber *55*
vernier scale Messschieber *63*
versatile vielseitig *34*
versatility Vielseitigkeit *108*
vertically senkrecht, vertikal *108*
vessel Gefäß, Behälter *78*
to vibrate vibrieren *65*
vice Schraubstock *55*
video card Videokarte *66T*
video-editing Videobearbeitung *66T*

187

Alphabetical word list

virtually praktisch, nahezu *10*
viscous zähflüssig *41*
visible sichtbar *39*
visionary Visionär/in *15*
vital wesentlich *57*
vocational beruflich, Berufs- *26*; ~ **college** Berufsschule *27*; ~ **training** Berufsausbildung *115T*
voltage Spannung *67*
volume Menge, Umfang *50*
voyage (See-)Reise *15*
vulnerable to empfindlich gegen *43*

W

walkway Laufgang, Fußweg *79*
wallpaper Tapete *22*
warehouse Lager(halle) *17*
warranty repair Garantiereparatur *112*
washer Waschanlage *10*
wasteland Ödland, Brache *42*
waste-water treatment plant Kläranlage *25*
water heater Warmwasserbereiter *100*
water supply Wasseranschluss, -versorgung *27*
water tap Wasserhahn *72*
waterbound wassergebunden *50*
waterproof wasserdicht *86*; ~ **tar paper** wasserdichte Dachpappe *58T*
watertight wasserdicht *102*
wave shape Wellenform *70*
weakness Schwäche *115T*
wear Abnutzung *50*
wearing course Deckschicht *50*
weed Unkraut *42*
weight Gewicht *16*
weird merkwürdig, seltsam *54*
to weld schweißen *21*
welder Schweißer/in *17*
welding visor (Schutzhelm mit) Visier, Schweißerschutzvisier *79*
well equipped gut ausgestattet *22*
wheel guard Radschutz, Schutzhaube *59*
wheel loader Radlader *82*
wheelbarrow Schubkarre *43*
whirring Surren *71*
width Breite, Weite *58T*
wind turbine chamber Windturbinenkammer *90*
window frame Fensterrahmen *10*
windscreen wiper Scheibenwischer *87*
to wipe (ab)wischen *21*
wire Draht *33*; ~ **cutter** Seitenschneider *62*; ~**lessly** drahtlos, per Funk *65*; ~ **stripper** Abisolierzange *62*
wiring Verkabelung, Leitungen *18*
within budget innerhalb des Finanzplans *25*
to withstand aushalten *50*
witness Zeuge/Zeugin *82*
wooden aus Holz, Holz- *21T*
work experience Berufs-, Arbeitserfahrung *26*
workbench Werkbank *21*
workforce Belegschaft *18*
working order Betriebsfähigkeit *99*
work-life balance Gleichgewicht zwischen Arbeit und Freizeit *109*
workload Arbeitsbelastung, -pensum *110*
workpiece Werkstück *60T*
worksite Arbeitsplatz *48*
World Fair Weltausstellung *15*
worn verschlissen, abgenutzt *71*
wound Wunde, Verletzung *83*
wrestling Ringen *52*
to write sb off sick jdn krankschreiben *83*

Y

Yours faithfully Mit freundlichen Grüßen *114*
Yours sincerely Mit freundlichen Grüßen *84*

Z

zinc Zink *91P*; ~-**coated** verzinkt *91P*

Basic technical vocabulary (German–English)

Berufe – Jobs

Ausbilder/in	training supervisor, instructor
Auszubildende/r	apprentice, trainee
Baukostengutachter/in	quantity surveyor
Dreher/in	turner
Elektriker/in	electrician, electrical engineer
Facharbeiter/in	skilled worker
Fließbandarbeiter/in	assembly line worker
Gabelstaplerfahrer/in	forklift operator
Gerüstbauer	scaffolder
Klempner/in	plumber
Maler/in	painter
Maschinenbauer/in	machine builder
Maurer/in	bricklayer
Mechaniker/in	mechanic
Mechatroniker/in	mechatronic systems engineer
Meister/in	foreman
Mitarbeiter	staff
Schweißer/in	welder
Stahlarbeiter	steelworker
Techniker/in	state-certified engineer
Technischer Zeichner/in	CAD engineer
Teilezurichter/in	metal dresser
Tischler/in	joiner
Werkstattleiter/in	workshop manager
Werkzeugmacher/in	toolmaker

Handwerkzeuge – hand-held tools

Bandsäge	bandsaw
Bügelsäge	hacksaw
Elektrobohrmaschine	electric drill
Feile	file
Flachrundzange	snip-nose pliers
Gewindebohrer	tap
Hammer	hammer
Hobelmaschine	planing machine
Innensechskantschlüssel	hex(agonal) key
Körner	centre punch
Maulschlüssel	open-ended spanner
Meißel	chisel
Schlagdorn	pin punch
Schubkarre	whelbarrow
Schraubendreher	screwdriver
Spitzsenker	countersink
Stichsäge	jigsaw
Wasserpumpenzange	waterpump pliers
Zapfensenker	counterbore

Werkzeugmaschinen – machine tools

Betonmischer	cement mixer
Bohrmaschine	drilling machine
Fräsmaschine	milling machine
Hubsäge	power hacksaw
Schleifmaschine	grinding machine
Drehmaschine	lathe
Planierraupe	bulldozer
Radlader	wheel loader
Winkelschleife	angle grinder
Steintrenner	block cutter

Materialien – materials

Bauholz	timber
Beton	concrete
Buntmetall	non-ferrous metal
Eisen	iron
Eisenmetall	ferrous metal
Holz	wood
Kalkstein, Kalk	limestone
Kies	gravel
Lehm, Ton	clay
Messing	brass
Pflastersteine	paving stones
Stahl	steel
Zement	cement
Zuschlagsstoff	aggregate

Aktionen – actions

(ab)schleifen	grind
(an)fasen	chamfer
befestigen	fasten, fix
biegen	bend
bohren	bore, drill
drehen	turn
ersetzen	replace
formen	shape
fräsen	mill
hartlöten	braze
lösen	loosen
montieren	assemble
nachfüllen	refill
ölen	oil
polieren	finish
rändeln	knurl
reparieren	repair
schmieren	grease
schweißen	weld
weichlöten	solder

Common irregular verbs

INFINITIVE, SIMPLE PAST, PERFECT PARTICIPLE

be	was/were – *been*	sein	**let**	let – *let*	lassen
beat	beat – *beaten*	schlagen; besiegen	**lie**	lay – *lain*	liegen
become	became – *become*	werden	**light**	lit – *lit*	anzünden
begin	began – *begun*	anfangen	**lose**	lost – *lost*	verlieren
blow	blew – *blown*	wehen, blasen	**make**	made – *made*	machen
break	broke – *broken*	(zer)brechen; kaputtgehen	**mean**	meant – *meant*	bedeuten
bring	brought – *brought*	bringen	**meet**	met – *met*	sich treffen
build	built – *built*	bauen	**overtake**	overtook – *overtaken*	überholen
buy	bought – *bought*	kaufen	**pay**	paid – *paid*	(be-)zahlen
catch	caught – *caught*	fangen	**put**	put – *put*	setzen, stellen, legen
choose	chose – *chosen*	auswählen	**read**	read – *read*	lesen
come	came – *come*	kommen	**ride**	rode – *ridden*	reiten
cost	cost – *cost*	kosten	**ring**	rang – *rung*	klingeln
cut	cut – *cut*	schneiden	**rise**	rose – *risen*	steigen
do	did – *done*	tun, machen, erledigen	**run**	ran – *run*	laufen
draw	drew – *drawn*	zeichnen	**say**	said – *said*	sagen
drink	drank – *drunk*	trinken, saufen	**see**	saw – *seen*	sehen
drive	drove – *driven*	fahren	**sell**	sold – *sold*	verkaufen
eat	ate – *eaten*	essen, fressen	**send**	sent – *sent*	senden, schicken
fall	fell – *fallen*	hinfallen	**set up**	set up – *set up*	aufbauen, einrichten
feed	fed – *fed*	füttern	**shake**	shook – *shaken*	schütteln
feel	felt – *felt*	sich fühlen	**shine**	shone – *shone*	scheinen; leuchten
fight	fought – *fought*	(be)kämpfen	**shoot**	shot – *shot*	schießen
find	found – *found*	finden	**show**	showed – *shown*	zeigen
fly	flew – *flown*	fliegen	**sing**	sang – *sung*	singen
forget	forgot – *forgotten*	vergessen	**sink**	sank – *sunk*	sinken; versenken
freeze	froze – *frozen*	(ge)frieren; einfrieren	**sit**	sat – *sat*	sitzen
get	got – *got*	bekommen, erhalten	**sleep**	slept – *slept*	schlafen
give	gave – *given*	geben	**speak**	spoke – *spoken*	sprechen
go	went – *gone*	gehen	**spend**	spent – *spent*	ausgeben, verbringen
grow	grew – *grown*	wachsen	**stand**	stood – *stood*	stehen
hang	hung – *hung*	(auf)hängen	**steal**	stole – *stolen*	stehlen
have	had – *had*	haben	**stick**	stuck – *stuck*	kleben
hear	heard – *heard*	hören	**swim**	swam – *swum*	schwimmen
hide	hid – *hidden*	verstecken	**take**	took – *taken*	nehmen
hit	hit – *hit*	schlagen, aufprallen auf	**teach**	taught – *taught*	unterrichten, lehren
hold	held – *held*	halten	**tear**	tore – *torn*	(zer)reißen
hurt	hurt – *hurt*	verletzen	**tell**	told – *told*	erzählen, mitteilen, sagen
keep	kept – *kept*	behalten	**think**	thought – *thought*	denken, meinen
know	knew – *known*	kennen, wissen	**throw**	threw – *thrown*	werfen
lay	laid – *laid*	legen	**understand**	understood – *understood*	verstehen
lead	led – *led*	führen, leiten	**wear**	wore – *worn*	tragen, anhaben
leave	left – *left*	verlassen	**win**	won – *won*	gewinnen
lend	lent – *lent*	(ver)leihen	**write**	wrote – *written*	schreiben

Be careful with:

burn	burnt – burnt burned – burned	(ver)brennen	**smell**	smelt – smelt smelled – smelled	riechen
dream	dreamt – dreamt dreamed – dreamed	träumen	**spell**	spellt – spellt spelled – spelled	buchstabieren
learn	learnt – learnt learned – learned	lernen, erfahren	**spoil**	spoilt – spoilt spoiled – spoiled	verderben

Bildquellenverzeichnis

Titelbild: Getty Images Jonathan Knowles

S. 7: 1/Shutterstock Pedro Salaverria, 2/Shutterstock Landov/Liu Haifeng, 3/dpa/Audi AG, 4 Shutterstock Luchschen, 5/Shutterstock Robert Cernohlavek, 6/dpa-Zentralbild/Jens Wolf Ressort, unten 1/Airbus, 2/VW, 3/MAN, 4/Hochtief, 5/Bayer; **S. 8:** 1/Rehau, 2/Rehau, 3/Rehau; **S. 9:** 1/Shutterstock shyshak roman, 2/Shutterstock photobank.ch, 3/Shutterstock Flashon Studio, 4/Shutterstock Yuri Arcurs, 5/Shutterstock Elena Elisseeva, 6/Shutterstock Yuri Arcurs; **S. 12:** Rehau; **S. 14:** Mercedes-Benz Classic; **S. 15** Mercedes-Benz Classic; **S. 16:** picture alliance DB Werksfoto Porsche; **S. 17:** 1/picture alliance Panasia/Yasushi Arishima, 2/Shutterstock Zastol`skiy Victor Leonidovich, 3/picture alliance dpa/MAN, 4/picture alliance dpa/Heinz von Heydenaber, 5/Shutterstock l i g h t p o e t, 6/Shutterstock Baloncici, 7/Shutterstock Pawel Papis; **S. 18:** fotofinder direktfoto; **S. 19:** picture alliance dpa/Boris Roessler; **S. 20:** 1/Shutterstock yui, 2/Shutterstock Alexander Ryabintsev; **S. 24:** 1/Shutterstock Zhukov Oleg, 2/Shutterstock Tobias Machhaus, 3/Shutterstock Juan Carlos Zamora, 3/Shutterstock Juan Carlos Zamora, 4/Shutterstock lexaarts, 5/Shutterstock Anke van Wyk, 6/Shutterstock Picsfive; **S. 27:** 1/Alamy © Image Source/Alamy, 2/Shutterstock CandyBox Images; **S. 30:** 1/Shutterstock Gemenacom, 2/Shutterstock Robert Kneschke, 3/Shutterstock Yuri Arcurs, 4/Shutterstock Lorraine Swanson 5/Shutterstock Kzenon, 6/Shutterstock Avava, 7/Shutterstock Dwight Smith; **S. 31:** Shutterstock archidea; **S. 33:** 1/Shutterstock Nikola Spasenoski, 2/Shutterstock Hal_P, 3/Shutterstock Sarunyu_foto, 4/Shutterstock Viktor Gladkov; **S. 35:** 1/SLV, 2/SLV, 3/Shutterstock StudioSmart; **S. 39:** 1/Daimler Werkfoto, 2/KENCKOphotography/Shutterstock.com; **S. 40:** Shutterstock cobalt88; **S. 41:** 1/Shutterstock mack2happy, 2/Shutterstock LesPalenik, 3/Shutterstock auremar, 4/Shutterstock Subbotina Anna, 5/Shutterstock pra_zit, 6/Shutterstock Bart_J, 7/Shutterstock Irina Konstantinova; **S. 46:** 1/Shutterstock Ali Ender Birer, 2/Shutterstock pedrosek, 3/Shutterstock John T Takai, 4/Shutterstock John T Takai, 5/Shutterstock dusit, 6/Shutterstock Ivelin Radkov; **S. 49:** Shutterstock Image Wizard; **S. 53:** 1/Shutterstock prism68, 2/Shutterstock auremar, 3/Shutterstock Kurhan, 4/Shutterstock thieury, 5/Shutterstock Dmitry Kalinovsky, 6/Shutterstock runzelkorn 7/Shutterstock Kurhan, 8/Shutterstock jordache; **S. 54:** Shutterstock Andrjuss; **S. 56:** Shutterstock Martynova Anna; **S. 57:** 1/Shutterstock mrHanson, 2/Shutterstock Ivanov, 3/Shutterstock Chas, 4/Shutterstock Ivanov, 5/Shutterstock tale, 6/Shutterstock alpturk33, 7/Shutterstock prism68, 8/Shutterstock Dusty Cline; **S. 59:** 1/Shutterstock m.bonotto, 2/Shutterstock olegbush, 3/Shutterstock Eimantas Buzas, 4/Shutterstock Milan Vasicek; **S. 60:** 1/Shutterstock Josef Bosak, 2/Shutterstock Coprid; **S. 62:** 1/Shutterstock R-photos, 2/Shutterstock Konstantin Yolshin; **S. 64:** 1/Shutterstock Repina Valeriya, 2/Shutterstock Sielemann, 3/Shutterstock Thorsten Schmitt, 4/Shutterstock sima, 5/Shutterstock marilyn barbone, 6/Shutterstock S_E, 7/Shutterstock Jovan Nikolic, 8/Shutterstock maska; **S. 68** Shutterstock Monkey Business Images; **S. 70:** 1/Shutterstock Konjushenko Vladimir, 2/Shutterstock Bragin Alexey, 3/Shutterstock Gordon Heeley, 4/Shutterstock Roberts; **S. 74:** Shutterstock Tyler Olson; **S. 76:** 1/Shutterstock Colour, 2/Shutterstock Garsya, 3/Shutterstock Ivaschenko Roman, 4/Shutterstock nito, 5/ODI, 6/Shutterstock Bragin Alexey, 7/Shutterstock Laborant, 8/Shutterstock LI CHAOSHU, 9/Shutterstock Hellen Sergeyeva, 10/Shutterstock aerogondo2, 11/Shutterstock Kalim, 12/Shutterstock Piotr Malczyk, 13/Shutterstock Winiki; **S. 77:** 1/Shutterstock Robert J. Beyers II, 2/Shutterstock Lack-O'Keen, 3/Shutterstock John Lock, 4/Shutterstock Barry Barnes, 5/Shutterstock Barry Barnes, 6/Shutterstock tony4urban, 7/Shutterstock Barry Barnes, 8/Shutterstock Yobidaba, 9/Shutterstock Barry Barnes, 10/Shutterstock Kaspri; **S. 79:** 1-16/Shutterstock Barry Barnes; **S. 82:** Shutterstock Mammut Vision; **S. 85:** Shutterstock Andreas G. Karelias; **S. 88:** 1/Alamy © Sean Spencer/Alamy, 2/Shutterstock akiyoko, 3/Shutterstock Huguette Roe; **S. 93:** Alamy © FLPA/Alamy; **S. 95:** 1/Shutterstock Rich Carey, 2/Shutterstock Huguette Roe, 3/Shutterstock Huguette Roe; **S. 97:** Shutterstock ponsulak kunsub; **S. 98:** 1/Shutterstock okicoki, 2/Shutterstock andrejco, 3/Shutterstock andrejco, 4/Shutterstock Ecelop; 5/Shutterstock Loren Rodgers; unten 1/Shutterstock Barry Barnes, 2/Shutterstock Ecelop, 3/Shutterstock cg-art 4/Shutterstock Ecelop, 5/Shutterstock cg-art, 6/Shutterstock cg-art; **S. 99:** 1/Shutterstock Ruslan Semichev, 2/Shutterstock Rob Wilson, 3/Shutterstock Gaja, 4/Shutterstock ssuaphotos, 5/Shutterstock Lisa S., 6/Shutterstock andersphoto, 7/Shutterstock Olivier Le Queinec, 8/Shutterstock magicoven; **S. 109:** 1/Shutterstock kolosigor, 2/Shutterstock Omer N Raja, 3/Shutterstock Sheftsoff, 4/Shutterstock vita khorzhevska, 5/Shutterstock Apollofoto, 6/Shutterstock Aaron Amat, 7/Shutterstock IKO, 8/Shutterstock Flashon Studio, 9/Shutterstock Christo; **S. 119:** Shutterstock Brian A Jackson

Illustrationen: alle Illustrationen Oxford Designers & Illustrators

Wir danken allen Rechteinhabern für die Abdruckgenehmigung. Da es uns leider nicht möglich war, alle Rechteinhaber zu ermitteln, bitten wir, sich gegebenenfalls an den Verlag zu wenden.